Text-Driven Preaching

Text-Driven Preaching

GOD'S WORD AT THE HEART OF EVERY SERMON

EDITED BY

**DANIEL L. AKIN, DAVID L. ALLEN
& NED L. MATHEWS**

B&H
ACADEMIC
Nashville, Tennessee

Contents

Part III: Preaching the Text-Driven Sermon

ABBREVIATIONS

BDAG	Bauer, W., F. W. Danker, W. F. Arndt, and F. W. Gingrich, *Greek-English Lexicon of the New Testament and Other Early Christian Literature*. 3rd ed.
BibSac	*Bibliotheca Sacra*
CBQ	*Catholic Biblical Quarterly*
CTR	*Criswell Theological Review*
ERT	*Evangelical Review of Theology*
ExpTim	*Expository Times*
FM	*Faith and Mission*
FN	*Filologia Neotestamentaria*
GTJ	*Grace Theological Journal*
JBDS	*Journal of Beeson Divinity School*
JETS	*Journal of the Evangelical Theological Society*
JP	*Journal for Preachers*
JSOTSup	Journal for the Study of the Old Testament: Supplement Series
NAC	New American Commentary
NCV	New Century Version of the Bible
NIDNTT	*New International Dictionary of New Testament Theology*
NovT	*Novum Testamentum*
NTOA	Novum Testamentum et Orbis Antuquus
RB	*Revue Biblique*
SBJT	*Southern Baptist Journal of Theology*
SJT	*Scottish Journal of Theology*
ST	*Studia Theologica*
SWJT	*Southwestern Journal of Theology*
TDNT	*Theological Dictionary of the New Testament*
TJ	*Trinity Journal*
TNIV	Today's New International Version of the Bible
TynBul	*Tyndale Bulletin*
UBS	*The Greek New Testament*, United Bible Societies
VTSup	Vetus Testamentum Supplements
WTJ	*Westminster Theological Journal*

INTRODUCTION

David L. Allen

O n any given Sunday in today's preaching pantheon, one can observe a diverse group of devotees, some paying homage to the chapel of "creativity," others sitting at the feet of the "culturally relevant." Some are transfixed at the nave marked "narrative," whereas others have their hearts strangely warmed at the chassé of "pop-psychology." There is never a shortage of worshippers at the "new homiletic" altar, and the "topical" shrine always receives its share of Sunday patrons. Fearful that some as yet undiscovered homiletical "method" might be missed, the gatekeepers of the pantheon have installed an altar inscribed "to the unknown preaching method." It is that method which the authors of this book declare unto you. Actually, the method itself is not "unknown" at all, and like the true church on earth, it has always had its practitioners in every era of church history. In fact, it is the oldest method in the preaching pantheon, having been used by the earliest preachers as far back as the apostolic era of the church. It is called "expository preaching."

But why has this time-honored method of preaching fallen into disuse in so many places and misuse in so many others? What has happened to engender so many substitute methods?

It should come as no surprise that the century that witnessed the greatest assault on biblical authority (the twentieth century) should also be the century that witnessed an unparalleled attack on expository preaching. At times, the assault was frontal; at other times, surreptitious. The sallies and sorties of her detractors, along with the niggling neglect of her friends, continue unabated. With everything from Harry Emerson Fosdick's 1928 harangue to Fred Craddock's "New Homiletic"; from the Hybel's/Warren's baby boomer "purpose-driven" sermonic church to the "great communicator" gurus Young/Stanley; from the "your-best-life-now" Osteens to the sometimes whacky misadventures of the emerging church; and from Buttrick's broadside to Pagitt's dialogical diatribe, expository preaching has come under attack these days. But somehow expository preaching manages to live on, refusing to give up the ghost. In fact, in some homiletical pockets of Christendom, it is experiencing something of a revival.

Paul Van Gorder, one-time assistant to Richard Dehann, remembers vividly a late-night telephone call his father received. When Van Gorder was a teenager, his father, the local Baptist pastor, received a phone call at 11:00 p.m. on Saturday, July 3, from the local Methodist pastor. It seems the pastor was so excited about his July 4 sermon, but he could not remember the location of the text in the Bible from which he wanted to preach. He wanted to know if he recited the text whether pastor Van Gorder might be able to tell him where to find it in the Bible. "What is the text?" Van Gorder asked. The pastor replied, "Give me liberty or give me death!"

We can at least be grateful the pastor thought he had a text, even if it came from the annals of American liberty and not the Bible. Whatever his sermon turned out to be on the following Sunday morning, it certainly was not "text driven."

What exactly is text-driven preaching? Is this merely another name for expository preaching? In one sense, yes. However, much that goes under the umbrella of exposition today is not really worthy of the name. While there are many books on the subject of preaching, those that promote an expository approach to preaching are few and far between. Of these, many treat the subject in more general and traditional ways. This book rests firmly on the biblical and theological foundation for exposition: God has spoken. God is not silent. He has revealed Himself in Jesus, who is the living Word, and in Scripture, which is the written Word. Therefore, the theological foundation for text-driven preaching is the fact that God has spoken!

It is the nature of Scripture itself that demands a text-driven approach to preaching. God is the ultimate author of all Scripture, according to 2 Tim 3:16 (NKJV): "All Scripture is given by inspiration of God, and is profitable for doctrine, for reproof, for correction, for instruction in righteousness." What Scripture says is indeed the Word of God.

Both the inerrancy and the sufficiency of Scripture serve as the theological ground for text-driven preaching. This is the testimony of Scripture itself. For example, it is interesting how "God" and "Scripture" are used as interchangeable subjects via metonymy when New Testament authors quote the Old Testament. Thus, God is viewed as the author even when He is not the speaker in Matt 19:4–5, and "Scripture says" is used when God Himself is the direct speaker of what is quoted, as in Rom 9:17. In three places, Scripture is called "God's speech" (Gal 3:8,22; Rom 9:17). In the words of J. I. Packer, "Scripture is God preaching."[1]

The best preaching throughout church history has always been expository preaching. Even before the advent of the church, Jewish preaching sought to make plain the meaning of a passage from the Torah. A clear quality of Jewish preaching in the synagogues was its text centeredness. This approach was continued by the apostles as well as by the early church fathers. In the patristic era, Origen, Chrysostom, Augustine, and others show painstaking exegesis and explanation of Scripture in

---

1. J. I. Packer, *God Has Spoken* (Grand Rapids: Baker, 1979), 97.

their preaching. Origen was the first to preach through books of the Bible. During this period, there were different methods of preaching, but there was never a time when exposition was not prized and practiced.

While preaching waned during the Middle Ages (Bernard of Clairvaux was one of the few exceptions), with the Reformation (the sixteenth century) came a recovery of expository preaching. The publication of Erasmus's Greek New Testament, along with other factors, contributed to the Reformers' rediscovery of Scripture in its original language and genuine Bible-centered preaching. Luther, Calvin, and Zwingli preached expositionally. The post-Reformation Puritans continued this heritage. Systematic exposition was practiced often in the churches. From that time of the Reformation until now, the best preaching in the churches has been preaching that is basically expositional in its character and method.

Now if this is the case, how is it that so much of the preaching that cascades over pulpits today is anything but an exposition of a text of Scripture? By what hubris do we think we could possibly have anything more important to say than what God Himself has said through Scripture? It is the height of arrogance to substitute the words of men for the words of God. So much modern-day preaching is horizontal in dimension rather than vertical; that is, it is man-centered preaching that appeals to so-called felt needs rather than what exalts God before the people as the One who alone can meet genuine needs.

The church today is anemic spiritually for many reasons, but one of the major reasons has to be the loss of biblical content in so much of contemporary preaching. Pop-psychology sometimes substitutes for the Word of God. Feel-good messages on "Five Ways to Be Happy" and "Three Ways to Love Your Mother" have become the steady cotton candy diet fed to the average church. Today's sermonic focus therefore is on application. But application, without textual warrant for such, does not "stick"; it needs the glue of textual meaning. Biblical content accordingly must precede application; how else can we possibly know what to apply? Thus, in the headlong rush to be relevant, *People* magazine and popular television shows have replaced Scripture as sermonic resources. There are other signs of this anemia: in some churches, the music portion of the worship service has lengthened, whereas the sermon time has diminished. No wonder so many spiritual teeth are decaying in our churches.

Eloquent nonsense abounds in many pulpits today; sometimes it is not even eloquent. The conjuring adroitness of many preachers who keep producing fat rabbit after fat rabbit out of an obviously empty hat is the marvel of much contemporary preaching. There is mounting evidence that people are beginning to grow weary of these trite pop-psychology sermons. Biblical preaching, especially when it is done in a creative way, will always meet the needs of people, felt or otherwise. In fact, it is our contention that *only* biblical preaching can meet the ultimate spiritual needs of people.

Preaching is a spiritual act. So much of its ultimate effectiveness depends on the role of the Holy Spirit and the spiritual life of the preacher. This topic is often neglected in books on preaching. No one has ever improved on Aristotle's rhetorical triad—*logos*, *pathos*, and *ethos*—as descriptive of the basic elements of powerful and effective communication. This book begins with these matters rather than plunging immediately into the nuts and bolts of the "how-to" of text-driven preaching. Dr. Paige Patterson masterfully outlines for us the Aristotelian triad and explains just how important this is for effective preaching. To give some historical perspective, Jim Shaddix takes us on a brief tour of some of the giants of text-driven preaching in the past. Bill Bennett and Ned Mathews follow up in this vein as well with chapters on the empowering of the Holy Spirit and the spiritual disciplines of a text-driven preacher.

These days it seems everything is "purpose driven." Glossing this valuable concept and applying it to preaching, we believe that true expository preaching should be "text driven." By this, we mean that sermons should not only be based upon a text of Scripture but should also actually expound the meaning of that text. Too often preachers take a text and then straightway depart therefrom in the sermon. The biblical text becomes for many not the source of the sermon but merely a resource. Many a preacher *uses* a text of Scripture, but the sermon that follows is not *derived* from a text of Scripture.

David Allen introduces part 2 with a survey of text-driven preaching's methodology and how that aids sermon preparation. Text-driven sermons deal with the actual structure of the text itself, and thus the role of exegesis, discourse analysis, genre analysis, and contemporary communication theory are explained and illustrated in this work in a practical way. The Bible is not monolithic in its genre or its structure. It contains narrative, poetry, gospels, epistles, and prophecy, among others. Text-driven preaching is not a monolithic, cookie-cutter approach to preaching. This book investigates ways in which the structure of the text should influence the structure of the sermon. Issues such as how a text-driven sermon differs in form and style from a narrative on a New Testament epistle are explored. These matters are taken up and illustrated well by David Black, Robert Vogel, and Herschel York.

Linguists now point out that meaning is structured beyond the sentence level. When the preacher restricts the focus to the sentence level and below, there is much that is missed in the discourse that contributes to its overall meaning and interpretation. The authors of this book believe the paragraph unit is best used as the basic unit of meaning in expounding the text of Scripture. Expositional preaching should at minimum deal with a paragraph (as in the epistles), whereas, in the narrative portions of Scripture, several paragraphs that combine to form the story should be treated in a single sermon since the meaning of the story itself cannot be discerned when it is broken up and presented piecemeal. Bottom line: the structure of the text itself should guide the structure of the sermon, since meaning is expressed by an author through the text itself.

This work also addresses issues of outlining, application, and sermon delivery. Many homiletics books focus more on preparation and devote little space to the importance of application and delivery. No preacher can fail to take account of how he says what he says. The "how" may not be as important as the "what," but it is important. Danny Akin is fond of saying, "What we say is more important than how we say it, but how we say it has never been more important." Jerry Vines takes us into his study and, from the reservoir of his more than 50 years of expositional preaching, teaches us about the delivery of a text-driven sermon. Danny Akin caps it all off with a chapter on the "how-to" of application in a text-driven sermon.

The authors of this book believe the following components are essential to text-driven preaching. First, God has spoken His final word in His Son, Jesus Christ (Heb 1:1–2). Second, because Scripture is authoritative, inerrant, and sufficient, our motto is always *Textus Rex*—"the text is king." Third, as Ned Mathews points out elsewhere,

> The preacher submits to the authority of the text. Therefore, he shuns the reader-response approach of the postmodern hermeneutic which manages the text in such a way that the biblical author's view is replaced by the reader's own perspective. The preacher, as interpreter, to the degree possible in humankind, seeks to empty his presuppositions, biases, and previous conclusions as he approaches the text. His goal is to come to the text, as if for the first time, in order to be instructed by the text rather than to instruct the text.[2]

The authors agree that text-driven preaching is not enslaved to artificial outlining techniques such as a three-point structure and alliteration. Expository preaching is a broad umbrella term that permits a wide variety of styles and structures to communicate the meaning of the text. The text-driven preacher strives to practice exposition, not imposition. Faulty hermeneutical

---

2. In personal correspondence with coeditors David Allen and Danny Akin concerning the need for this book.

methods such as spiritualizing and allegorizing the text are avoided. The preacher's goal is to allow the text to stand forth in all its uniqueness and power. Text-driven preaching is driven by the text, not by theology. Theology serves the text, not the other way around. It is first the text, then theology. Biblical theology therefore precedes systematic theology. Text-driven preachers also believe that creativity ultimately resides in the text itself. The first place to look for creativity to use in preaching is often the last place that many preachers look: the text. All the creativity in the world is of no value if the text itself is neglected, obscured, or ignored in the process of preaching.

The authors of this book are not claiming that only text-driven preaching has these components. Rather, we claim that there cannot be text-driven preaching without these components. A text-driven sermon is a sermon that develops a text by explaining, illustrating, and applying its meaning. Text-driven preaching stays true to the substance of the text, the structure of the text, and the spirit of the text.

Some preachers, instead of expounding the text, skirmish cleverly on its outskirts, pirouetting on trifles to the amazement of the congregation. Text-driven preachers refuse to let the congregation walk away without understanding what God is saying to them through the text. It is in this way that people encounter God. It is not outside of the text of Scripture but *through* the text of Scripture that people encounter God. Jesus said to the disciples on the road to Emmaus, "O foolish men and slow of heart to believe in all that the prophets have spoken! . . . Then beginning with Moses and with all the prophets, He explained to them the things concerning Himself in all the Scriptures" (Luke 24:25–27 NASB).

The authors of this book are committed to helping you fulfill Paul's mandate to Timothy in 2 Tim 4:2 (NKJV): "Preach the Word!"

PART I

THE PREACHER AND TEXT-DRIVEN PREACHING

1

ANCIENT RHETORIC: A MODEL FOR TEXT-DRIVEN PREACHERS

Paige Patterson

Although I recall none of the content of those early sermons, I have been hearing preaching almost from the time of my conception. Charmed, motivated, convinced, convicted, humbled, amused, bored, angered, and exasperated are just a few of the ways I have been affected on this long rhetorical journey. Somewhere on this verbal pilgrimage, I began to evaluate sermons, to compare preachers, and to study methodologies and approaches. Having the unabated confidence of youth mixed with just enough knowledge to confuse a whiff of insight with the taste of perception, I decided that sermons and preachers could be easily assessed. Someone pointed me to Aristotle's canons of rhetoric, and I concluded that I had discovered the prism of discernment.

With maturity came the revelation that Christian preaching was a mystery defying all attempts to bottle any formula for good preaching. First, I observed it in others. A message that to me seemed pedestrian at best, to my astonishment, would appear to be used of God profoundly. On the other hand, an eloquent discourse abounding in insight, wonderfully illustrated, and rich with pregnant metaphor would produce no spiritual energy and little response among the listeners. The latter sometimes engendered a certain admiration, but the former often generated changed lives.

Then, I observed this phenomenon in my own attempts to preach. Often when I thought I had come close to the achievement of preaching a good sermon, little happened of spiritual significance. Then, mystery wrapped in enigma, I would falter and, to my way of thinking, utterly fail, only to witness the mighty hand of God at work. I learned that it is "not by might nor by power, but by My Spirit, says the LORD" (Zech 4:6 NKJV). I can only conclude that the greatest failure in preaching and in books on preaching is the failure to invoke the anointing of God on the preacher and his message. Minus this touch, the preacher may achieve eloquence, but his message will never be like a two-edged sword, "piercing even to the division of soul and spirit," and become "a discerner of the thoughts and intents of the heart" (Heb 4:12). Only God can affect that, and He often does so through paltry human examples.

Leaving a famous church one Sunday morning, I encountered a godly saint who had been sitting nearby as we were immersed in the eloquence of the new preacher. "Now that was a great speech," my friend opined. He meant no uncharitable criticism. He simply gave a startling testimony on the effect of the preacher's sermon. In the process, this perennial occupier of pews taught me afresh the most important lesson of Homiletics 101, namely, that great oratory does not necessarily translate into effective preaching. Arduous human effort and critical, rhetorical assessment count for little when the needs of the human heart are addressed by a man of God bringing the prophetic, inspired word of God.

To recognize that another—indeed the most critical—dimension lies beyond human artifice is not to conclude that one is justified in abandoning preparation—academic and spiritual—or assessment. Consequently, a serious preacher will contemplate his art just as ardently as any other artist but with full knowledge that if he is faithful and true, he can anticipate the intervention of God, which is largely unknown to the practice of rhetorical arts in any profession or era.

This chapter recognizes that the ancients who first brooded over the art of rhetoric provide contemporary preachers priceless insights into the art of effective public declamation. Armed with these insights, a faithful man of God labors under the promised guidance of the Holy Spirit to form the text into instruction and inspiration for the people of God. Now, like Elijah on Carmel, he must pray for the fire to fall. Elijah's altar was doubtless well constructed and all preparations carefully considered. But when the moment of truth came, Elijah understood from whence fire would fall and called on God, who alone could answer from heaven.

This chapter will now consider what can be learned from the ancients about good "altar construction." However, one must not forget that the fire fall comes only from God. Nevertheless, good altars have value, and this value the preacher must seek.

RHETORIC AND DEMOCRACY

The city-state network of the Hellenistic world depended on a participatory society in which citizens exercised greater influence than could ever be the case in monarchies. Essential to such budding democracy was communication. And since perspectives differ, the ability to convey one's view effectively became a substantive value.

Classical rhetoric began and always remained primarily a system of training young men how to speak effectively in a court of law; and it was developed for the needs of participatory democracy, especially in Athens. Under the Athenian

democracy, reaching its most radical form in the fifth and
fourth centuries BCE, there was no public prosecutor and
there were no professional lawyers; criminal indictments,
like civil suits, were brought by an interested person. In both
criminal and civil cases, prosecutor and defendant were ordi-
narily expected to speak on their own behalf, though if they
were unable to do so an advocate could speak for them. Since
women were not allowed to speak in court, they had to be
represented by a male family member. Any evidence of witnesses was taken down in writing before the trial and read
out by a clerk, and prosecutor and defendant were expected
to deliver a carefully planned speech, without interruption
by the court. There was no presiding judge to ask questions,
interpret the law, or establish relevance, only a clerk to organize proceedings; both fact and law were judged by a panel of
jurors (*dikastai*) numbering at least 201 and, in some major
cases, several thousand persons, chosen by lot from among
male citizens. To make an effective case before such large
juries required considerable rhetorical skill and confidence.[1]

According to John Henry Freese, the island of Sicily is the
birthplace of rhetoric.[2] After the expulsion of tyrants from Syra-
cuse (467 BC), returning exiles made claims for recovery of
property and made use of skilled orators to argue their cases.
On the other hand, Aristotle focuses on Empedocles, whose
pupil was said to be Gorgias, a famous rhetor. Plato uses the
word *rhētorikē* in Gorgias (385 BC).[3] Regardless of origins,
by the time Aristotle wrote his *Art of Rhetoric* (c. 330 BC) in
Athens, the practice of rhetoric was a *known* and, to some, a
respected part of the life of the cities. Reputations were made or
at least sustained through the use of rhetoric and discussions
about its nature and use. Cicero (106–43 BC), Quintilian (30–
100 BC), Demosthenes (384–322 BC), Isocrates (436–338 BC),

1. T. O. Sloane, ed., *Encyclopedia of Rhetoric* (Oxford: Oxford University Press, 2001), 94.
2. J. H. Freese, *Aristotle XXII; Art of Rhetoric* (Cambridge, MA: Harvard University Press, 1926), xii.
3. Sloane, *Encyclopedia of Rhetoric*, 94.

Anaximenes (588 BC), and Aristotle are just a few of the participants in this art. Demosthenes had few natural abilities and overcame serious handicaps in order to excel,[4] whereas Hermogenes of Tarsus (AD 160–230) had by age 15 already "achieved such mastery of the art of oratory that he aroused the admiration of the emperor Marcus Aurelius with his declamations and improvised lectures."[5]

Not everyone in the ancient world or since that time has been a fan of rhetoric. Wayne Booth, in his excellent volume *The Rhetoric of Rhetoric*, mentions the opposition voiced in Plato's *Phaedrus* by Socrates, who scolded the Sophists by commenting, "He who would be a skillful rhetorician has no need of truth." Booth then cites a typical definition of rhetoric, which he says "concentrates on the pejorative."

> Rhetoric: n. the theory and practice of eloquence, whether spoken or written, the whole art of using language to persuade others; false, showy, artificial, or declamatory expression; rhetorical: oratorical; inflated, over-decorated, or insincere in style; rhetorical question: a question in form, for rhetorical effect, not calling for an answer.[6]

Doubtless, the objective of ancient rhetoric was to persuade. The fact that the issue was neither truth nor accuracy does not, however, render the art valueless for the preacher. To the contrary, if the preacher is armed with the truth of God, then the art of rhetoric becomes a tool for righteousness in his hands. Nazi physicians' misuse and abuse of the scalpel did not render scalpels morally suspect. In addition to the logic of that conclusion is the example of Paul, who regularly sought to "persuade" his listeners (Acts 13:43; 18:4; 19:8; 26:28; 28:23; 2 Cor 5:11). The

---

4. *Encyclopedia Britannica* (Chicago: William Benton, 1768), 229.
5. H. Cancik et al., eds., *Brill's New Pauly Encyclopedia of the Ancient World* (Leiden, The Netherlands; Boston: Brill Academic, 2005), 6:224.
6. W. C. Booth, *The Rhetoric of Rhetoric* (Malden, MA: Blackwell, 2004), x.

preacher's task is to persuade sinners to repent and to believe the saving gospel of Jesus, the Christ. He is to exhort (a form of persuasion) the saints to continue to follow Christ, to maintain orthodox views, to love the brethren, to be morally and ethically pure, among other things.

Robert L. Dabney first published his *Sacred Rhetoric* in 1870. Dabney notes the importance of speech:

> The gift of speech is the most obvious attribute which distinguishes man from the brutes. To him, language is so important a handmaid of his mind in all its processes that we remain uncertain how many latent faculties, which we are now prone to deny to the lower animals, may not be lying inactive in them, because of their privation of this medium. It is speech which makes us really social beings; without it our instinctive attraction to our fellows would give us, not true society, but the mere gregariousness of the herds. It is by speech that the gulf is bridged over, which insulates each spirit from others. This is the great communicative faculty which establishes a communion between men in each other's experience, reasoning, wisdom, and affections. These familiar observations are recalled to your view, in order to suggest how naturally and even necessarily oral address must be employed in the service of religion. If man's religious and social traits are regarded, we cannot but expect to find a wise God, from the beginning, consecrate His gift of speech to the end of propagating sacred knowledge and sentiments.[7]

In fact, the ancients and their contributions to rhetoric provide much grist for the preacher's mill. One can learn the value of avoiding long, unbroken narrative from Demosthenes. The infrequent but masterful use of metaphor can be grasped here also. Quintilian's emphasis on the building of the speaker's character as well as his intellect is essential for the preacher. Cicero's canons of rhetoric are invaluable to the preacher.

---

7. R. L. Dabney, *Sacred Rhetoric, or a Course of Lectures on Preaching* (Chatham: W&J Mackay Limited, 1870), 20–21.

Anaximenes championed extemporaneous speaking, an art that may be observed in many gifted preachers. Space limitations preclude such extensive forays into the literature and practices of famous rhetoricians. Rather, the focus here will be on the three famous rhetorical means of persuasion provided by Aristotle in his *Art of Rhetoric*. These, in order of consideration for the preacher, are *ethos, logos*, and *pathos*. Although there are a number of good methods to assess the value of a sermon, my thesis is that, from the point of view of simplicity and yet sufficient comprehension to cover the matter, these three canons of rhetoric, though born in a pagan context, are both adequate and remarkably serviceable. We turn to this consideration.

Ethos

Aristotle's simple definition of rhetoric is the launchpad for this discussion. "Rhetoric then may be defined as the faculty of discovering the possible means of persuasion in reference to any subject whatever."[8]

Books I and II of the volume *Art of Rhetoric* focus on the subject of *dianoia* or thought. The *Oxford Encyclopedia of Rhetoric* calls this rhetorical invention, the counterpart to *dialectic*. Rhetoric concerns itself with particular cases, whereas *dialectic* addresses general issues.[9] In Books I and II, Aristotle describes the nature of "rhetorical invention."

> Means of persuasion are either nonartistic—laws, witnesses, contracts, or oaths, used but not invented by the speaker—or artistic, the invention of the speaker. Artistic means of persuasion take three forms, which have come to be known as ethos, the presentation of the character of the speaker as a person to be trusted; pathos, the emotions of the audience as

---

8. Freese, *Art of Rhetoric*, 15.
9. Generally, in dialectic the focus is on issues that are not in need of proof, whereas rhetoric addresses issues that need to be proven or believed.

stirred by the speaker; and logos, logical argument based on evidence and probability.[10]

Elsewhere in this book, attention is devoted to the non-artistic means of persuasion, though not necessarily with that nomenclature. This chapter will focus on the artistic means of persuasion, since these are too often neglected in text-driven preaching. Aristotle presents these three: "Now the proofs furnished by the speech are of three kinds. The first depends upon the moral character of the speaker, the second upon putting the hearer into a certain frame of mind, the third upon the speech itself, in so far as it proves or seems to prove."[11]

The first of these "artistic" demonstrations can be termed *ethos*, the moral character of the speaker. Aristotle observes that when a speaker delivers a speech in such a manner that he is thought worthy of confidence, such an impact is greater than the sum of other aspects of the declaration.[12] For Aristotle, this *ethos* must arise from the speech itself rather than from preconceived ideas about the speaker. While this may sometimes be the case, a "small world technology" of the modern era increasingly adds significance or credibility to a contemporary speaker. But we may certainly agree with the conclusion of the sage when he declares, "Moral character, so to say, constitutes the most effective means of proof."[13] Such virtues as justice, courage, self-control, magnanimity, magnificence, goodness, goodwill, liberality, gentleness, and both practical and speculative wisdom are among the virtues extolled. "Virtue, it would seem, is a faculty of providing and preserving good things, a faculty productive of many and great benefits, in fact, of all things in all cases."[14]

10. Sloane, *Encyclopedia of Rhetoric*, 99.
11. Freese, *Art of Rhetoric*, 17.
12. Ibid.
13. Ibid.
14. Ibid., 91.

When the preacher begins his message, the auditors tend to make instantaneous judgments about him and, therefore, to some degree, about his message also. Listeners, for example, may decide almost instantly whether they think the preacher will be boring or interesting. The preacher lacks experience to know that of which he speaks. His training is apparently quite limited. He is bombastic but not very profound. He is a salesman, and I would never buy a "previously owned" automobile from him. All of these judgments relate to the credibility of the preacher. As the message continues and reaches a conclusion, congregants continue verifying or revising those initial judgments.

Factors establishing credibility are too many for this chapter, but the subject can be approached under two basic categories: preparation and character. Preparation entails both tangible and intangible factors. Three will be mentioned here.

The Preacher's Walk with God

Although no one is party to the private devotions of the preacher, the Scriptures are often eloquent in their note of genuine men of God. In 2 Kgs 4:9 (NKJV), the Shunammite woman tells her husband, "I know that this is a holy man of God, who passes by us," and suggests that a room be added for his visits. Of Stephen, it is observed that when they looked at his face, it was "as the face of an angel" (Acts 6:15). Moses found himself forced to veil his face because of the radiance of God's presence reflected thereon (Exod 34:29–33).

To walk with God is to study His character, meditate on His words, search for His purpose, and converse with Him in prayer. The more one walks with God, marinates his messages in the presence of Jesus, and seeks the guidance of the Holy Spirit in both life and message, the more obvious it becomes to people of discernment that the preacher is a messenger straight from the throne room of the Lord. No single factor is more compelling than a challenge from a man who apparently walks closely with God. When the radiance of heaven is discernible in the messenger's life and face, even those outside of Christ are frequently touched. God can certainly use a dirty vessel because the gospel remains true regardless of the failure of preachers. But God's delight assuredly is in the effective blessings upon the labor of a pure and holy vessel, and He is under no constraint to bring anything other than judgment regarding soiled vessels.

Venturing into the unthinkable in a casual age, even dress is part of *ethos*. Formal dress has never been a personal joy for me. I am happier in my jeans, boots, western shirt, and hat. Moreover, informal ways seem to me less likely to become pretentious than the more stately and formal. Even though I have come to admire a pretty tie, I still suspect that the inventor of such an article was probably hanged by a tie by those forced to wear one. All of this notwithstanding, the casual dress of so many ministers may say more than they intend. If invited to the Oval Office by the president, my hunch is that most preachers would don their best, short of a tux. Yet when appearing before God or His people, some pay little respect to either. Now I want to make clear that not all occasions or contexts call for formal dress. The world of the cross-cultural missionary (whether internationally or in North America) immediately leaps to mind. The issue for the minister is one of honor and respect for God, whom he represents before the people. The preacher always should show respect for Christ and His church—at the very least, the same respect he would deem appropriate for dignitaries of the world. Otherwise, his *ethos* will also suffer.

The Preacher's Study

Listeners do not have to persevere long to ascertain whether the minister has done his homework. If the preacher has grappled with the passage until he understands it, he will be able to stake out the significance of the text and apply it fruitfully to the assembly. If the preacher struggles to make the text come to life, seems confused by portions of the text, or is clearly unaware of its possibilities, the public will rapidly discern his inadequacy to expound the biblical message. Often-used and dated illustrations and dependence on the work of other well-known ministers will quickly erode the *ethos* of the man of God. There is no substitute for spiritual preparation, and failure in rigorous study is surely a sin second only to the failure to prepare spiritually. Arduous study is simply not optional. Paul, in 2 Tim 2:15, demands the following of the young pastor: "Be diligent to present yourself approved to God, a worker who does not need to be ashamed, rightly dividing the word of truth." The verb *diligent* is the translation of the Greek term *spoudazō*, a vivid concept of giving oneself zealously to be an unashamed worker, unashamed because he has learned rightly to divide the word of truth. The vast majority of preachers in the contemporary era are unaware of the obligatory nature of rigorous study of God's Word.

The Preacher's Observable Life

Drugstore cowboys have cowboy hats, boots, and jeans. One might even have a rope or a saddle. He may talk about the ranch and even spout *cowography*, but put him on a horse and in less than a nanosecond you will discover that he is, though looks are to the contrary, not a cowboy. The preacher may be eloquent, dress professionally, have appropriate credentials, and know his way around the ministerial world. But if his life fails to magnify what he preaches, his *ethos* will vanish like the dew of the grass under the gaze of the midmorning sun.

Paul's instructions to Timothy (1 Tim 3:1–7; Titus 1:5–9) regarding the character and qualification of elders emphasize the exemplary demands for the preacher-teacher. In 1 Tim 4:12 the apostle encourages his youthful disciple, "Let no one despise your youth, but be an example to the believers in word, in conduct, in love, in spirit, in faith, in purity." All these instructions for the young minister focus on a life open to the gaze of the saints and, for that matter, the observing world. In so doing, the preacher establishes credibility or *ethos*, which lends credibility to his message.

A preacher's response to anger, misrepresentation, judgment of motives, abuse, unkindness, and so on are verification or falsification of his exhortations. The chasteness of his language and life, the comparison of his life and actions, and the affections of his heart either add vitality to his sermons or else sap them of holy energy. The sanctity of his union with his wife and the joy of wise and faithful parenthood render his pleas from the pulpit doubly persuasive. Godly *ethos* is thus established. The character of the preacher may lie beyond the observatory abilities of the parishioner but will not, thereby, escape such conclusions. At least two factors will be at play here.

Respect for Auditors

The saints make judgments about speakers just as speakers evaluate the congregation. One of the first observations will focus on whether the speaker shows respect for the audience.

Because contemporary preachers are so acclimated to sizing up the audience, they tend to forget that the same process is happening in reverse. Here are some of the questions being asked, mostly unconsciously, about the preacher's respect for the listener. Does he think I am a child with his firm affirmation of the obvious or his constant repetition? Why is he browbeating me? Is he attempting to impress me with all those sesquipedalian words? Oh, my! You would think he would at least find a new illustration. I have only been a Christian for two years, and I have heard that one six times. He is just here for a big offering. He is entertaining, but he is wasting my time because there are superior entertainers on television. Any analysis of the speaker's *ethos* includes an assessment of whether his character is such that he can respect the assembly, even if he disagrees with most or all of them.

Possession of Virtues

The basic attributes of honesty, integrity, and justice make up the primary armor for a great preacher. I once asked my father for his impression of George W. Truett, far-famed pastor of the First Baptist Church of Dallas, Texas, from 1897 to 1944: "Truett, in retrospect, was not a great preacher," he replied. Continuing, he added, "But he was a man of such unparalleled integrity that you were awed almost as if in the presence of God." That is *ethos*. Of another famous preacher, I once heard it said in a Texas way: "He is as strong as goat's breath, but, you know, he is always so painstakingly fair." This is justice. Or again, someone said adroitly about my own father, "Have you noticed that all of his illustrations are apparently true?" While this was a fine observation of Dad's *ethos*, I sometimes shudder when I think about what the statement implied about preachers in general. In commentaries it is not unusual to find a section in the introduction on the integrity of the text. But if the preacher's *ethos* does not merit a similar trust, the message of the text may be broken apart on the slippery racks of character flaws in the speaker.

Logos

Logos references the speech or sermon itself. The concept of *logos* boasts philosophical roots stretching to the virgin days of Greek thought. B. G. Kerford observes,

> Earlier attempts to trace a logical progression of meanings in the history of the word are now generally acknowledged to lack any secure foundation, and even to try to trace out the history of a single "logos doctrine" in Greek philosophy is to run the risk of searching for a simple pattern when the truth was much more complex. But the extreme importance of the

"logos doctrines" of different thinkers is clear, and there certainly were relationships between the ways in which successive thinkers used the term.[15]

Kerford goes on to comment that the *logos* doctrine of Hereclitus was both famous and obscure, combining the three ideas of human thought about the universe, the rational structure of the universe, and the source of that rational structure. *Logos*, he says, was for the Sophists both arguments and what arguments were about, whereas for Stoics, *logos* was the principle of all rationality and as such often identified with God. Of course, from *logos* comes the English term "logic," and the extent of the influence of the word may be observed by its frequency in taxonomy of sciences—geology, psychology, sociology, biology, zoology, and so on—or in the categories of theology such as hamartiology or ecclesiology.

For the Christian, the importance of the concept is located in the *logia tou theou*, the "oracles of God" (Rom 3:2). Here words are more than mere terms. The Bible constitutes the very utterances of God. Even more fascinating is the Johannine employment of the idea to express the mysteries of the preexistence of Christ, His deity, and His incarnation. In the prologue to John's Gospel, "In the beginning was the *logos*, the *logos* was with God, and the *logos* was God" (John 1:1). Again, "the *logos* became flesh and dwelt among us" (John 1:14). This is sufficient to demonstrate that both in the writings of the Greek philosophers and in the Greek New Testament, *logos* was a term of significance.

Recent advocates of narrative preaching are unsure about this *logos*. David Buttrick says, "So the Bible offers meaning—not in every little passage; some Bible passages may be largely irrelevant or even sub-Christian—the Bible offers meaning by handing out a story with a beginning and an end and, in between, a narrative understanding of how God may interface

---

15. B. G. Kerford, "Logos," in *Encyclopedia of Philosophy*, vols. 5 & 6 (New York: Macmillan, 1967), 83.

with our sinful humanity."[16] The case is actually even worse. Buttrick discloses, "There is no pure gospel; no, not even in the Bible! To be blunt, the Christian scriptures are both sexist and anti-Semitic."[17] There is no *logia tou theou*—just religious testimony, much of which is in error. Buttrick and others have given away the farm. They have jettisoned the gospel. If we have no certain word from God to expound, then listening to CNN or Fox, depending on one's preference, will prove more entertaining than preachers and just as compelling.

When one asks about the *logos* of a particular sermon, he is inquiring about its logic as well as its content. As to the logic of a message, one asks first, does the message make sense? This is not just a broad, general query but rather an attempt to ascertain whether the message has thoughtful purpose, orderly progression, and convincing conclusion. Does it "hang together" and is the purpose clear and powerful? Are there apparent or actual contradictions in the sermon; and if there are intentional paradoxes, are these defended at least regarding the rationale for leaving matters unresolved? Do the propositions, postulates, points (whatever you wish to call them) follow logically and develop the overall theme, or are they unrelated to each other and tangential to the text?

Not so many moons have passed since a great preacher, in the process of preparing for a conference on preaching, placed this intriguing query before me: "Who are the great Bible preachers today?" He was not searching for preachers who had texts but for texts that had preachers! As Jeff Ray so poignantly stated the matter,

> I know that genuine expository preaching is almost as rare as the once multitudinous buffalo on our Texas prairies. If you

---

16. D. Buttrick, *A Captive Voice: The Liberation of Preaching* (Louisville: Westminster/John Knox, 1994), 17.
17. Ibid., 75.

ask me why, I can tell you. I found it not in a book nor by observation of other preachers. I found it out by personal, practical experience. When I am to make a sermon, I have found it an easy job, quickly performed, to deduce a topic and dress it up in platitudinous superficialities and palm it off as a message from the Word of God. But I have found it difficult, laborious, and time-consuming to dig out an adequate interpretation of a passage of Scripture and coordinate the results of that patient digging in an effective, logical outline. Because I have allowed so many little "higglety-pigglety" inconsequential enterprises to break in on my time, I have felt it necessary to follow the line of least resistance and thus have I, and doubtless thus have you, formed the habit of preparing mainly topical sermons. I am an "old dog" now and they tell me that it is hard to teach an antiquated canine a new trick, but I say to you solemnly that if I could call back fifty years, I should make it a life's ambition to be a real expositor of the Word rather than a rhetorical declaimer on topics and mottos.[18]

Slavish adherence to what is generally termed "exposition" is not the concern. Learning three conventional categories of sermons—topical, textual, and expository—is a helpful discipline. Particularly, exposition should be mastered in its classical form. However, the concern here is not that the preacher always selects an extended text, taking all major "points" and subheadings from that text. My own conclusion is that good preaching consists in helping people to read the Bible. A preacher may be a persuasive orator; but if only that, how is he superior to Greek rhetoricians? On the other hand, as a Bible preacher, the text-driven prophet explains, illustrates, and applies the text. The pericope under scrutiny ought to have much in common with Ezekiel's dry bones. The skeletal parts sort themselves out and come together. Sinew, ligament, and skin cover what is still merely a corpse until the refreshing gusts of the presence

---

18. J. Ray, *Expository Preaching* (Grand Rapids: Zondervan, 1940), 81–82.

of the Spirit vivify the sermon, and the words of the text leap from the pages of Holy Writ to electrify the hearts of listeners.

Too many contemporary practitioners of the homiletical art are bored with the task. They fret about what they will preach next Sunday, and somewhere in the hidden recesses of the soul they know their messages are vacuous—sound and fury about little more than human opinion and pop psychology. As the inimitable Spurgeon cautioned, "Estimated by their solid contents rather than their superficial area, many sermons are very poor specimens of godly discourse . . . verbiage is too often the fig leaf which does duty as a covering for theological ignorance."[19] Others seem actually to enjoy themselves as they engage merrily in homiletical dog-paddling on the religious surface, whereas the beauty of the depths is neither discovered by the preacher nor exhibited to the saints and sinners who have come to hear from God but too often depart having only been entertained. As a scuba diver, I can assure you that however intriguing you may find the breakers and horizons of the ocean surface, the radiance of the coral reef, the majesty of the effortless "wings" of the manta ray, and the sheer magnitude of the whale shark, together with the other mysteries of the depths, far exceed the surface.

The sermon should be the crowning moment of the preacher's week. Spurgeon said,

> Draw a circle around my pulpit, and you have hit upon the spot where I am nearest heaven. There the Lord has been more consciously near me than anywhere else. He has enraptured my heart while I have been trying to cheer and comfort His mourners. Many of you can say the same of your pew where you like to sit. It has been a Bethel to you, and the Lord Jesus has revealed Himself to you in the midst of His people.[20]

---

19. C. H. Spurgeon, *Lectures to My Students* (Grand Rapids: Zondervan, 1972), 71–72.
20. C. H. Spurgeon, *The Mourner's Comforter* (Columbia, MD: Opine, 2007), 110.

Ezra pioneered text-based preaching, reading the Torah to the great congregation (Hb. *qāhāl*) from a pulpit, whereas Levitical preachers "explained the law to the people as they stood in their places" and gave them the meaning (Neh 8:1–12 HCSB). Predictably, when the *logos* was explained, the people first wept over their sins and then rejoiced about God's grace and forgiveness and then celebrated the whole event with "dinner on the grounds" (Neh 8:10–12). Most contemporary preaching seems still to inspire the potluck dinner, but *logos*-light proclamation produces little repentance and consequently a paucity of either gratitude to God or joy.

A similar event is captured by an observant physician who rehearsed a breathtaking stroll shortly after the resurrection of Jesus. Joining the two morose disciples journeying to Emmaus, Luke notes that "beginning at Moses and all the Prophets, He [Jesus] expounded to them in all the Scriptures the things concerning Himself" (Luke 24:27 NKJV). The word translated "expounded" (Gk. *diermēneusin*) is at the root of the English word "hermeneutics." *Hermēnuō* is related to *Hermes*, the messenger of the gods, whose dubious mythological responsibilities included clarifying the sentiments of the gods to humans—and to each other! *Hermes* was needed because sometimes these capricious gods were not on speaking terms with one another.

Jesus explained Moses and the prophets (which together make up the Hebrew canon) in a Christological way—a model for all genuinely Christian preaching. There were two measurable results. First, the *logos* of the preaching of the eternal *logos* set their "hearts ablaze" (Luke 24:32). Only *logos*-based preaching has much of a chance to produce this effect. Second, the two wayfarers returned to Jerusalem and excitedly shared their experience with the risen Lord (Luke 24:33–35). *Logos*-based (text-based) preaching will generate hearts ablaze and chronic witness.

Concerning the content of the message itself, one must determine first whether the preacher has understood the text and grasped his subject. A biblical preacher must not only comprehend the broad purpose of his text, as well as other insights available about the text, but he must also have a sufficient theological comprehension and an above-average grasp of the Bible as a whole to set his text properly in the theological milieu. Great preachers are cognizant of the necessity to be able to do exegesis and exposition within a historical setting of which they are constantly aware. How little actual grasp of scriptural knowledge is present in most North American preachers is reflected in the relative biblical illiteracy and theological misapprehensions of most congregations.

Now, the listener might ask himself, am I learning as a result of this sermon? Am I not only growing in my knowledge of the text itself, but am I also developing in my own abilities "rightly to divide the word of truth"? And, finally, is what is being proclaimed here of any substantive significance for life and eternity? If these questions can be positively answered, then the preacher's *logos* is probably far above average.

Pathos

In the New Testament documents, *pathos* often appears as a descriptive word for the vileness of sin (Gal 5:24; Rom 7:5). But Michaelis notes that the word has positive meanings (2 Cor 1:5; 1:7) and is essentially neutral in its history. He suggests that the central motif of *pathos* is "experience."[21] Liddell and Scott, in their monumental lexicon of classical Greek, confirm this judgment, even though their first meaning suggested is "that which happens to a person or thing."[22] Eventually, almost all lexicographers get around to the more commonly accepted meaning of

---

21. W. Michaelis, *"sphazō," TDNT* 7:926–30.
22. H. G. Liddell and R. Scott, comp., *A Greek-English Lexicon* (London: Oxford University Press, 1966), 1285.

"emotion." Whenever most people think of *pathos*, emotion is likely the understanding evoked. In Aristotle, the intent seems to be to evoke emotion in the listener. But this can seldom be achieved without *pathos* in the preacher.

For the purpose of estimating the effectiveness of the sermon, Acts 1:3 may be the best text to assist in ascertaining the most helpful meaning of the word. Here the Bible reads, "To whom He also presented himself alive after His passion [Gk. *pathein*] by many infallible proofs." Here the word clearly references the suffering of Jesus in His atoning death. The idea of experience or what happens to a person is at the base of this suffering. But the "passion" of Christ was not passive. Cries from the cross, added to those of Gethsemane, are evidences of a purposeful and passionate plan that motivated Jesus to pursue this course. His purpose "to give His life a ransom for many" (Mark 10:45) was expressed vividly and often. He said, "But I have a baptism to be baptized with, and how am I straitened until it be accomplished!" (Luke 12:50). The Greek word (*sunechō*) translated "straitened" in this text literally means "constrained, held prisoner, or hemmed in." The baptism Jesus faced was His passion.

This passion, this constraint that motivated Jesus to move toward the cross, is close to what is intended by *pathos* in preaching. Jesus was not out of control. Emotions and sentiments did not drive Him. He was "emotional" but only in a way totally engaged with His mental and spiritual understandings. Thus the cross was not just suffering, whether physical, emotional, or spiritual. The atonement was a purposeful, thoughtful, determined, but highly motivated, even passionate, act of supreme sacrifice. *Pathos* captures in part the understanding of what Jesus did at Calvary. And this in turn assists us in comprehending *pathos* in preaching.

Pathos may then be defined as passion in preaching. The preacher is not simply making a speech. He is not making a living. If there were no compensation, he would still preach because "woe is me if I do not preach the gospel" (1 Cor 9:16). The eternal destinies of men and women are at stake every time he preaches. The ability to cope with life and to find meaning and happiness constitutes the fabric of his preaching; and he is driven, knowing the difference that obedience to the truth of God can generate. Like Jeremiah, there will be times when the preacher, because of his own humanity, will not want to speak for God; but he will find that God's word is a fire in his bones and he cannot remain silent (Jer 20:9).

Throughout my own life, I have been the recipient of the goodness of God so far beyond what I ever could have dreamed. I have traveled extensively and attempted almost everything I ever dreamed. But without reservation, I can report that opening the Word of the Lord for an assembled congregation, expounding the text, and pleading for the souls of men are not only my favorite activities in life but also the passions of my soul. If passion or *pathos* is not deeply ingrained in the preacher's message, even if his content is good and his life credible, his listeners may well conclude that whatever does not grip the preacher's soul may not be particularly important.

A major key to *pathos* is learning to live in the text until the text comes to life in the preacher's heart. Doing one's homework in the lexicon, commentary, and other sources is critical; but having completed the academic task, armed with his grasp of meaning and possibilities, the preacher must now transport himself to the world and environment of the text. He has to join the troops and march around the walls of Jericho. Or he must tag-team with Jacob at the river Jabbok and wrestle with God until he enters the pulpit walking with a limp. He has to sit on a Galilean hillside and watch in startled amazement as Jesus breaks a few chunks of bread and a few small fishes, and the more He breaks, the more there is. In a didactic text, he has to get inside the mind of Paul as the apostle pens Romans and imagine himself chained beside him in the Mamertine Prison as Paul writes 2 Timothy. The Apocalypse will leap to life with incredible *pathos* if the preacher can make a mental journey to Patmos, that rock quarry in the Aegean Sea, and witness the visions of the beloved disciple.

Pathos grows naturally from living in the text, from the sacredness of the assignment, and from the awareness of potential for temporal and eternal transformation in the lives of the hearers. These three elements operate together to produce a holy anticipation of high-stakes adventure in the preacher. Finding lion and cape buffalo in Africa, diving with the sharks in the Andaman Sea, or, as a boy, preparing for a big football game under the lights, the adrenaline rush, the adventure, the awareness of high drama and higher stakes—these have always thrilled my soul. But in many sacred occasions, all of these have been subordinated to the drama of opening the Word of God and watching with awe as the Holy Spirit opened the hearts of people to the Lord. There is nothing in life to parallel this adventure.

One should also note that the ability to illustrate cogently may assist not only in the *logos* of the message but also with the *pathos* of the sermon. Illustrations serve several important functions. They give brief respite to the listeners in which the mind relaxes for a moment from following the *logos* of the sermon. Appropriately selected illustrations constitute another way of illuminating the *logos*, since they often provide concrete examples of what is otherwise abstract truth. The best sources for illustrative material are the narrative portions of Scripture. The Bible itself declares this to be the case. "Now all these things happened to them as examples, and they were written for our admonition, upon whom the ends of the ages have come" (1 Cor 10:11). While the preacher must be careful not to overuse personal and family anecdotes, these, nevertheless, make it easy for the auditors to find common ground and, hence, comprehension of vital truth. Integrity in the use of the preacher's own experiences is also critical and ties to the subject of the minister's *ethos*.

Another source of illustration develops from the broad, extensive reading that hopefully composes the regimen of the preacher. Biography and history are the most productive areas for mining illustrative gems. Wide reading with a view to illustration as well as to the general acquisition of knowledge and wisdom is crucial for anyone who takes seriously the preaching task. A system may be designed to store these nuggets for the moment of need. Great preachers are almost always good storytellers, and my father always insisted that the better preachers boasted some of the abilities of the actor as well. Both of these skills are important, but the preacher must remember that he does not have the luxury of untruthful embellishment without the sacrifice of credibility.

What about show and tell? The contemporary church is the era of PowerPoint, big screens, minidramas, and other artifice. These are more often used by that genre of preachers who are less concerned with the text than by those whose purpose is to explain the text. This is unfortunate. Every honest means for assisting in the successful launch, flight, and landing of the text-driven preacher is not only acceptable but also desirable. However, when the use of such artifice becomes monotonous, predictable, or the essence of the message, its legitimacy is sacrificed. Too often, contemporary pulpiteers use such devices as a substitute for significant *logos* or for the incarnational and prophetic mandate achieved by a genuine man of God whose *ethos* is unquestioned. But as illustrations of the teachings of the Bible, such tools in the hand of the preacher become the scalpel and sutures of his profession of spiritual healing. Of course, entertainment for its own sake is never the purpose of the Christian preacher.

As a part of the process of *pathos*, though also essential to *logos*, application and exhortation are likewise the preacher's tasks. If the preacher assumes that the lesson is complete without concrete application, he assumes too much. The bridge from the text to applications to the *Sitz im Leben* of the congregation is a vital part of both *logos* and *pathos* in preaching. Otherwise, the proclaimer may well have expounded the truth of Scripture, bringing the congregation to view the promised land on the far bank but leaving them with Moses at Nebo rather than revealing how to cross Jordan and arrive in the land.

Exhortation is a crucial aspect of Christian preaching. *Pathos* is primary in exhortation, though *logos* and *ethos* figure prominently as well. Paul insisted that Timothy "preach the word! Be ready in season and out of season. Convince, rebuke, *exhort*, with all longsuffering and teaching" (2 Tim 4:2). This also was Peter's practice: "And with many other words he testified and *exhorted* them saying, 'Be saved from this perverse generation'" (Acts 2:40). Judas and Silas "*exhorted* and strengthened the brethren with many words" (Acts 15:32).[23] "Exhort" is a translation of the Greek *parakaleō*, meaning "to call to one's side." My own favorite translation betrays my revivalist and evangelistic background, but I translate the word as "extending an invitation or appeal." Pleading for the souls of men or consistently pleading for believers to follow the Lord should be the climax of every text-driven sermon. Extending this appeal must use *pathos* in its primary nuance of "passion," though controlled emotion is not thereby excluded.

CONCLUSION

A surface observation might adjudicate the preaching enterprise as essentially simple. A man stands before an assembled body and gives testimony to the grace of God. But if the man of God wants to make an optimal presentation, if he wishes to advance mere talk to an art of preaching, then he recognizes that he must begin with his own life. In fact, Paul warned about making an elder of a "novice" because lacking a life of experience and testimony, such a one would be more likely to be "puffed up with pride" and "fall into the same condemnation as the devil" (1 Tim 3:6). Armed with a credible and saintly life, which renders the preacher "above reproach" (1 Tim 3:2 ESV), the servant of the Lord is now prepared to travail in study until the sermon based on the text is formed in his mind and heart.

---

23. See also Acts 11:23, 14:22, and 20:2 for additional uses of *parakaleō* in the apostolic community.

Having prepared arduously, the prophet opens the Word of God to the people. Text-based preaching or exposition is the only really appropriate form of Christian preaching. This is true because the preacher is to be an "able teacher" (1 Tim 3:2 HCSB). However, this is also the case because if God has spoken on any issue, is it not ultimate chutzpah for the preacher to substitute even the noblest of human formulations for the thoughts and utterances of God? And if God did not address the subject, then why would the preacher's choice of subject be more important than the subject that God has chosen to address? After all, is the preacher a servant of the world or is he a spokesman for God? With *ethos* established, the preacher now explains the *logos* of the will and purpose of God in Holy Scripture.

One would hope this task is pursued with *pathos*, that is, with passion. Shouting is neither included nor excluded in *pathos*. The same is true for tears. Disengagement from emotion "run amok" is essential but not wholesale disregard of emotion, since "feeling" is a vital part of what it means to be human. If preaching were compared to the flight of an airplane, *ethos* would represent the trained, reliable pilot; *logos* the cargo to be delivered; and *pathos* would be the trim on the wings and tail of the plane. All of this that is to be used of God must be borne along on the zephyr winds of the Holy Spirit.

Preaching is not simple but complex. Like salvation, the basic concept is simple so that all may profit. But beneath the surface, both salvation and preaching are complex issues. The ancient Greeks had no intention of making a contribution to Christian preaching. Classical rhetoric, no matter how persuasive, can never approach the transforming impact of Spirit-endowed preaching. But Aristotle's three criteria for rhetoric are still invaluable for today's minister. *Ethos*, *logos*, and *pathos* in Christian, text-driven, Spirit-inspired preaching are, in fact, lifted to a level that Aristotle himself might have envied.

2

A HISTORY OF TEXT-DRIVEN PREACHING

Jim Shaddix

The history of text-driven preaching essentially is the history of expository preaching. For the most part, men who have been faithful to allow their sermons to be driven by the text of Scripture are the same men who have sought to interpret the biblical text rightly and then expose and apply its intended meaning to their listeners. Such proclamation has been the lifeblood of preaching throughout the history of the church. James F. Stitzinger wrote, "Indeed, great value results from understanding those who have given themselves to a life of biblical exposition. The current generation whose history has yet to be written can learn much from those whose history is now complete. Time yet remains to change, refocus, improve, and be moved to greater accomplishment."[1]

---

1. J. F. Stitzinger, "The History of Expository Preaching," in J. MacArthur Jr. and The Master's Seminary Faculty, *Rediscovering Expository Preaching*, ed. R. L. Mayhue (Dallas: Word, 1992), 37–38.

A cursory study of the history of text-driven preaching provides at least two benefits. First, it provides a filter through which we can distinguish what is fleeting from what will last. Second, it possibly can motivate a preacher toward greater confidence in the biblical text and faithful proclamation of it in his own generation. In the words of John Stott, he will glimpse "the glory of preaching through the eyes of its champions in every century."[2]

THE PROPHETS, JESUS, AND THE APOSTLES

It should never be denied that preachers in the Bible like the Old Testament prophets, Jesus, and the apostles practiced what has been called *revelatory* preaching—they proclaimed God's Word as He revealed it for the very first time. They often had no text from which to work because they spoke information from God never before revealed. But equally true is that they also did *explanatory* preaching based on what God had already revealed and inspired to be written. They frequently provided explanation and application of God's previous revelation that had been recorded and accepted as written Scripture.[3]

Among the earliest examples of the combination of revelatory and explanatory preaching are Moses' sermons in the book of Deuteronomy, where he expounded on God's law and exhorted the people to obey it. The two farewell addresses of Joshua also offered to his people not only profound words of revelation from God but also clear explanation of Moses' previously recorded words (Josh 23:2–16; 24:2–27). Additionally, David and Solomon gave profound examples of revelatory and explanatory preaching of God's Word in poetic form, revealing and explaining His nature and character in the Psalms and Proverbs.

---

2.   J. R. W. Stott, *Between Two Worlds: The Art of Preaching in the Twentieth Century* (Grand Rapids: Eerdmans, 1982), 47.

3.   J. Shaddix, *The Passion Driven Sermon* (Nashville: Broadman & Holman, 2003), 71–72.

Perhaps the greatest examples of Old Testament preaching are found among the prophets. Their messages not only were characterized by the familiar predictions of the future (e.g., Isaiah 9, 53), but they also provided explanation of God's previous written revelation. Some examples include Josiah's command to repair and reform the house of the Lord (2 Kgs 22–23); Ezra's study and teaching of the law (Ezra 7:10); Nehemiah's comments about the law (Neh 8:1–8); and Daniel's explanation of his vision of the 70 weeks (Daniel 9). Prophets who spoke of their work as instruction are Samuel (1 Sam 12:23), Isaiah (Isa 30:9), Jeremiah (Jer 32:33), and Malachi (Mal 2:9). After a body of revelation had been given in the Old Testament, the people would return to it with a need to have it expounded or explained. Old Testament preaching provided necessary clarification of the recorded text.[4] Even the preaching of John the Baptist had a text-driven nature as he bore witness to Christ and called men to repentance and faith by identifying Jesus as the fulfillment of Old Testament prophecy (John 1:15,29).

Text-driven preaching also was part of the repertoire of Jesus' proclamation ministry. In one sense, segments of the Sermon on the Mount have an expositional flavor as Jesus referenced what the people had been taught and then proceeded to clarify the intended meaning of each principle (cf. Matt 5:21–48). His numerous references to Old Testament passages suggest His intent to clarify the intended meaning of each text. On the road to Emmaus, He obviously displayed His practice of allowing the text to determine His message, "beginning with Moses and all the Prophets, he interpreted to them in all the Scriptures the things concerning himself" (Luke 24:27 ESV).

Following Jesus' ministry, sermons that were driven by the text of Scripture continued to feature in apostolic preaching. The Pauline epistles are riddled with implications that such was the conviction in the early church. The great apostle instructed

---

4. Stitzinger, "The History of Expository Preaching," 39–40.

young Timothy to "devote yourself to the public reading of Scripture, to exhortation, to teaching" (1 Tim 4:13 ESV). The foundational exposition of Old Testament Scripture in early synagogue worship gave way to the practice of the early church wherein a public reading from the Old Testament text or the apostolic writings was followed by an exposition of the same. Stott clearly underscored the role of text-driven preaching during this period when he said, "It was taken for granted from the beginning that Christian preaching would be expository preaching, that is, that all Christian instruction and exhortation would be drawn out of the passage which had been read."[5]

Without a doubt, preachers during the biblical period were the first text-driven preachers, allowing the text of written Scripture to determine the content and theme of their proclamation. By the end of the period, text-driven preaching had become the norm. As the closing of the canon of Scripture marked the end of God's revelation of new truth, preaching naturally evolved to being exclusively explanatory in nature. The "apostles' doctrine" (e.g., Acts 2:42; Eph 2:19–21) combined with the Old Testament Scriptures to form our Bible, and every preacher in subsequent generations was relieved of the responsibility of introducing *new* information from God and given the mandate of explaining and applying the biblical text and persuading listeners to embrace it in the power of the Holy Spirit.[6]

THE EARLY CHURCH (AD 100–476)

Although a strong foundation for text-driven preaching had been laid during the biblical period, its practice was all but abandoned for almost a century and a half after the apostolic age. Such a contrast was merely reflective of the rapid deterioration

---

5. J. R. W. Stott, *Guard the Truth* (Downers Grove: InterVarsity, 1996), 22.
6. Shaddix, *The Passion Driven Sermon*, 72.

of New Testament Christianity in all areas, including the shift of the ordinances from symbolism to sacrament and the perversion of church leadership from elders and deacons to a hierarchy of priests and apostolic succession. The importation of Greek philosophy, logic, and rhetoric into Christian thinking by the church fathers caused most preachers to abandon the actual text of Scripture in preaching and strive to master the "art of the sermon" that was more involved with rhetoric than with truth.[7] Thus, the Greek concept of the "sermon" was born out of the syncretistic fusion of the biblical necessity of teaching with the notion of Greek rhetoric.[8] The tradition of the Christian sermon quickly took on a life of its own, with little emphasis on the biblical text.

A few faithful men, however, did carry the torch even during this dark period. John Chrysostom (347–407), whose name means "golden mouthed," was one of the leaders of the Antiochene school and arguably the most significant expositor of the early Christian church. He rejected the common allegorical approach to interpretation and emphasized grammar and history in eloquent verse-by-verse and word-by-word expositions of numerous biblical texts. Among his works were homilies on Genesis, Psalms, Matthew, John, Acts, Romans, 1 and 2 Corinthians, the other Pauline epistles, and Hebrews. Historian Philip Schaff even concluded that Chrysostom wrote commentaries on the entire Bible.[9] Serious study of the biblical text became the impetus for the sermons of others in the fourth century (c. 325–460) as well. Notable preachers included Basil, Gregory of Nazianzen, Gregory of Nyssa, Ambrose, and Augustine. In addition to his theological writings, Augustine (354–430) produced over 600 sermons, including

---

7. K. Craig, "Is the 'Sermon' Concept Biblical?" *Searching Together* 15 (Spring/Summer 1968): 25.
8. Ibid., 28.
9. P. Schaff, *A Selected Library of the Nicene and Post-Nicene Fathers*, repr. (Grand Rapids: Eerdmans, 1983), 9:17.

expositions of the Psalms, homilies on John's Gospel, 1 John, and the Gospels.[10]

THE MIDDLE AGES (AD 476–1500s)

If the period of the early church was sparse when it came to text-driven preaching, the Middle Ages—or medieval period—was a famine. James Philip provides a sad commentary:

> The influence of the scholastic theology of the universities, which from the beginning were clerical institutions, took over, and the combination of theology and philosophy, and the application of Aristotelian logic to the interpretation of Scripture, with its speculation, analysis and ratiocination imposed an intolerable incubus upon preaching which virtually destroyed it as an effective means for communicating the gospel. It is not surprising, therefore, that hardly any counterparts to the comprehensive patristic expositions of complete books of the Bible are to be found in medieval ecclesiastical literature.[11]

Obviously, the absence of the practice of biblical exposition during the era reflected the minimal role of the text of Scripture in sermons.

Only a few gifted men arose to counter the influence of scholastic theology and Aristotelian logic in biblical interpretation. Prereformers like John Wyclif (1330–84) and William Tyndale (1494–1536) denounced the preaching of their days and rejected preaching that did not significantly treat the biblical text and interpret it literally. Others, like John Huss (1373–1415) and Girolamo Savonarola (1452–98), also were known as credible students of the biblical text who allowed it to directly influence

---

10. G. W. Doyle, "Augustine's Sermonic Method," *WTJ* 39 (Spring 1977): 215, 234–35.
11. J. Philip, "Preaching in History," *ERT* 8 (1984): 300.

their sermon subjects. Although never embracing faithful exposition of the text, even some humanists like Erasmus (1469–1536) and John Colet (1466–1519) helped lay the groundwork for later expositional preaching through the study of the Greek New Testament via *Novum Instrumentum* (1516) and *NovT* (1518).[12]

THE REFORMATION (AD 1500–1648)

The most significant reemergence of the biblical text in preaching took place in response to the glaring abuses of the indulgence system in Germany at the beginning of the sixteenth century. Text-driven sermons were a primary vehicle for the prophetic voices that directly ignited the Protestant reformation. Although the sixteenth century was a great period for preaching in just about all areas, probably the most significant quality was the revival of biblical preaching in which expository sermons driven by the text of Scripture replaced the mere telling of stories of saints, martyrs, and miracles. These sermons were characterized by the employment of better methods of interpretation and application, a combination that fostered a much-needed revival of reverence for the biblical text in preaching. The mantra of Christian preachers became *sola scriptura*— "the freedom of Scripture to rule as God's word in the church, disentangled from papal and ecclesiastical magisterium and tradition."[13] This conviction viewed Scripture as supreme over tradition and the sacraments.

Martin Luther (1483–1546) heads the list of great reformers who called the church back to Scripture alone as the authority for faith as well as the subject of preaching. After being

12. F. R. Webber, *A History of Preaching in Britain and America*, 3 vols. (Milwaukee: Northwestern, 1957), 1:150.
13. D. F. Wright, "Protestantism," in *Evangelical Dictionary of Theology*, ed. W. A. Elwell (Grand Rapids: Baker, 1984), 889.

appointed as professor at the University of Wittenberg in
1510, the Augustinian monk traveled to Rome the following
year, where he witnessed widespread corruption and worldli-
ness among the clergy. Convinced of the need for reform, he
returned to Wittenberg and began lecturing on the texts of
Psalms, Romans, Galatians, and Hebrews. After his conversion,
Luther's opposition to the abuses of the indulgence practices
prompted him to post his historic 95 theses on the church door
at Wittenberg on October 31, 1517. The reformation proper had
begun, and there is no doubt that text-driven preaching helped
to usher it in and laid the foundation for the Protestant tradition.

Other great reformers came alongside of Luther and approached their pulpits with firm convictions about the role of
the biblical text in preaching. In 1519 in Zurich, Ulrich Zwingli
(1484–1531) almost single-handedly launched the Swiss Reformation with his expository series through the book of
Matthew. He studied the Bible carefully in its original languages
and applied to the text his "considerable linguistic and exegetical abilities."[14]

After the publication of his famous *Institutes of Christianity*
in 1536, John Calvin (1509–64) also became firmly established
as one of the leading reformers. His sermons were not only
driven by the biblical text but also consumed with it. Although
his exile interrupted an expositional series through the book of
Acts, he returned to his pulpit three years later and picked up
with the very next verse where he had stopped! His commitment to exposing the text of Scripture, earnest presentation,
love of the truth, and devotion to duty made him one of the
greatest preacher-theologians of all time. His incredible treatment of one biblical text after another in sequential expositions
of Bible books is unparalleled in church history.

Calvin spent his life expounding the text of Scripture. As
senior minister of Geneva, he preached twice each Sunday

14. G. R. Potter, *Zwingli* (Cambridge: Cambridge University, 1976), 92.

and every weekday on alternating weeks from 1549 until his death in 1564. He preached more than 2,000 sermons from the Old Testament alone. He spent a year expositing Job and three years in Isaiah.[15] Maybe Calvin's perspective on the importance of the text in preaching is best summarized by his words, "Let us not take it into our heads either to seek out God anywhere else than in his Sacred Word, or to think anything about him that is not prompted by his Word, or to speak anything that is not taken from that Word."[16]

MODERN TIMES (AD 1649–1970)

Text-driven preaching continued to play a vital role in the church's life at many critical junctures, not the least of which was the dawn of modernity. During the latter part of the six-teenth and most of the seventeenth centuries, the Puritans made the biblical text central in Christian worship and cham-pioned true preaching, which they defined as the exposition of the text of Scripture. To the Puritans, "true preaching is the exposition of the Word of God. It is not a mere exposition of the dogma or the teaching of the church. . . . Preaching, they said, is the exposition of the Word of God; and therefore it must control everything."[17]

William Perkins (1558–1602) was one of the early Puritan preachers who did much to emphasize the role of the text in preaching. He developed his views in *The Art of Prophesying*, the first manual of its kind for preachers in the Church of England. Perkins identified certain principles to guide the preacher in his work, including reading the text distinctly out of the canonical

---

15. M. Anderson, "John Calvin: Biblical Preacher (1539–1564)," *SJT* 42 (1989): 173.
16. J. Calvin, *Institutes in Christian Classics*, 1:13:21 (1, 146).
17. D. M. Lloyd-Jones, *The Puritans: Their Origins and Successors* (Edinburgh: Banner of Truth, 1987), 379.

Scriptures, and then giving the sense and understanding of it by allowing other Scripture to interpret it.[18]

Some other major Puritan preachers who demonstrated reverence for the biblical text and great ability as expositors were Joseph Hall (1574–1656), Thomas Goodwin (1600–1680), Richard Baxter (1615–91), John Owen (1616–83), Thomas Manton (1620–77), John Bunyan (1628–88), Stephen Charnock (1628–80), and William Greenhill (1581–1677). Although their styles were diverse, they were tied together by the "thread of commitment to a faithful explanation of the text."[19]

Although the evangelistic preaching during the First Great Awakening was largely topical, several text-driven preachers were influential as well. Of note were John Gill (1697–1771) and Matthew Henry (1662–1714), both of whom were heavily influenced by the Puritans. The following 50 years featured other notable exceptions to topical preaching like the ministries of Andrew Fuller (1754–1815), Robert Hall (1764–1831), John Brown (1784–1858), John Eadie (1810–76), and Alexander Carson (1776–1844). The latter part of the nineteenth century also produced influential biblical expositors in Britain and America, including James H. Thornwell (1812–62), John A. Broadus (1827–95), John C. Ryle (1816–1900), Charles J. Vaughan (1816–97), Alexander Maclaren (1826–1910), and Joseph Parker (1830–1902).[20]

Although Charles Haddon Spurgeon (1834–92) is considered one of history's greatest preachers, whether he should be categorized as a pure text-driven preacher is debatable. Without a doubt, his *Treasury of David*—in which he provides a careful verse-by-verse exposition of the Psalms along with "hints to preachers"—is genuinely expositional in form and content.[21]

18. M. W. Perkins, *The Works of that Famous and Worthy Minister of Christ in the University of Cambridge*, 3 vols. (Cambridge: John Legate, 1608–9), 2:762.
19. Stitzinger, "The History of Expository Preaching," 53.
20. Ibid.
21. Ibid., 55–56.

However, in his overall preaching ministry his practice of exegesis is at times difficult to reconcile with his interpretation. As opposed to studying a text, probing it, and drawing out of it the truths that were in it, Spurgeon seemed to reverse the process by selecting a text and then grouping around it closely related Bible truths. At times he would stress meanings that were somewhat foreign to the text under consideration.[22] It is probably no surprise that Spurgeon viewed George Whitefield as a hero and a preaching model, given that Whitefield was more topical and theological than expositional.[23] Regardless, Spurgeon's life and ministry is a testimony of strong convictions about the Bible and its role in preaching.

Bridging the nineteenth and twentieth centuries, the ministry of G. Campbell Morgan (1863–1945) at the Westminster Chapel in London provided a resounding voice for text-driven preaching. He truly was one of the great Bible expositors of all time, and his sermons were permeated with the biblical text. His works are rich not only in explanation but also in textual illustration and exegetical interpretation based on the whole Bible. Regarding the relationship between preaching and the biblical text, Morgan said,

> The Word is not something that I have found out by the activity of my own intellectual life. The Word is something which my intellectual life apprehends, because it has been expressed. . . . And that is what we have to preach. God's revelation, the truth, as it has been expressed. We must enter upon the Christian ministry on the assumption that God has expressed Himself in His Son, and the Bible is the literature of that self-expression. The minute we lose our Bible in that regard, we have lost Christ as the final revelation. . . . Every

---

22. Webber, *History of Preaching*, 1:602.
23. H. Davies, "Expository Preaching: Charles Haddon Spurgeon," *Foundations* 6 (1963): 17–18.

sermon that fails to have some interpretation of that holy truth is a failure. . . . Preaching is not the proclamation of a theory, or the discussion of a doubt. . . . Speculation is not preaching. Neither is the declaration of negations preaching. Preaching is the proclamation of the Word, the truth as the truth has been revealed.[24]

Morgan's numerous and masterful published expositions are a testimony of the work to which he dedicated his life.

Morgan was succeeded at Westminster Chapel by his associate, D. Martyn Lloyd-Jones (1899–1981), who continued his mentor's practice. Lloyd-Jones viewed weekly preaching in the church as simply picking up in the text where he left off the previous week in his ongoing exposition of a Bible book. His preaching stemmed from careful exegesis and featured a careful setting forth of the meaning and application of each Bible passage. He knew of no substitute for the task of expounding the biblical text in the church. Although he identified three types of preaching—evangelistic, instructional teaching, and purely instructional—he contended that all preaching must be expository, both in its preparation and in its presentation to the people.[25]

Along with Morgan and Lloyd-Jones, several other notable Bible expositors in the first part of the twentieth century shared similar convictions about the role of the text in preaching. Among them were H. A. Ironside (1876–1951), Donald Grey Barnhouse (1895–1960), James M. Gray (1881–1935), William Bell Riley (1861–1947), James Denney (1856–1917), William Graham Scroggie (1877–1958), W. A. Criswell (1909–2002), and James Montgomery Boice (1938–2000).

24. G. C. Morgan, *Preaching* (New York: Revell, 1937), 17–21.
25. D. M. Lloyd-Jones, *Preaching and Preachers* (Grand Rapids: Zondervan, 1971), 63, 75–76. See also R. L. Penny, "An Examination of the Principles of Expository Preaching of David Martyn Lloyd-Jones" (D.Min. diss., Harding Graduate School of Religion, 1980).

POSTMODERNITY (1970–PRESENT)

Designating an end to the modern period, as well as identifying the following time period, is incredibly subjective and arbitrary. The term "postmodernity" often is used to describe the present social, cultural, and economic state. The designation is used by philosophers, social scientists, and social critics to refer to aspects of contemporary culture, economics, and society that are the result of the unique features of late twentieth- and early twenty-first-century life twenty-first century life and are a reaction to the perceived failures of modernism. But its influence on religion—and preaching—are evident enough to merit a separate consideration of the period.

We must always be careful when interpreting contemporary history because the ministries of its representative preachers are yet to be completed. But one thing is certain to this point: in general, the postmodern era has been robbed of the biblical text in preaching. The specific influences of this trend, however, predate the era itself. One must go back to the Christian psychological preaching of Harry Emerson Fosdick in the early part of the twentieth century, which gave birth to the power of positive thinking championed by Norman Vincent Peale. His philosophy paved the way for the neoorthodoxy of Robert Schuller, whose preaching ultimately conceived the seeker-sensitive movement that has influenced evangelical preaching in the contemporary age to unprecedented degrees.

Probably the most overlooked philosophical shift informing this movement has been in the area of corporate worship. Many contemporary pastors champion corporate worship experiences in the church that are focused on communicating to unregenerate seekers as opposed to leading the church in authentic worship of God. In other words, the evangelistic thrust of these churches—although very sincere and often evangelistically effective—has digressed to a "come and hear" mentality as opposed to the "go and tell" emphasis in the New Testament. This focus naturally lends itself to a de-emphasis on many classic Christian values in corporate worship, including the use of the biblical text in preaching and the subsequent maturing of the body of Christ. Embracing the belief that the needs of the hearers are paramount and that preaching must be relevant to them, many proponents of this philosophy use inductive sermons that begin where people are and go back to Scripture to find appropriate texts.[26]

One popular approach born out of this strand of influence has been the "life application" preaching that seeks to address real and felt needs using multiple verses of Scripture from various parts of the Bible. However, a careful analysis of the sermons of many preachers who have adopted the approach reveals a great amount of liberty with the biblical text in exegesis, interpretation, and application. Preaching hailed as "verse with verse"—while obviously making some attempt to maintain a loose identity with the "verse-by-verse" description associated with expository preaching—appears to be little more than veiled topical preaching that rearranges the biblical text and uses selected verses merely as support for addressing particular subjects and providing practical application. Furthermore, criticisms of expository preaching—which come frequently from some life application preachers—seem to be more reaction to *abuses* of exposition than to weaknesses of exposition itself.

Even in its dark hour of de-emphasis on the biblical text, however, the postmodern era still has been graced with the counterinfluence of text-driven preaching. It has not been dormant even in a historical period characterized by relativism, pluralism, and tolerance, or in a church era assaulted by the depreciating and diminishing of theology and the authority of Scripture. Motivated with a conviction that spiritual growth can never take place apart from knowing and understanding God's truth (see Neh 8:2–3,8; Rom 12:2; Eph 4:22; Col 3:10),

---

26. M. Quicke, "History of Preaching," in *The Art and Craft of Biblical Preaching*, ed. H. Robinson and C. B. Larson (Grand Rapids: Zondervan, 2005), 64.

an increasing number of preachers are delivering sermons that are driven by and consumed with the biblical text. Describing them as "teacher preachers," Michael Quicke says,

> Such preachers stay close to the text and explain its meaning deductively. Typically doctrinal and instructional, this preaching examines verses in logical order. Some examples of teacher preachers are John Stott, John Ortberg, Timothy Keller, Jack Hayford, and John MacArthur. Often cerebral in style, teacher preachers want to get information across. A sermon form often used by teacher preachers is verse-by-verse preaching.[27]

Obviously, these text-driven preachers embrace a belief that all true preaching must involve teaching and that teaching for understanding is a prerequisite for right application to people's lives.

Bridging the modern and postmodern eras, John R. W. Stott (1921–) has emphasized the need to handle the text properly in preaching in order to expose its truth. He said,

> To expound Scripture is to bring out of the text what is there and expose it to view. The expositor prys open what appears to be closed, makes plain what is obscure, unravels what is knotted and unfolds what is tightly packed. The opposite of exposition is "imposition," which is to impose on the text what is not there. But the "text" in question could be a verse, or a sentence, or even a single word. It could be a verse, or a paragraph, or a chapter, or a whole book. The size of the text is immaterial, so long as it is biblical. What matters is what we do with it.[28]

Stott contends that all true Christian preaching is expository preaching when understood in light of the treatment of the text.

---

27. Ibid.
28. Stott, *Between Two Worlds*, 92.

John MacArthur Jr. (1939–) arguably has emerged as the most notable American expositor at the end of the twentieth century. His stated goal is "always to have deep fellowship with the Lord in the understanding of His Word, and out of that experience to explain to His people what a passage means. . . . The dominant thrust of my ministry, therefore, is to help make God's living Word alive to His people."[29] MacArthur sees expository preaching as concerned primarily with the content of the biblical text, reflecting the objective of explaining and applying Scripture.[30]

To Quicke's list of representative teacher preachers we might add other men whose sermons are driven by the biblical text. John Piper is one of the great theological preachers of the contemporary era. His expository preaching can be described as "intercanonical" in nature as he systematically expounds on the great doctrinal themes of the Bible from key texts of Scripture. James MacDonald is the founding pastor of Harvest Bible Chapel in Illinois and is well known for his radio ministry, *Walk in the Word*. MacDonald faithfully expounds God's Word—usually through Bible book series—with passion, humor, integrity, and contemporary flare.

Mark Driscoll and David Platt are among the younger generation of passionate text-driven preachers, both of whom pastor megachurches filled with young people who are sitting under the exposition of Scripture every week. Driscoll preaches systematically through Bible books in view of building a Christian "city within a city" in Seattle, Washington. At one time a proponent of the early emerging church movement, he began to disassociate himself from its adherents when some of his friends

---

29. J. F. MacArthur Jr., *Matthew 1–7*: The MacArthur New Testament Commentary (Chicago: Moody, 1983–), vii.
30. B. E. Awbrey, "A Critical Examination of the Theory and Practice of John F. MacArthur's Expository Preaching" (Th.D. diss., New Orleans Baptist Theological Seminary, 1990), 17; cf. R. K. Willhite, "Audience Relevance and Rhetorical Argumentation in Expository Preaching: A Historical-Critical Comparative Analysis of Selected Sermons of John F. MacArthur, Jr., and Charles R. Swindoll, 1970–1990" (Ph.D. diss., Purdue University, 1990).

"began pushing a theological agenda that greatly troubled me . . . referring to God as a chick, questioning God's sovereignty over and knowledge of the future, denial of the substitutionary atonement at the cross, a low view of Scripture, and denial of hell."[31] Platt—still in his twenties at the time of publication— uses weekly expository sermons to challenge and equip his northeast Alabama congregation to embrace God's world mission of disciple-making.

One of the great testimonies of text-driven preaching in the postmodern era has emerged out of the conservative resurgence within the Southern Baptist Convention, the world's largest Protestant denomination. After a theological struggle centering on the inerrancy and authority of the Bible that spanned more than three decades, Southern Baptists have taken great strides toward restoring text-driven preaching in the pulpits of their local churches as well as the classrooms of their theological institutions. One of the by-products of the return to conservative theology and classic Christian doctrine has been the reestablishment of expository preaching as the primary fare in the homiletics departments in just about all of the denomination's seminaries. Certainly their desired end is the raising up of a generation of text-driven pastors, preachers, and missionaries who will influence the world with the supernatural truth of God's Word.

LOOKING AHEAD

One of the great tragedies of human nature is that we have a tendency to use perceived "success" in church growth to validate preaching philosophy and practice. In other words, if a church has experienced numerical growth, then the preaching approach of the pastor must be right and worthy to be

---

31. See Mark Driscoll's blog at http://theresurgence.com/?q=node.

modeled. Certainly, such is not the case. God does not call His preachers to *success*, especially what is measured by worldly standards. God calls His preachers to *faithfulness*, and faithfulness includes the careful handling of His revealed Word with the utmost of integrity. And besides, we will never know how much more effective some of the "successful" preachers—past and present—could have been had they been faithful to allow the biblical text to drive their sermons.

In time, the postmodern era may prove to be more of a fad than an actual period by which we interpret history. The reason is that everything exhausts itself faster in our explosive media environment because we run everything to its limit at a more rapid pace. We exhaust everything faster through television, radio, cell phones, PDAs, iPods, the Internet, and blogs. This world experienced thousands of years of premodernism but only hundreds of years of modernism. We will have a few years of postmodernism, and by the time these words are published, something else will come along if it has not already.

The same brevity likely will characterize the preaching trends that define the era. The more recent the trend, the shorter its existence will be. Each one will have a shorter shelf life than the one preceding it. In my opinion, every nontraditional preaching philosophy that is not driven by the text of Scripture will expire. It will run its course and fade away. Postmodern preaching—along with its "textless" sermons—likely will prove to be faddish. Just like the passing fads of psychological preaching and positive thinking, each philosophy will have its day in the sun and then will set quietly on the horizon of evangelicalism. And when the dust settles, I anticipate that text-driven preachers will still be standing and faithfully proclaiming Holy Writ.

3

THE SECRET OF PREACHING
WITH POWER

Bill Bennett

*My speech and my message were not in plausible words
of wisdom, but in demonstration of the Spirit and of
power.*

—1 Cor 2:4 ESV

In our day we often hear the statement, "We need more
good preaching." I agree we need more "good" preaching, but we need more than good preaching. "Good"
preaching in the popular mind is that which is well-crafted
homiletically, verbally and grammatically correct, cleverly illustrated, concluded with a moving poem, and skillfully delivered.
However, there is a tragic absence that may accompany such
preaching. It is preaching that is *without power*. Our seminaries
prepare their students well to deliver "good" sermons as I have
described, but I fear there is too little emphasis on preaching
with Holy Spirit power.[1]

---

1. I rejoice that our Southern Baptist Seminaries are beginning to address the
    need of the power of the Holy Spirit in preaching. Dr. Daniel Akin, president of

What we desperately need is not more performers who deliver a well-prepared and skillfully delivered speech but rather a passionate and powerfully delivered plea with a "Thus saith the Lord" that rends the hearts of the hearers. Preaching is not primarily an explanation or a lecture and certainly not an apology. It is a heralding, a heart cry, a bold declaration with the urgency of the Master Himself ringing out through His anointed, yielded vessel.[2] It is what I call apostolic preaching, commended in the New Testament, and exemplified in the preaching of men like Amos, John the Baptist, Stephen, Peter, and Paul in the Bible, and in history, John Chrysostom, Girolamo Savonarola, John Knox, Jonathan Edwards, John Wesley, George Whitefield, Charles Spurgeon, Shubal Stearnes, Jack Wilder, Charlie Howard, Finny Mathews, Billy Graham, Johnny Hunt, and Adrian Rogers.

The apostle Paul describes such preaching in terms like these: "For our gospel came not unto you in *word* only, but also in *power*, and in the Holy Ghost" (1 Thess 1:5 KJV, italics added). As a pastor, Paul expressed his unwavering determination not just to preach "good messages, . . . with enticing words of man's wisdom," but in the "demonstration of the Spirit and of power, that your faith should not stand in the wisdom of men, but in the power of God" (1 Cor 2:4–5). Paul reiterates his resolve to preach with power rather than mere words two chapters later: "I will come to you . . . not [with] the speech of them which are puffed up [as with Greek oratory], but the power. For the kingdom of God is not in *word*, but in *power*" (1 Cor 4:19–20, italics added).

Before a preacher prepares a manuscript, he must meditate on his text until, like Jeremiah, he senses a "fire in his bones."

Southeastern Baptist Theological Seminary, wrote me these words, "Southeastern Seminary is committed to engaging exposition that is Spirit anointed and Christ focused. Expounding the text accurately and applying the text clearly are twin goals that guide our approach to preaching the Holy Scriptures."

2. Joe Durai, SermonCentral.com.

As the prophet put it, "His word was . . . as a burning fire shut up in my bones" (Jer 20:9). Before we stand to preach the Word of God, we must pause before we deliver it, humble ourselves before Almighty God, desperately pray that the Holy Spirit will enable us to do what the text says, and then look up to God and confess, "I can do all things through Christ who strengthens me" (Phil 4:13 NKJV).

Do we have Holy Spirit–empowered preaching in our day? I believe that there is very little of it from what I hear and read. Dr. Martin Lloyd-Jones, considered by many to be one of "the last of the great preachers," lamented the scarcity of powerful preaching, saying that "the greatest essential" in preaching today is the anointing of the Holy Spirit.[3] Dr. Jerry Vines, an adroit homiletician himself, makes an impassioned plea for the preacher to seek the anointing constantly:

> We must seek the Spirit's anointing. Ask Him to come on you and your message. Allow Him to manifest His power in and through you. Never be satisfied with anything less in your sermon delivery. You may not always experience the power of the Holy Spirit upon your preaching in equal measure. For reasons in the realm of the mysterious, there are times when the anointing comes upon us in larger measure than at other times. . . . But there should be such a surrender of life to the Spirit that every time we preach there is evidence of God's blessings upon us.[4]

The stalwart old Methodist preacher Dr. Robert P. Shuler, noting the loss of power in the pulpits of his own denomination, wrote these words to describe the tragedy of the absence of the power of the Holy Spirit: "The church of this tragic hour has

---

3. B. Bennett, *Thirty Minutes to Raise the Dead* (Nashville: Thomas Nelson, 1991), 175–76.
4. J. Vines, *Practical Guide to Sermon Preparation* (Chicago: Moody, 1985), 162–63.

more wire stretched and less juice on it than in any other day I have ever known. We have superlative equipment without any vitalizing force to bring it into action. We are continually building sanctuaries that are often as devoid of spiritual life as tombs. Our altars are no longer places of penitential tears and the birth of new souls."[5]

The late Dr. Carl Bates, former president of the Southern Baptist Convention and professor of preaching at Southern Seminary, said to me, "Bill, if the Holy Spirit were suddenly withdrawn from the world, 90 percent of Southern Baptist churches would not notice it and carry on as usual." Dr. R. G. Lee said, "The Southern Baptist church is so cold at 11:00 a.m. Sunday that you could skate down the aisles as if on ice."

Dr. Scott Pace, my former student and fellow, and a Ph.D. graduate in preaching at Southeastern Baptist Theological Seminary, wrote in his superb dissertation, "The subject of the Holy Spirit and His role in preaching lacks adequate consideration among evangelicals."[6]

James Forbes notes, "If a greatly improved quality of preaching is to be experienced in our times, it will stem from the renewing power and presence of the Holy Spirit." Significantly, Forbes goes on to say that the issue is not ignorance. He writes, "It is not that preachers do not know the place of the Spirit, rather it is that those attitudes which urge silence and privacy regarding the role of the Spirit in our preaching also tend to rob us of the full empowerment crucial for all who preach the Word."[7]

Arturo G. Azurdia goes even further and avows that the deficiency of Holy Spirit power in the preacher makes his preaching

5. Robert P. Shuler, *What New Doctrine Is This?* (Nashville: Abingdon, 1956), 115–16. Robert P. Shuler is not to be confused with Robert Shuler of Garden Grove Community Church, Garden Grove, California.
6. S. Pace, "Hermeneutics and Homiletics: A Case for the Necessity and Nature of Contextual-Theological Application in the Expository Sermon" (Ph.D. diss., Southeastern Baptist Theological Seminary, 2007), 144.
7. J. Forbes, *The Holy Spirit and Preaching* (Nashville: Abingdon, 1989), 11, 26.

powerless. "It is my deep conviction that the greatest deficiency in contemporary expositional ministry is powerlessness; in other words, preaching that is devoid of the vitality of the Holy Spirit." He then adds, "Apart from the quickening power of the Holy Spirit in the act of proclamation, even the best and most essential technique falls miserably short of transforming those to whom we preach."[8]

Dr. Greg Heisler, professor of preaching at Southeastern Baptist Theological Seminary, indicts the field of preaching for its superficial treatment of the role of the Holy Spirit in preaching. He notes, "Preachers often talk about the Spirit with vague generalities and tip their theological hats to acknowledge their need of the Spirit, but when it comes to specifics and theological depth, you find few satisfying explanations. . . . Homiletics textbooks lack consensus and clarity as well."[9]

I heard the North Carolina evangelist Vance Havner lament, "You can be as straight theologically as a gun barrel and at the same time as spiritually empty." So the question, then, is this: what will it take to bring back powerful preaching? I wish to share one essential, the absolutely necessary requirement, in my judgment, that will restore powerful preaching to our pulpits in our day. I do so not only humbly and cautiously but also confidently, because this essential is clearly set forth in the Scriptures. It is also a reality that I observed in the preaching of my own father, who, though limited in formal education, preached with incredible power, which I humbly believe I have experienced enough to recommend to others.

When I began to preach, I knew very little about the Holy Spirit, but I was hungry and open to know more about Him. Thus I began to search the Scriptures; read some good books, especially Dr. Ralph Herring's classic, *God Being My Helper;* and prayed earnestly that I might know and experience His power in

---

8. A. Azurdia, *Spirit Empowered Preaching* (Fern, Scotland: Christian Focus Publications, 1998), 12–13.
9. G. Heisler, *Spirit-Led Preaching* (Nashville: Broadman & Holman, 2007), 129.

my life and ministry. In the early years of my ministry, I served as state chairman of evangelism of the North Carolina Baptist State Convention. Though limited in my understanding of the Holy Spirit but convinced of His primacy in evangelism, I often preached on the Holy Spirit, and my brothers in the convention referred to me as "The Holy Spirit Preacher." Unfortunately, the Holy Spirit, at that time, was a "strange" doctrine in the minds of some brothers, belonging only to the Pentecostals, so they thought. Some years later, Oral Roberts was intrigued when he heard that I, a Southern Baptist, had a deep interest in the Holy Spirit. So he asked me to visit with him. The first question he asked me was, "Have you been baptized by the Holy Spirit?" I replied, "Yes, I was baptized in the Spirit the day I was saved." He then, pointing to his stomach, asked, "Did you have rivers of water flowing out of your belly?" I answered, "No." Then he said to me, "Well you are a Jesus man," implying I was not a Holy Spirit man. I replied, "Yes, indeed I am a Jesus man and a Holy Spirit man. I do not separate the two." He finally said, "Well, it is obvious that God has already used you mightily in His kingdom, but if you would go on and experience the 'baptism' of the Spirit, He would use you to change the world." At this time I saw the crucial difference in my understanding of the Holy Spirit and that of the Pentecostals. I have never thought of my infilling with the Holy Spirit as a "second work" of grace but as the last part of the first blessing, for the Holy Spirit who came into my life when I was saved was the same Holy Spirit who filled me years later.

God accomplishes His purposes in the believer's life by two instruments: the Word and the Spirit. The words of this familiar saying sum it up: "All Word and no Spirit, you dry up. All Spirit and no Word, you blow up. Combine the Word and the Spirit, you will grow up." Therefore, the basis of powerful preaching is the "internalization of the Word."[10] But the Word, without

---

10. Internalization of the Word is much more than reading and studying it. "Internalization" means four things: (1) *know* it in the head by diligent study,

the Holy Spirit, will not work the miracle of God's grace in the human heart. We see this very clearly in the experience of the new birth. Jesus commands that we must be born of the water and the Spirit in order to enter the Kingdom of God (John 3:5). I believe water speaks of the Word of God (Eph 5:26) and the Spirit means the Holy Spirit. It is when the Word of God and the Spirit of God come together in the heart, by the faith of the believer, that the miracle of a new life begins.

The Word of God and the Spirit of God share a dynamic relationship and interdependence. Ezekiel 37 describes this relationship in graphic terms. Here is the situation of Israel spiritually in those days: She is as dead as "dry bones." So God commands Ezekiel to prophesy to these bones. The effect of the Word prophesied was immediate and powerful: "The bones came together, bone to his bone." But if the story ended there, all we would have would be lifeless skeletons. Next, God told Ezekiel to call forth the Holy Spirit, and by the power of the Word and Spirit, the bones "lived and stood up upon their feet" (Ezek 37:10). Inspired by Ezekiel 37, I named my book on expository preaching *Thirty Minutes to Raise the Dead*. What an awesome task for the preacher—to raise the spiritually dead in a 30-minute sermon—but what a glorious reality when the Word and the Spirit work together.[11]

However, the new birth is but the beginning of the work of the Holy Spirit in human experience. When one repents and turns to Jesus as Lord and Savior, the Holy Spirit enters immediately and permanently into that person (Rom 8:9b; 1 Cor 6:19). We call this His indwelling. Simultaneously, the Holy Spirit baptizes the believer into the body of Christ once and for all (1 Cor 12:13). This is the real baptism of the Holy Spirit. All these divine acts are inseparable, and they occur at the moment one truly surrenders to Jesus as Lord and Savior.

---

(2) *stow* it in the heart by memorization and meditation, (3) *show* it in one's life by obeying its teaching, and (4) *sow* it in one's world by our witness.

11. Heisler, *Spirit-Led Preaching*, 61.

These events do not conclude the work of the Holy Spirit in the believer. Beyond these, God categorically commands, through the apostle Paul, that every believer be continually filled with the Holy Spirit. We read, "And do not be drunk with wine, in which is dissipation; but be filled with the Spirit" (Eph 5:18 NKJV). The question naturally arises then, why do we need to be filled (controlled) by the Holy Spirit if we already have His indwelling and His baptism? The answer is clear: you can have the Holy Spirit, but the Holy Spirit may not have you. That is, the Holy Spirit may be *present* in you, but He demands to be *President* in you so that He can fill and control your life. Let me bring all this truth together under three major headings.

First, there are two main reasons to be filled: The first is that God commands it. "Be filled [literally "be being filled"] with the Holy Spirit" (Eph 5:18b). Please notice four facts about this command:

1. This command is in the *imperative* mood. This means it is not optional. To be filled is to obey God and thus reap His blessings; to fail to be filled is to disobey God and miss His blessings. It has been widely reported that on one occasion Billy Graham went to preach in a certain Baptist church, and upon arrival the pastor told Billy that the church had recently revoked the ordination of three deacons. Billy then asked, "What reason did you have for doing this?" The pastor replied, "Because they were drinking alcoholic beverages." Then Billy retorted, "Well, you were certainly Scriptural in doing so, but I want to ask if you revoke the ordination of those deacons who are not filled with the Holy Spirit?" The pastor answered, "We never thought of that," to which Billy replied, "You are very inconsistent, for the same Scripture which forbids that we be not drunk with alcoholic beverages also commands every believer to be filled with the Holy Spirit, and certainly above all the deacons."
2. This command is *plural* in number. This means that this command is given to every believer, not just spiritual giants, super saints, pastors, elders, or deacons.
3. This command is in the *passive* voice, which means we cannot fill ourselves, but filling comes from an outside source—the Holy Spirit. Our responsibility is to put ourselves in a position where the spirit of God can control us.

4. This command is in the *present* tense. Unlike the new birth and baptism of the Holy Spirit, which happens only once in a believer's life, the filling of the Holy Spirit is a repeated event. In essence, the text commands, "Be ye being filled *continually* with the Holy Spirit." I have heard both James Merritt and the late Adrian Rogers make this statement: "It is a far greater sin for a child of God not to be filled with the Holy Spirit than for a person to get drunk on alcoholic beverages." I agree.

The second reason to be filled is that the demands of the Christian life require it. These demands cannot be met by our natural willpower but only by the supernatural power of God released in our lives through the Holy Spirit. Who in his natural power can preach with mighty power (1 Cor 2:4)? Who within his own power can "love his enemies" (Matt 5:44)? Who in his own power can "rejoice evermore" (1 Thess 5:16)? Who in his own power can fulfill the righteous requirements of the law (Rom 8:2–4)? Who in his own power can go the second mile and then some (Matt 5:41)? Who can overcome the law of sin and death (Rom 8:1–4)? D. L. Moody allegedly said, "You might as well try to hear without ears, or breathe without lungs, as try to live a Christian life without the Spirit of God in your heart."[12]

There is a second major point to be made about the filling of the Spirit: there are requirements to be filled. It has been said, "The kingdom of God does not belong to the well-meaning but to the desperate." Candidates for the infilling and anointing must "mean business" with the Lord. The casual Christian and the average Sunday morning attendee do not qualify.

1. You must have been born of the Holy Spirit before you can be filled.
2. You must desire with all your heart to be filled. Only those who "hunger and thirst will be filled." "Blessed are those who hunger and thirst for righteousness, for they shall be filled" (Matt 5:6 NKJV). Jesus cried out to the multitude, saying, "If anyone thirsts, let him come to Me and drink. He who believes in Me, as the Scripture has said, out of his heart will flow rivers of living water. But this He spoke concerning . . .

---

12. D. L. Moody, *Notes from My Bible* (Grand Rapids: Baker, 1979), 155.

for the Spirit was not yet given, because Jesus was not yet glorified" (John 7:37–39).

3. You must believe that God *will* fill you, not just God *can* fill you.
4. You must denounce all known sin in your life. You must do more than confess sin (i.e., admit it); you must abandon it. "He who covers his sins will not prosper, but whoever confesses and forsakes them will have mercy" (Prov 28:13).
5. You must dethrone self and enthrone Christ as Lord of all. This means that you would release your control over your life and turn it over to the living Christ.
6. You must, by faith, ask the Holy Spirit to fill you. "If you then, being evil, know how to give good gifts to your children, how much more will your heavenly Father give the Holy Spirit to those who ask Him!" (Luke 11:13).
7. You must accept the fact that He has filled you and live with total dependence on Him saying, "Lord God, I yield control of my life to you today. Just show me what to do." This would mean that you are walking in the Spirit. "Walk in the Spirit, and you shall not fulfill the lust of the flesh" (Gal 5:16).

In a word, you must surrender your life to Jesus Christ as your Lord. Please notice that I did not say "commit" your life but "surrender" it. When you commit, you choose the things you will commit; when you surrender, the Lord determines the things you will surrender. Commitment would be like taking a plain sheet of paper and writing on that paper the things you would commit to the Lord and then signing your name at the bottom. Surrender would mean something entirely different. You would not write anything on the blank sheet of paper, but you would sign your name at the bottom and ask the Lord Jesus Christ to fill in the rest. Be sure not to confuse surrender with the "time-honored" rededications that take place in many churches with little continuing results. Rededications are the very opposite of surrender, as is commitment, and will never result in the filling of the Holy Spirit and the anointing that follows.

There is a third major point to be made about the filling of the Spirit. The results of being filled will be evident to all, for the person who is filled will overflow with the fruit of the Holy Spirit as confirmed by Scripture: "But the fruit of the Spirit is love, joy, peace, longsuffering, kindness, goodness, faithfulness, gentleness, self-control. Against such there is no law" (Gal 5:22–23). These are some of the results:

1. The person who is filled will have an intimate "Abba Father" relationship with his Father in heaven. "For you did not receive the Spirit of bondage again to fear, but you received the Spirit of adoption by whom we cry out, 'Abba, Father'" (Rom 8:15).
2. The person who is filled will be a bold witness to the ends of the earth. "But you shall receive power when the Holy Spirit has come upon you; and you shall be witnesses to Me in Jerusalem, and in all Judea and Samaria, and to the end of the earth" (Acts 1:8).
3. The person who is filled with the Holy Spirit will have victory over indwelling sin. "For if you live according to the flesh you will die; but if by the Spirit you put to death the deeds of the body, you will live" (Rom 8:13).
4. The person who is filled with the Holy Spirit will be enabled to exercise his gifts in the power of God. "Most assuredly, I say to you, he who believes in Me, the works that I do he will do also; and greater works than these he will do, because I go to My Father" (John 14:12).
5. The person who is filled with the Holy Spirit will be powerful in prayer. "And when they had prayed, the place where they were assembled together was shaken; and they were all filled with the Holy Spirit, and they spoke the word of God with boldness" (Acts 4:31). The person who is filled with the Holy Spirit will have a deeper understanding of the Bible. "But as it is written: 'Eye has not seen, nor ear heard, nor have entered into the heart of man the things which God has prepared for those who love Him.' But God has revealed them to us through His Spirit. For the Spirit searches all things, yes, the deep things of God" (1 Cor 2:9–10).
6. The person who is filled with the Holy Spirit will worship God in Spirit and in truth. "God is Spirit, and those who worship Him must worship in spirit and truth" (John 4:24).
7. The person who is filled with the Holy Spirit will carry out his duties in his home, "submitting to one another in the fear of God" (Eph 5:21). "Husbands, love your wives, just as Christ also loved the church and gave Himself for her. . . . Children, obey your parents in the Lord, for this is right" (Eph 5:25; 6:1).
8. The preacher filled with the Holy Spirit will be anointed to preach the gospel with life-changing power.

But there are hindrances to being filled with the Holy Spirit:

1. Ignorance or misunderstanding of the Bible
2. Associating the Holy Spirit with religious fanaticism
3. Laziness and lukewarmness
4. Men-pleasers rather than God-pleasers
5. Prayerlessness
6. Desire to be popular rather than prophetic and biblical
7. Unhealthy influence of former pastors
8. Unhealthy influence of parents
9. Denominational teaching contrary to Scripture
10. Exalting self-life rather than the Savior

The anointing follows the infilling. I want to describe the anointing and my personal experience of the anointing as best I can. I once read of a certain deacon who often prayed publicly for his pastor with these words, "Dear Lord, please unctionize or anoint our pastor." After hearing this prayer time and time again, the pastor asked his deacon, "Brother, what do you mean by unction?" To which the deacon replied, "Brother Pastor, I don't know what it is; but whatever it is, I know you ain't got it." To describe the anointing is impossible, but one thing is clear: when the anointing is present, the people know it; and when it is absent, the people also know it.

The question then is this: what is the anointing? The powerfully anointed Spurgeon admitted he could not explain the anointing. "What is it?" Spurgeon asked. "I wonder how long we might beat our brains out before we could plainly put in words what is meant by preaching with unction; yet he who preaches knows its presence and he who hears can detect its absence; such is the mystery of the anointing; we know but we cannot tell others what it is."[13]

Dr. Tony Sargent, in his superb book *The Sacred Anointing*, describes the experience the anointed preacher enjoys.

---

13. C. H. Spurgeon, *Lectures to My Students* (Carlisle, PA: Banner of Truth, 1979), 50.

It is the afflatus of the Spirit resting on the speaker. It is "power on high." It is the preacher gliding on eagle's wings, soaring high, swooping low, carrying and being carried along by a dynamic other than his own. His consciousness of what is happening is not obliterated. He is not in a trance. He is being worked on but is aware that he is still working. He is being spoken through, but he knows he is still speaking. The words are his, but the facility with which they come compels him to realize that the source is beyond himself.[14]

Pastor Kent Hughes describes the "unnatural silence" that accompanies anointed preaching:

There are times when I am preaching that I have especially sensed the pleasure of God. I usually become aware of it through the unnatural silence. The ever-present coughing ceases and the pews stop creaking, bringing an almost physical quiet to the sanctuary—through which my words sail like arrows. I experience a heightened eloquence, so that the cadence and volume of my voice intensify the truth I am preaching. There is nothing quite like it—the Holy Spirit filling one's sails.[15]

The great English preacher, W. E. Sangster, whom Billy Graham proclaimed to be the greatest preacher of the twentieth century, gave this enigmatic explanation of the unction or anointing:

Unction is the mystic plus in preaching which no one else can define and no one with any spiritual sensitivity at all can mistake. Men have it or they do not have it. It is a thing apart from good sermon outlines, helpful spiritual insights, wise understanding or eloquent speech. It can use all these media—and dispense with them. It is rare, indefinable and unspeakably precious.[16]

---

14. T. Sargent, *The Sacred Anointing* (Wheaton, IL: Crossway, 1994), 29.
15. R. K. Hughes and B. Chapell, *1 and 2 Timothy and Titus*, Preaching the Word Series (Wheaton, IL: Crossway, 2000), 13.
16. W. E. Sangster, *Power in Preaching* (New York: Abingdon, 1958), 106.

Greg Heisler, in *Spirit-Led Preaching*, sets forth four results of anointed preaching: (1) freedom, (2) vitality, (3) power, and (4) possession.[17] To these, I would add five more: (1) joy, (2) confidence, (3) boldness, (4) authority, and (5) endurance.

I like the way Stephen Olford and Adrian Rogers describe the infilling and anointing. "As the filling suggests an inward working of the Spirit, the anointing stresses the outward clothing with the power."[18] "The anointing is the special touch for the special task."[19]

Perhaps it would help for me to describe a special event where I believe the anointing was powerfully manifest. I was preaching on Elijah's revival on Mount Carmel, my subject being, "God's Answer by Fire," my text being 1 Kgs 18:1–40. I concluded my message by quoting loudly and powerfully 1 Kgs 18:38: "The fire of the Lord fell." When I spoke these words, the "fire" of the Holy Spirit fell upon me and the entire congregation. People rushed forward and filled the altar. One "dead" soul was resurrected from the dead. He grabbed me and began to drag me across the church, and several hardened sinners were gloriously converted. This event was the prelude to the greatest revival I ever witnessed in a local church. So manifest was the power upon that church that 21 laymen arose within a year to preach three revivals at Sixteenth Street Baptist Church (now North Pointe), Greensboro, North Carolina, and ushered in an unprecedented prayer revival and growth of the church.

Dr. R. G. Lee, my neighbor and friend in Memphis, shared an experience with me that occurred when he was pastor of a church in New Orleans. He said there was one Sunday when he "flopped" in the pulpit and asked the chairman of the deacons, "Brother deacon, what happened to me today?" The deacon

17. Heisler, *Spirit-Led Preaching*, 139–40.
18. S. Olford, *Anointed Expository Preaching* (Nashville: Broadman & Holman, 2003), 217.
19. Heard on tapes of sermons preached at Bellevue Baptist Church, Memphis, TN, 1972–2004.

asked, "Do you really want to know?" Dr. Lee answered, "Yes," and the deacon replied, "Pastor, you laid the foundation of a skyscraper and proceeded to build a chicken coop on top of it." So it has been for me and, at times, I believe, for every preacher. However, the very day I "flopped" in the morning service, I soared to the heavens in the evening service under the anointing of the Holy Spirit.

Although I have not often experienced such a "fire fall" as I described earlier, I have often had the feeling that I was not actually doing the preaching. I was just looking on in astonishment. It was not my effort. I was just the instrument, the vehicle and channel the Holy Spirit was using.

The effect of anointed preaching upon hearers is equally amazing. In their excellent book *Power in the Pulpit*, Dr. Jerry Vines and Jim Shaddix describe the impact of the anointing on both preacher and people. They write,

> Spirit anointed preaching does something to both the preacher and the people. The anointing keeps the preacher aware of a power not his own. In the best sense of the word, he is "possessed"—caught up in the message by the power of the Spirit. He becomes a channel used by the Holy Spirit. At the same time, the people are gripped, moved and convicted. When the Holy Spirit takes over the preaching event, something miraculous happens.[20]

The question naturally arises, what are the requirements of the preacher for the anointing? The Bible does not give a step-by-step formula for experiencing the anointing, but I would summarize what I believe to be the key in three statements: These men lived a life of holiness, a life of prayerfulness, and a life of yieldedness.[21] The anointing is something that must be sought day by day in the preacher's walk with God—in his

---

20. J. Vines and J. Shaddix, *Power in the Pulpit* (Chicago: Moody, 1999), 66.
21. Olford, *Anointed Expository Preaching*, 218–19.

study, preparation, and the preaching event itself. E. M. Bounds wrote, "This anointing comes to the preacher not in the study but in the closet."[22]

Furthermore, if you ask me, "From whence comes the anointing?" I would point you to the place of the Word of God. The Holy Spirit has bound Himself to the living and written Word of God. Consequently, as a preacher binds himself to the Word by "internalizing" it into his life, he is binding himself to the Holy Spirit and His power. Thus the anointing is within the grasp of every God-called preacher and provides the power by which he engages in powerful preaching.[23]

I was saved at the age of nine. Thus, I possessed the presence of the Holy Spirit in my body, as I was baptized into Christ's body by the Holy Spirit (1 Cor 12:13). I was gloriously called to preach at age 26, but I was not filled with the Holy Spirit until I was 34 years old. This encounter with the Holy Spirit occurred at a time of deep desperation and after I had been fasting, repenting, praying earnestly, and hungering profoundly to experience the power of God in my life and ministry. It happened on the streets of Greensboro, North Carolina.

The experience was far more moving than I can describe. It was not an emotional experience primarily but an experience of revelation. I saw no angels. I did not speak in tongues, and I did not go into a trance or lose consciousness. I was not slain in the Spirit but rather awakened to the greatest reality of my life—a new life of freedom and joy, of consistent fellowship with the risen Christ, consistent victory over sin and discouragement, consistent power for witnessing, and glorious power in preaching. The Holy Spirit joined me on Davie Street in Greensboro. The result was the release of a power I had never known before. Above all, it enabled me to experience preaching with great power and exceedingly great freedom and joy.

22. E. M. Bounds, *Power through Prayer* (Grand Rapids: Baker, 1991), 76.
23. J. Shaddix, *The Passion Driven Sermon* (Nashville: Broadman & Holman, 2003), 81–82.

Prior to the earlier experience, I tended to think of the Holy Spirit as a feeling, but now I knew He was as much a person as God the Father and God the Son—a person I could know and with whom I could have fellowship. In fact, I experienced the Holy Spirit in exactly the same way Jesus described Him to His disciples before Pentecost—He became to me the *Parakletos* (John 14:16)—the One coming alongside me to be my Helper, my Companion, my Comforter, my Motivator, my Lover, my Best Friend. What a glorious discovery! I knew I was no longer alone but that the All-Sufficient One was as close as my breath. I began to experience a power, a freedom, a joy I had never known in my preaching, as I was released from discouragement, tiredness, anger, and frustration.

In fact, before my encounter, I felt relieved each Sunday evening, knowing I would not have to preach for another week. After the infilling and anointing, I desired to preach every day and night—a desire I still have many years later. There was a quickening in my physical body and a notable increase in my physical strength.

I do not mean to imply that I have never experienced low moments and even a few dark nights of the soul, but I have never doubted the sufficiency of the Holy Spirit to meet those needs as I have constantly asked the Holy Spirit to refill me. Powerful preaching of the Word of God will only take place when men of God are filled and anointed with the Holy Spirit. Such preachers not only will preach "good" sermons from a homiletical and exegetical standpoint, but they also will preach in that power above all power, the power of our Risen Lord, the power that raises the dead, the power that is able to save and able to sanctify.

D. L. Moody said,

> We believe firmly that if any man . . . has been cleansed by the blood, redeemed by the blood, and been sealed by the Holy Ghost, the Holy Ghost dwells in him. And a thought I want to call your attention to is this, that God has got a good many

children who have just barely got life, but not power for service. You might say safely, I think, without exaggeration that nineteen out of every twenty of professed Christians are of no earthly account so far as building up Christ's kingdom, but on the contrary are standing right in the way, and the reason is because they have just got life and have settled down and have not sought the power.[24]

I became acquainted with Adrian Rogers in 1971, and we remained close friends until his death in 2004. In my opinion, he was the most powerful preacher Southern Baptists produced in my lifetime. The secret of his power was not primarily in his use of words, of which he was a master, but in the filling and anointing of the Holy Spirit. So in closing, I feel it relevant and appropriate that I share his testimony concerning the desperate need of every believer to be filled and anointed by the Holy Spirit, but especially the preacher of God's Word. Here is what Dr. Rogers wrote:

I want you to imagine a man who has bought, for the first time in his life, a brand-new automobile. He's never driven before, never had an automobile, and what he does not understand is that it has an engine in it. He is proud of the car. He invites his friends over and shows them how beautiful the paint job is, how soft the seats are. And he says, "See how nice this is, what a sleek automobile this is." But everywhere he goes, he has to push it. Sometimes when he is going downhill, he can get in and coast, but that doesn't excite him too much because he knows for every hill that he coasts down he's got to push that thing up the next hill. While he's proud of his automobile and in some ways grateful that he has it, in other ways he secretly wishes he didn't have it. Rather than being a blessing to him, it became a burden to him. Rather than it carrying him, he has to push it. And then somebody says, "I want to show you something. See that thing. That's called an ignition key. Put it right in there and turn it. 'Vroom!'" "What's

24. V. R. Edman, *They Found the Secret* (Grand Rapids: Zondervan, 1973), 76–77.

that?" "That's a thing called the engine. Now take that lever right there and put it where it says 'D' and then press that pedal," and that automobile begins to surge forth with power. "Hey," he says, "this is wonderful, this is glorious, this is amazing. Why didn't somebody tell me before? Why didn't somebody show me about this before?" You say, "That's foolish. Nobody could be that dumb." You're right, unless it is the Christian who does not understand the power of the Holy Spirit of God. Many Christians don't understand that when they got saved, God put an engine in their salvation. I don't mean to speak disrespectfully about the Holy Spirit by calling Him an engine, but He is the dynamism, the power of our Christian life. Many people are somewhat proud of their Christianity, but it's almost a burden to them. Rather than it carrying them, they are pushing it. And they're just grinding out this matter of being a Christian because they have not made the discovery of the wonderful Spirit-filled life. Ephesians 5:18 has a command of God: "And do not be drunk with wine, in which is dissipation; but be filled with the Spirit." When you are filled with the Spirit, it will turn the drudgery to dynamism. Rather than making your Christianity a burden, it will become an empowering blessing to you.[25]

John MacArthur recently observed,

There is certainly no shortage of preachers today who are all emotion and no content . . . preachers whose content is just fine, but whose delivery is flat and passionless. . . . Such preachers usually do not even realize the damage they do to the cause of truth. They may truly love the Word of God and have a high regard for sound doctrine, but what their dispassionate delivery actually communicates is apathy and indifference. In the end, they under mind the very work they believe they are called to advance. The world (and the church) would be better off without such preaching.[26]

---

25. A. Rogers, *What Every Christian Ought to Know* (Nashville: Broadman & Holman, 2005), 168–69.
26. A. Montoya, *Preaching with Passion* (Grand Rapids: Kregal, 2000), 7.

What is wrong with such preachers? Could it be that they are simply not saved or not called to preach in the first place, or could it be they are not filled with the Holy Spirit?

In closing, I wish to make one thing clear above all: I do not expect anyone to have the same experience with the Holy Spirit that I have had. But there is one question I must lovingly ask every God-called preacher of the gospel on this earth: "Brother, are you filled with the Holy Spirit?" If not, admit it, and surrender all to Jesus and be filled today. Text-driven preachers must also be Spirit-filled preachers.

4

THE DISCIPLINES OF A
TEXT-DRIVEN PREACHER

Ned L. Mathews

Watch your life and doctrine closely.

Persevere in them, because if you do, you will save both yourself and your hearers.

—1 Tim 4:16 NIV

All preachers have in common the resources of text and speech. Not all, however, seem dedicated to the notion that they must live by the same principles that they so readily proclaim to others. After all, if listeners are obliged to apply what they hear, are not those who preach expected to do the same? Shall not he who is text driven in the preparation and delivery of sermons also be text driven in thought and deed?

The preacher, like his hearers, must be a conscientious "doer of the word," for he who fails in that will not only deceive himself but also others (Jas 1:22). Such deception is well known in church and culture, leaving the appeal of the gospel greatly weakened, even unattractive, to many. Thus, there is common acknowledgment that sermons, no matter how well prepared or eloquently delivered, even if to much praise, are virtually powerless to convict the minds or hearts of listeners once it is known that the actions of the preacher are in conflict with what he proclaims.

Should not the God who is Himself holy be represented by those who are also holy? The answer, of course, is resoundingly affirmative. Therefore, the preacher is to look first to his own walk with God, then to the walk of those to whom he preaches (1 Tim 4:16). As Doug Webster puts it, "The best preachers are those who preach first to themselves and then to others."[1]

The preacher therefore not only must be holy in his walk with God; he also has a mandate to "keep a close watch on [his] doctrine." The reason is clear. The members of the body of Christ are to be fed by the teaching of the word of God, for that is their nourishment" (1 Tim 4:6 NASU). It is the spiritual food that is essential to their spiritual growth. It is the means by which the followers of Christ are discipled. Thus the pastor, who is also designated in Scripture as elder and bishop, is expected primarily to "feed the flock of God" (1 Pet 5:2 KJV). Indeed, he must give even more careful attention to this duty because of the presence of those who teach doctrinal error. To fail at this is inexcusable in a bishop because he is expected to protect the flock from such predators. The apostle Paul exercised that role when he warned the Ephesian elders of the danger they faced from false teachers, whom he called "fierce wolves," who would "come in among" them (Acts 20:28–30 ESV). On the other hand, the flock of God, when led by a godly shepherd, is able to feed on the word of God without concern of being misled by false teachers.

---

1.   D. Webster, "Walking with John Chrysostom," *JBDS* (Spring 2009): 14.

In our time there is widespread antipathy toward doctrine or, for that matter, toward anything deemed ideological. Some would say that this antipathy borders on revulsion. For example, the so-called mainline denominations consider doctrine divisive, thus a threat to church unity and a hindrance to their much-vaunted progressivism. As for a growing number of evangelicals, how can they keep a close watch on something they apparently have trouble seeing? In the film *O Brother, Where Art Thou?* the protagonists are known as the Foggy Bottom Boys. Is this not descriptive of the current situation among many evangelicals? They appear to be dwelling in the swamp of a foggy bottom concerning the issue of doctrine. The result is that questions are now being asked that, in other times, would have seemed odd, even perplexing. Is doctrine really essential for church music?[2] Is doctrine even "relevant" to the problems that people of this generation face?[3] These are important questions, of course, but there is another more important one. Shall we tailor our worship experiences, our preaching, and our teaching to suit the temperament of the age or the God of eternity? Unfortunately, many have decided, as their actions indicate, that they prefer the temperament of the age.

A godly preacher, however, must have another agenda. It is personal and it is urgent because it affects the health of Christ's church. The agenda is clear: "Keep a close watch on *yourself* and on *the teaching. Persist* in this, for by so doing you will save both yourself and your hearers" (1 Tim 4:16 ESV, italics added). Persistence is a major part of the agenda. The preacher must realize that it is not enough for him to be occasionally committed to such vital matters. To be around a preacher who is a

---

2. See Eph 5:19–21 and Col 3:16. The issue is not one of traditional or contemporary church music but whether either style uses the wealth of scriptural doctrine available for lyrical content.
3. See 2 Tim 4:3–4. The age of which Paul wrote has arrived. Many of our contemporaries seem to prefer entertainment, defined by Paul as "the tickling of the ears," and preachers who teach only what they deem relevant to the interests and "felt needs" of their listeners.

poor example of the faith and ungodly in behavior is a cause of much aggravation and disappointment for believers. Will the *real* preacher please stand up?[4] The scriptural commands under consideration also provoke a sense of urgency because they resound with an alarm that lives hang in the balance for time and eternity (John 5:24). Thus, godly living "saves" or delivers a spiritual leader from the displeasure and judgment of the Lord to whom he "must give an account" (Heb 13:17 NIV). Moreover, sound doctrinal teaching "saves" or delivers those who hear it and accept it.[5] A preacher who is godly and faithful in the proclamation of doctrine therefore has a powerful influence on his generation, with an impact that will endure for future generations as well. One thinks of the legacy of Luther, Calvin, Wesley, Whitefield, Moody, Billy Graham, and a host of others. If we are lacking such men in our day, could it be because we are not being led by text-driven men to the same degree?

But how will such a commitment to being text-driven in conduct and ministry come to pass? Only he who is serious about it needs to apply. Paul compares the mandate for developing a godly life and effective teaching of sound doctrine to the world of athletics, to long practice sessions in a gymnasium, with athletes stripped only to their essential garments in pursuing the objective of excellence in the chosen event. He states that such physical effort, however, is of "a limited benefit," whereas "godliness is beneficial in every way, since it holds promise for the present life and also for the life to come" (1 Tim 4:8 HCSB).

What is godliness? Is it just an attitude or is it something that can be observed? It is both. Paul implored the Philippian believers: "Let this [attitude] be in you which was also in Christ Jesus." Then he followed that by reminding them of the Lord's

---

4. See Gerald Kennedy. He thinks that "eventually even the most obtuse member of the congregation must see the quality of the person who is doing the speaking." *The Seven Worlds of the Minister* (New York: Harper & Row, 1968), 2.
5. See Ezek 33:9 for a reference that the apostle Paul may have had in mind. Those who warn the wicked man to turn from his evil way deliver or save their own souls from the judgment of the Lord.

obedience to His Father as He humbled Himself and gave up His life on the cross (Phil 2:5–8 NKJV). Godliness is therefore both attitude and action. It is, in essence, as Paul reminds us, Christlike character. Thus the preacher is to exhibit a pattern for godly living "in speech, in conduct, in love, in faith, in purity" (1 Tim 4:12 ESV). The display of this pattern, like the beautiful tapestry of Christlikeness that it is, will give credence and power to the words proclaimed from pulpits, Bible study classes, and other venues.

In this context, a preacher should expect that he will have to discipline himself in order to excel in developing Christlikeness and in teaching sound doctrine. It will require daily and relentless practice. He will have to work at it and stay with it.

DRIVEN TO EXCEL IN DEVELOPING GODLY CHARACTER

The bottom line for personal integrity is character. What the man of God says in his sermons and how he conducts himself before the public cannot be separated. Certainly, more is required of him than this, such as pastoral care and oversight of his work, but no less is expected. No matter how corrupt the culture becomes, character still matters. There is nothing about this that is time bound or relative to evolving moral standards. The apostle Paul makes this quite clear to the young pastors, Timothy and Titus, in the Pastoral Epistles.[6]

Some pastors like to imagine that they will one day come to be known as great preachers, constantly in demand on the conference circuit. Yet even if for a while, people think that certain

---

6. See 1 Tim 3:2 and Titus 1:7. The bishop or pastor is to be "blameless," that is, he is to be "above reproach." Literally, he should be one who "cannot be laid hold of" and charged with blame. To Titus, Paul adds that his teaching should "show integrity [and] dignity" (Titus 2:7 ESV). The apostle thus raises the bar of ethical and spiritual qualification very high for the preaching and teaching responsibilities of the pastor.

men preach with unusual power, they cease to be impressed once it is known that they are involved in scandalous behavior. Character still matters. History confirms this. In every generation, Christian leaders have arisen who call for holiness in all those who preach the word of God. John Wycliffe (1324–84) was one of them. He is reported to have said, in a play on words, that there are "two things necessary" for the pastor: "the holiness of the pastor and the wholesomeness of his teaching."[7]

Of course, the wider the circle of influence, the more crucial it is that those who attain status as outstanding preachers-teachers be careful to maintain their reputations as men of godly character. For example, shock waves are still being felt in the churches of America because of the recent highly publicized scandals of certain well-known evangelical ministers. Moreover, such perverseness, including the numerous cases of Roman Catholic priests engaging in the reprehensible practice of pedophilia, provokes revulsion in the society at large and even widespread rejection of the Christian message. These reports discourage and depress the followers of Christ.

Every generation has examples of widely influential pastors who have fallen in disgrace. One of the more highly publicized accounts involved Henry Ward Beecher, son of Lyman Beecher, for whom the Yale Lectures on Preaching was named. Henry was regarded as a great preacher. He "had immense public stature in the 1870s. . . . [His] powers to inspire lifted him to new heights of public admiration."[8] But rumors began to circulate that he was having an adulterous affair with his best friend's wife. In 1875, the matter was taken to trial and created a national sensation. For six weeks, the proceedings of the trial were printed in the nation's leading newspapers. Beecher was tried for "alienating the affections of Elisabeth Tilton" for her husband, and in

---

7. J. Wycliffe, cited in J. MacArthur, ed., *Rediscovering Pastoral Ministry* (Dallas: Word, 1995), 48.
8. G. Dorrien, *The Making of American Liberalism 1805–1900* (Louisville: Westminster John Knox, 2001), 234.

that day, such was considered a criminal offense.[9] Though the case ended in a mistrial, the evidence against Beecher was voluminous and the sensational charges followed Beecher for the rest of his life. His notoriety remains to this day, but his reputation as a preacher of integrity is seriously discredited. Beecher eventually "seemed to grasp that the cultural basis of his fame had changed. He was admired for his sparkling celebrity, not for his goodness."[10]

On the other hand, John ("Golden Mouth") Chrysostom (545–407) was a powerfully effective preacher who is revered to this day. He labored hard in study and preparation and excelled in sermon delivery. He also gave special attention to developing godly character. Many agree that he "ranks not only as the foremost preacher of the Greek Church, but also as a pastor of the highest reputation."[11] He had a reputation for holiness, though he lived all his life in fear that he might, in the end, still be found wanting in meeting the approval of the Chief Shepherd, Jesus Christ.[12]

God demands holiness of all who are in covenant with him (Lev 20:7), but He especially expects it of preachers. Of course, the same is true of a congregation as well. Thus, there remains the unspoken but troubling question in the minds of those who listen to sermons, especially when news breaks of disgraced preachers: "Does *this* preacher practice what he preaches?" The question reminds us that a sermon is not only heard; it is also seen. Richard Baxter was certain of this. Thus, he admonished his fellow pastors of the Worcestershire Association:

> It is not likely that the people will regard the doctrine of such men, when they see that they do not live as they preach. They

---

9. Ibid., 244.
10. Ibid., 247.
11. A. Purves, *Pastoral Theology in the Classical Tradition* (Louisville: Westminster John Knox, 2001), 33.
12. J. Chrysostom, *On the Priesthood, A Treatise in Six Books* (Westminster, MD: The Newman Bookshop, 1945), 36–39.

will think he doth not mean as he speaks, if he doth not live as he speaks. They will hardly believe a man that seemeth not to believe himself. . . . As long as men have eyes as well as ears, they will think they *see* your meaning as well as *hear* it; and they are apter to believe their sight than their hearing, as being the more perfect sense of the two. All that a minister doth is a kind of preaching; and if you live a covetous or a careless life, you preach these sins to your people by your practice.[13]

If the preacher's own life is inconsistent with his message, the public is quite justified in questioning whether there is any credibility in what he says. On the other hand, the preacher whose life is an open demonstration of the principles he proclaims has a lasting salutary effect on his listeners. Many rightly assume, in such circumstances, that the preacher functions, like his Lord, as a model for what he proclaims (1 Cor 11:1). A message to a pastor from one of his former church members provides support for this claim:

I appreciate all of the time you spent in bringing your messages to us as I was growing up. It has had a profound impact in my life and many others as well. I've been very fortunate to sit under the leadership of some fine godly men in ministry. Both you and my current pastor have been *great examples to me* of what a Christian should be. . . . Thanks for your faithfulness in bringing God's word to folks for all of these years (Italics provided).[14]

Luke, the author of Acts, must have seen the importance of deeds that fit with one's message when he wrote the opening words of his gospel. The order of the verbs in his remarks about Jesus are particularly significant. "In the first book, O Theophilus, I have dealt with all that Jesus began *to do* and

---

13. R. Baxter, *The Reformed Pastor* (Carlisle, PA: The Banner of Truth Trust, 1974), 84.
14. Used by permission of the writer.

teach" (Acts 1:1 ESV, italics added). This sequence of acts and speech, in that order, is especially consistent with the practice of making disciples. The teacher models the principles of holy character lest what he teaches is undermined by what he does. Jesus sums up the importance of this in this timeless axiom: "A disciple is not above his teacher, but everyone when he is fully trained will be like his teacher" (Luke 6:40). It was the deeds of the Lord in his praying, sometimes through the night, that led his disciples to ask him to teach them how and what to pray (Luke 11:1). Likewise, it is what we learn from the deeds and words of Jesus that shapes our lives as disciples and, in large part, forms the content of what we teach as text-driven preachers.

Moreover, the terms "deeds" and "words" are not exclusive of each other, the importance of which is underscored when we realize that some words actually function as deeds. Language theorists have long considered such a phenomenon under the rubric of performative speech or speech acts (e.g., John L. Austin, John R. Searle, and others). For example, the loud cry of "Fire!" will empty a public building quickly. The words "I do," when spoken by bride and groom, moreover, cause the officiating minister to declare them married. Presumably they would remain unmarried if one or the other had been silent.

By this light, a preacher's sermons, when they are shaped by the power of the words of Scripture, have the same effect on those who listen to him as they have on him. This is why effective expository preachers, especially with longevity in a particular church, find that the members, over time, begin to take on the persona of the pastor (thus confirming again the truth of Luke 6:40). Moreover, their confidence in him as a leader is confirmed because they see that what he requires of them, in obedience to the Lord, is backed up by his own life. This is more likely to happen, however, when the preacher's mind and heart remain firmly fixed on the word of God through thoughtful reflection and meditation in the Scriptures (see Ps 1:2). In this way, the power of the truth of Scripture affects his life continually so that he becomes wise in the ways of God. This is indeed a life-changing experience as the examples that follow demonstrate.

To this day, the students of Bluefield College in Virginia hear stories of the beloved fifth president of that institution, Dr. Charles Harman (1946–71). He was regarded by all as a man of deep devotion to God, a man who loved the Scriptures, and one who possessed the highest ethical standards and character. He held that office during my student days in that institution, and I observed firsthand his fidelity to the teachings of Scripture, his acts of wisdom, and his gentle Christian grace. It is good to remember the life of one whose deeds so well matched his words.

On the other hand, religion based on something other than the power of the word of God produces some strange aberrations. Simeon Stylites, who died in AD 459, was an ascetic who spent 36 years of his life living on the top of a pillar east of Antioch. He and others like him were considered by many to be "spiritual athletes." He is "said to have touched his feet with his forehead 1,244 times in succession."[15] The impact of a man like that on the lives of others had the effect of being nothing more than mere entertainment for the masses, fascination with a religious oddity, or an example, in the extreme, of "trivial pursuit." Contrast that, however, with the preaching power of the Puritan divine William Gouge. Unlike the public spectacle of Stylites perched on a pillar, he went into the privacy of his prayer chamber every day. Instead of the physical (deemed "spiritual") athleticism of "touching his feet with his forehead 1,244 times," he applied his mind to the Scriptures and his feet to shoe leather so that he could walk about to tell others of the gospel's life-changing power. He filled his mind with the word of God so much that he became known for his encyclopedic knowledge of the Bible. It is said of him that he "read through 16 chapters of

---

15. K. S. Latourette, *A History of Christianity* (New York: Harper & Brothers, 1953), 228.

the Bible every day, after his 6:00 A.M. morning prayers."[16] And his impact on others was notable. He received acclaim in his time as being one of the most effective preachers of England.

Let there be no misunderstanding, however. There are at least two fallacies that those who pursue the exemplary text-driven life must avoid.

The first fallacy is one of long standing in church history. It is the idea that one's life makes for a better sermon than one's words. It is well to remember, instead, that the preacher's life, when godly in character, only confirms the gospel; it does not *replace* it. Some in the Emergent Church movement, such as Dan Kimball, seem to think otherwise. Michael Horton sees this as part of the "alternative gospel of the American church." He rightly rejects such reductionism:

> Like many Emergent Church leaders, Kimball invokes a famous line from Francis of Assisi that I also heard growing up in conservative evangelicalism: "Preach the gospel at all times. If necessary, use words." Kimball goes on to say, "Our lives will preach better than anything we can say" (We encountered a nearly identical statement from Osteen . . .). If so, then this is just more bad news. . . . I am not an exemplary creature. . . . I am a Christian not because I think that I can walk in Jesus' footsteps but because he is the only one who can carry me. I am not the gospel; Jesus Christ alone is the gospel. . . . We do not preach ourselves but Christ. The good news . . . is that what we *say* preaches better than our lives, at least if what we are saying is *Christ's* person and work rather than our own.[17]

A variation of the argument by Kimball is the oft-repeated dictum of liberal theologians that "Christianity is a life, not a doctrine." This dichotomy is well refuted by J. Gresham Machen in his classic book *Christianity and Liberalism* and needs not take up space in this discourse. Instead, we return to Paul's word to

16. C. M. McMahon, "The Life of the Preacher." Online: http://apuritansmind.com/ Pastoral McMahonLifePreacher.htm.
17. M. Horton, *Christless Christianity* (Grand Rapids: Baker, 2008), 117.

Timothy that the believer is to take heed to his life *"and* to the doctrine" (1 Tim 4:16 NKJV, italics added). Being text-driven in one's life, therefore, is a means to an end, not the end itself. The intention is to see to it that we do not allow ourselves to live in such a way that our deeds have the effect of silencing or distorting the message we preach.

The second fallacy is sheer misrepresentation. It is the charge that those who are text driven in life and message somehow become worshippers of the biblical text itself. The pejorative term is "bibliolatry." This distortion must not be allowed to stand. Moses did not worship the text, though it is apparent that few were more text driven than he. Down from Mount Sinai he came with two tablets of stone in his hand, containing the Ten Commandments, "written with the finger of God" (Exod 31:18 ESV). As he descended, his face was shining, apparently because of his nearness to the presence of God. Although he did not know it at the time, his face was shining not because of the tablets, nor the text inscribed on them, but "because he had been talking *with* God" (Exod 34:29 ESV, italics added). In like manner, therefore, text-driven preachers are not idolaters of the biblical text. Instead, text-driven preaching is always teleological in nature; that is, the purpose of the reading and exegesis of the text is to drive the preacher and his listeners into the presence of God to worship Him alone.

The biblical text, because it is the "God-breathed" word from God (2 Tim 3:16 NIV), has the power, therefore, to place both preacher and listener in the very presence of God.[18] Billy Graham has long seemed to know this as he demonstrates in his oft-repeated phrase: "The Bible says. . . ." The text-driven preacher then is one whose encounter with the word of the

---

18. See Ps 119:169–76. This *Taw* section of the longest psalm clearly sums up the value of the text for the psalmist. The statutes of the text drives him to life-changing experiences with the Lord. Even when he wanders away, he desires nothing more than to be recovered by his shepherd Lord for he is ever mindful of the commandments of the Torah (vv. 171 and 176).

Lord provides content for that from which he should "flee" and to that which he should "pursue," in the former case, all kinds of evil, and in the latter, "righteousness, godliness, faith, love, perseverance and gentleness" (1 Tim 6:6–11 NASB).

DRIVEN TO EXCEL IN DOCTRINAL FIDELITY

I begin this section with some "What ifs?" What if somewhere, sometime, a man called of God to preach the gospel became convinced that he should give himself unreservedly to the study, memorization, and meditation of Scripture? And what if he did so, not as preparation for sermon delivery, but because he, like Paul (Phil 3:10), longed to know better the truth that led him to know Christ in the first place? And what if, as a result, his soul were to become aflame with a passion to declare to others what the Holy Spirit had revealed to him, as he mused upon the message of the texts he studied? And what if, like Jeremiah the prophet, he became a man with "a fire shut up in [his] bones" so that he could not forbear until he delivered his message (Jer 20:9 NKJV)? And what if that, in turn, resulted in changed lives so that the community in which this preaching and teaching occurred was transformed all the way down to its cultural roots? This, however, is not mere speculation. It actually happened.

The man aflame was Richard Baxter. The community was Kidderminster, England. The time was the seventeenth century. In the introduction of the book *The Reformed Pastor*, J. I. Packer explains what happened to the town when the pastor gave his life to his people. Baxter himself said that "on the Lord's Day . . . you might hear an hundred families singing Psalms and repeating sermons as you passed through the streets." He continued that when he arrived in the town of 2,000 people, there was not "one family in the side of a street that worshipped God." Others reported later that, at the end of his ministry, "there was not one family in the side of a street that did not do so."[19] Could

---

19. Baxter, *The Reformed Pastor*, 12.

what happened to him and to those who were transformed by his messages happen again? Why not? If other preachers were to follow the same pattern, is it not possible that there could be a similar outcome?

Any preacher, then, who becomes a text-driven man will not only become more fired up to proclaim what he has experienced in his close study of biblical texts; he also will *stay on message* in his preaching. Accordingly, he will be less likely, for fear of the consequences, to dilute the force of prophetic preaching or to ignore the essentials of the gospel message. Such examples include Jesus' radical demands of his disciples (Mark 8:34) and the primacy of the preaching of the cross of Christ (1 Cor 2:2). In short, he will be less likely to shape or fashion his message in such a way as to assure his own popularity and public acclaim. Instead, because his way of thinking, his personal goals, and his ways are exposed and judged daily by his study of the Scriptures, he finds himself inevitably brought under conviction of his waywardness by the Holy Spirit. Moreover, when he is thus humbled by that experience and willing to be compliant with the Spirit's direction for his life, he is also inevitably changed in character and conduct. And if such is the outcome in his life, he is accordingly determined to preach this same truth to his people so that *they too* may be convicted to put the Lord's way and glory above their own ambitions.[20] The text-driven preacher therefore stays on message because he knows that only the Bible gives him the authority to declare the truth that every generation so desperately needs.

It is, after all, the Bible that bears witness to Christ from beginning to end (Luke 24:27). And it is He whom we preach. So then, why do not all preachers give themselves to such a

---

20. See Heb 4:12. The Word of God is "living" and piercing to the soul of the reader so as to render one wounded and exposed before the eye of God. Compare this with Isa 55:8–11. The "thoughts and intents" of the heart are thus revealed so that an experience of genuine worship may occur. If the preacher is *not* subjected to this life-changing power in his own life, how can he justifiably demand it of others?

life-changing study of Scripture? John R. W. Stott accurately also points out the reason. It is because they seem to forget that Christ "is accessible only through the Bible, as the Holy Spirit brings to life his own witness to him in its pages."[21] Stott puts it this way:

> It is certain that we cannot handle Scripture adequately in the pulpit if our doctrine of Scripture is inadequate. Conversely, evangelical Christians who have the highest doctrine of Scripture in the Church should be conspicuously the most conscientious preachers. . . . If Scripture were largely a symposium of human ideas, though reflecting the faith of the early Christian communities, and lit up an occasional flash of divine inspiration, then a fairly casual attitude to it would be pardonable. *But in Scripture we are handling the very words of God*, "words not taught by human wisdom but taught by the Spirit" (1 Cor. 2:13), God's words through men's, his own witness to his own Son, then no trouble should be too great in the study and exposition of them (italics added).[22]

If what Stott advocates were to take hold among evangelical preachers on a broad enough scale, is it possible that today's churches would cease lurching from one ecclesiological fashion to another in what seems to be a never-ending quest for relevance to the culture? We are told that cultural changes such as generational differences, pluralism, and multiculturalism require us to move from a traditional outreach ministry structure to a postmodern one such as the emerging church, or from classical worship to "seeker sensitive" services or to "relevant" services designed solely for the interests of those who attend such. However, not one of these highly acclaimed changes has proven effective in transforming culture into anything resembling the evangelical Protestant hegemony that once prevailed in America. Accordingly, the seeker-sensitive model is now

---

21. J. R. W. Stott, *Between Two Worlds, the Art of Preaching in the Twentieth Century* (Grand Rapids: Eerdmans, 1982), 98.
22. Ibid., 99.

being revamped because its leaders have confessed its inadequacy for making disciples. To his credit, Bill Hybels, the founder of that movement, has been candid in admitting that the Willow Creek Church has made some serious errors in their approach to reaching people. He said, "Some of the stuff that we have put millions of dollars into thinking it would really help our people grow and develop spiritually, when the data actually came back, it wasn't helping people that much. Other things that we didn't put that much money into, and didn't put much staff against, is stuff our people are crying out for."[23] In fairness to Hybels, however, it should be admitted by all that the same judgment may be made against the traditional approach to making disciples. It has failed also. One evidence of this is that the major Christian denominations of America have been in serious numerical decline for years if not decades. Yet it remains true that when strong, dynamic exposition of Scripture is practiced in the churches, it is always effective in making and maturing disciples with results, over time, similar to those experienced by the people of Kidderminster.

David Wells, in his outstanding assessment of the current situation in American Christianity, believes that he sees a shift away from culturally driven distortions of authentic Christianity. Here is part of that assessment:

> There is a yearning in the evangelical world today. We encounter it everywhere. It is a yearning for what is real. Sales pitches, marketed faith, the gospel as commodity, people as customers, God as just a prop to my inner life, the glitz and sizzle, Disney Land on the loose in our churches—all of it is skin deep and often downright wrong. It is not making serious disciples. It cannot make serious disciples. It brims with success, but it is empty, shallow, and indeed unpardonable.[24]

---

23. B. Hybels, "Willow Creek Repents?" Online: http://blog.christianitytoday.com/outofur/archives/2007/10/willow_creek_re.html.
24. D. Wells, *The Courage to Be Protestant* (Grand Rapids: Eerdmans, 2008), 57–58.

Wells is right. It is obvious that the church has swerved off track. If it is going to get back on track, it will have to be led by pastors who once again "take heed to the teaching," as Paul put it to Timothy (1 Tim 4:16). The content of the teaching, of course, is sound doctrine that presents a far different faith than the one that has become popular in the early part of the twenty-first century. That faith is in the Jesus of the Bible who is a radical Christ with uncompromising demands for kingdom living. This is not going to change no matter what cultural trends come and go. In regard to the seeker-sensitive approach and the corresponding market-driven paradigm that created it, the gospel is not a product for sale and the masses are not customers. It will always be difficult to sell a call to Christian discipleship that requires execution.[25]

All this raises the question, how far have we drifted from our moorings as text-driven preachers? Marsha G. Witten is a sociologist who has done some studies on this and related issues. While listening to a Good Friday concert of Bach's St. Matthew Passion on the radio, the mail came and with it a mass mailing of a local Baptist church in the process of formation. What a contradiction, she thought, between the rendition in the music of the suffering and fallen Messiah and the mass-mailing brochure. She writes, "Mimicking the slick direct mailing of a credit card or insurance company, the letter contains a cheerful, practical list of the social and psychological pleasures one might receive from affiliation with its church—with no mention of faith or God, let alone suffering or spiritual striving."[26] She sees "an incongruity" in these messages.[27] The remarkable thing about her insight is that she is not a Christian.

---

25. See Mark 8:34. It is a radical Christ the New Testament presents. His demands for those who would follow Him seem far away indeed from what is being offered in His name in many contemporary churches.

26. M. G. Witten, *All Is Forgiven, the Secular Message in American Protestantism* (Princeton: Princeton University Press, 1993), 4.

27. Ibid.

Witten's study is based on the texts of 47 sermons on the Prodigal Son (Luke 15:1–32). These sermons "were preached between 1986 and 1988 by a sample of pastors within the Presbyterian Church (U.S.A.) and the Southern Baptist Convention."[28] Twenty-one are from Southern Baptists and 26 from Presbyterians.[29] Witten uses the structure of discourse analysis of the sermons to draw her conclusions. There are limitations to the study, of course. She discusses these on pages 14 to 17 of her book. The bottom line of her research is not very encouraging for any who may believe that text-driven preaching, which we champion in this book, is a common practice. For the 47 preachers who participated in the study, Witten's research reveals that these preachers are driven more by the conclusions of psychology than the message of Scripture. The preachers in the study used the secular language of psychology in focusing on "the subjective states of individuals [the younger and elder sons and the father in the parable] such as feelings and needs."[30] Witten concluded that if the preaching of these men is representative of current Protestant preaching, we now have "Christian psychology" in the pulpits of America. The key ideas deemed worthy of preaching by these men are "self awareness, self exploration, self knowledge, and self expression."[31] As we can see from this study, the need for a recovery of text-driven preaching is a desperate one.

HOW THE PREACHER BECOMES A TEXT-DRIVEN MAN

It is not a single or even an occasional dramatic encounter with the Word of God that makes one a text-driven preacher,

28. Ibid., 13.
29. Ibid.
30. Ibid., 20.
31. Ibid.

though such encounters are inspiring to us all. One thinks of Augustine's touching experience in the garden as he heard the voice of a child repetitively urging him to "take and read" followed by his reading of Rom 13:13–14, which changed his life forever. Or one may think of John Wesley's remarkable conversion at Aldersgate when, upon hearing Luther's commentary on Romans, his "heart was strangely warmed." But becoming a text-driven man is more pedestrian than that. It is the day-by-day exposure to the Word of God in disciplined study that makes the difference. As Gerald Kennedy put it, "It is immersing oneself in the atmosphere of the Bible until that world whose God is real is active in your world"[32]

Becoming a text-driven man is not easy. Paul made that clear to Timothy. The young pastor would have to work at it. It will always be a struggle. Some may find the challenge either unappealing or undesirable. This must have been the case in the early days of the church or else why would Paul have felt it necessary to deliver such a strict challenge to Timothy to strive for it? But it can be done. Paul himself was such a man, as his epistles attest. So, the bottom line is this: a preacher must *want* to be a text-driven man. Given that desire, here are some suggestions of how that can happen.

First, the preacher will need to work through any doubts, if he has them, of the desirability of a text-driven life and ministry. For some, this may take a crisis of faith. Does he really believe that such preaching is what our generation needs, given the cultural upheaval and the various ways that many are now "doing church"? If so, let him get on with the crisis of faith and seek to resolve it. This is what happened to Billy Graham. Richard Foster explains,

> Billy had to face the issue of the Bible as the focus of his life again just prior to the famous 1949 Los Angeles Crusade.

---

32. Kennedy, *Seven Worlds of the Minister*, 22.

Chuck Templeton, a close friend and able preacher in his own right, had been attending Princeton Seminary and was challenging some of Graham's most cherished beliefs about the inspiration and authority of Scripture. Graham indicated little inclination or patience for abstract intellectualism. "Bill," Templeton retorted, "you cannot refuse to think. To do that is to die intellectually." The rebuke stung, and the debate in his soul intensified. Finally, the issue came to a head at Forest Home, a Christian retreat centre in the San Bernardino Mountains near Los Angeles. Struggling over the intellectual questions his friend had raised, Billy went out alone into the pine forest to think, to pray. With his Bible spread open on a tree stump he dropped to his knees. "O God!" he prayed. "There are many things in this book I do not understand. There are many problems with it for which I have no solution. . . . Father, I am going to accept this as Thy Word—by FAITH! I'm going to allow faith to go beyond my intellectual questions and doubts, and I will believe this is Your inspired Word."[33]

As the late Paul Harvey would have put it, "Now we know the rest of the story." On the other hand, Templeton (1915–2001), the man who prodded Graham to reject the authority of Scripture, also struggled with his faith. But it was not the text of Scripture that provided the crisis. Instead, the crisis for Templeton came through his reading of other texts, especially those of Charles Darwin.[34] He accepted Darwin's position on "the origin of the species" and rejected Scripture's account, thus his appeal to Graham "to think." He started down another path and eventually became an agnostic. Ironically, many felt that, in earlier years, he had been a better preacher than Billy, especially during their college days. In those years, he and Billy worked together as associates of Youth for Christ International. It is reported that his preaching drew larger numbers of people to their special rallies and mass meetings than

---

33. R. Foster, *Streams of Living Water* (San Francisco: HarperCollins, 2001), 210.
34. Radio interview with Torrey Johnson as reported in http:/www.wheaton.edu/bgc/archives/trans/285t04.htm.

did Billy's. His preaching was dynamic. Yet according to fellow evangelist Torrey Johnson, Templeton once preached a sermon on the cross without providing a single scriptural reference.[35] Templeton was not text driven. He did *not* "closely watch [his] life or [his] doctrine." In the end, he was neither able to "save himself" or those who heard him (again, see 1 Tim 4:16).

Second, a text-driven life and a faithful proclamation of sound doctrine will not come by osmosis. A Bible placed under the preacher's head while he is sleeping will not, during the night, seep into the synapses of his brain. It requires effort through spiritual exercise. Is the preacher willing to discipline himself to seek the Lord in the fellowship of prayer and in his study of the Scriptures? Does he follow that up by Scripture memory drills and meditation? This is not the dry dust dullness of medieval scholasticism or mere religious ritual. He keeps the appointment time with the Lord in prayer and in Bible study not because it is a religious duty imposed on him by his conscience or religious tradition but because, through these means, he knows that he may encounter the Lord Himself as did the two disciples on the road to Emmaus (Luke 24:32). He seeks *Him* in this discipline. He knows, as those two men learned, that when the Word of God is opened, the Lord seems to show up.

Jesus spoke plainly to His detractors when He told them that they did not have His word "abiding" in them (John 5:38). Moreover, He told them that they did not have the love of God in them either (John 5:42). Then He revealed to them why their Bible study was fruitless. "You search the Scriptures because you think that in them you have eternal life, and *it is they that bear witness about me*" (John 5:39 ESV, italics added). The text-driven life leads us to Christ. This is the real life that Jesus promised (John 10:10).

Third, none of this will produce godliness without persistence. "Keep a close watch on yourself and on the teaching. *Persist* in

---

35. T. Johnson, "Collection 285 - Torrey Johnson. T4 Transcript." Online: http://wheaton.edu/bgc/archives/trans/285t04.htm.

this" (1 Tim 4:16, italics added). What is persistence? It is learning how to begin again. Victor Hugo wrote, "People do not lack strength, they lack will." Yesterday's text-driven life will not suffice for today's need. Have we, day by day, the will to persist in keeping "a close watch on ourselves and on the doctrine"? Most preachers live and die in relative obscurity, but any preacher can be just as text driven as another.

EXAMPLES THAT INSPIRE ONE
TO BE A TEXT-DRIVEN PREACHER

What does a text-driven preacher look like? Three examples follow, one from New Testament times, one from church history, and the other from my own experience.

Apollos was proclaimed a man "mighty in the Scriptures" (Acts 18:24 NKJV). His understanding of the text, however, was deficient until he received "instruction in the way of the Lord." Aquila and Priscilla "explained to him the way of God more accurately" (Acts 18:25). The word "accurately" translates the word *akribōs*. Louw and Nida point out that this word pertains "to strict conformity to a norm or standard, involving both detail and completeness." Text-driven preachers, as we can see in Luke's comments about Apollos, want to get it right.

That Apollos was text-driven, both in his life and in his preaching, was also made plain by his use of the Scriptures in debates. Luke points out that "he powerfully refuted the Jews in public, showing *by the Scriptures* that the Christ was Jesus" (Acts 18:27–28 ESV, italics added). It was the Scriptures, expounded boldly by him, that convinced them. This is life-changing preaching. Many of his listeners were not the same after hearing him.

John Bunyan was a text-driven man. His classical allegory, *The Pilgrim's Progress*, comports with Scripture at every point. In Bedford, England, where he spent many years in prison because he refused to procure a license from the state church to preach the gospel, stands his statue. On its back panel are the words Bunyan wrote, as in his account of "the House of the Interpreter." There Christian saw this scene: "A very great person hung against the wall and this was the fashion: eyes lifted up to heaven, the best of books in his hands, the laws of truth was written on his lips, the world was behind his back; he stood as if he pleaded with men; a crown of gold did hang above his head."[36]

Another that belongs in that portrait was the late James Leo Green, Old Testament professor at Southeastern Baptist Theological Seminary (c. 1960s). Dr. Green's forte was his scholarly work on the prophets. Students of yesteryear will remember, as do I, those days when Dr. Green was often "carried away" when lecturing on the prophets, particularly Amos of Tekoa. He would begin calmly, in a pedantic fashion, slowly and methodically, but then would come the transformation, when as one student put it, "the professor *became* the prophet." His voice would rise in passionate pitch and resonant cadences of poetic fervor until he himself seemed transfixed by the ardor and power of his own words. Teaching for him in those moments became fervent proclamation. Its effect on his listeners was palpable. The heat of early summer had caused the students to raise the windows, and the scene inside of rapt listeners, hanging on every word, was replicated outside as students, on their way to their classes, would stop enthralled under the windows of Old Appleby to listen to the enraptured professor. Others, on the sidewalks, farther from the building, hurried to listen in as well.

Most of us have long forgotten the lecture points of that day, but we will not soon forget the love of the Scriptures, fervor of proclamation, and the clarity of exposition of our beloved professor. What was then transitory in its effect on us as students has the potential now of becoming permanent for those who, like Dr. Green, develop both a text-driven life and a text-driven message.

---

36. As cited by W. A. Criswell in *Guidebook for Pastors* (Nashville: Broadman, 1980), 23.

In a way, 1 Tim 4:16 is the Magna Carta of Preaching. Like the document signed by King John in 1215, which guaranteed the basic liberties of England, this passage of Scripture, when signed onto by pastors who are text driven, frees the people of God from the tyranny of spiritually corrupt leadership. They are thus set free to follow the guidance of pastors who practice what they preach and teach others, by their example, to do the same.

What does it mean then to be a preacher who has a text-driven life? It means that such a man is under the influence of Scripture not only in his private devotions and public proclamation but also in his thoughts, his deeds, and his worldview. Go forth, pastors, as text-driven men!

PART II

PREPARATION AND
TEXT-DRIVEN PREACHING

5

PREPARING A TEXT-DRIVEN SERMON

David L. Allen

TEXT-DRIVEN PREACHING: A BIBLICAL AND THEOLOGICAL FOUNDATION

The method of preparing text-driven sermons is under-girded by certain biblical and theological convictions. Accordingly, John Stott insightfully comments that the essential secret of preaching is not "mastering certain techniques, but being mastered by certain convictions."[1] The biblical and theological foundation for all preaching is the fact that God has revealed Himself.[2] God is a God who speaks. Hebrews 1:1 states it clearly: "God, having spoken in times past to the fathers by the prophets in many portions and in many ways, has in these last days spoken to us in his Son." God's speech through

---

1. J. Stott, *Between Two Worlds* (Grand Rapids: Eerdmans, 1982), 92.
2. For an excellent short treatment of a theology for expository preaching, consult P. Adam, *Speaking God's Words: A Practical Theology of Expository Preaching* (Downers Grove: InterVarsity, 1996), 15–56.

the prophets was verbal as they declared, "Thus says the Lord." God's speech is written in that it has been inscripturated into the text we call the Bible. God's speech is personal via the incarnation of Jesus Christ. God is the ultimate author of all Scripture: "All scripture is given by inspiration of God, and is profitable for doctrine, for reproof, for correction, for instruction in righteousness" (2 Tim 3:16 NKJV). The phrase "all scripture" in the Greek text connotes that every individual part of Scripture is the word of God. We call this "verbal plenary" inspiration; that is, all of the words of Scripture are inspired by God. The very words of Scripture are the words of God. Two principles critical for homiletics emerge from this understanding of biblical authority: the inerrancy of Scripture and the sufficiency of Scripture.

It is instructive to observe just how the New Testament authors quote the Old Testament. Often, the words "God" and "Scripture" are used interchangeably as subjects with the verb "to speak." In Matt 19:4–5, God is said to be the author of Scripture although He is not directly the speaker. In Rom 9:17, we read, "Scripture says," even though God Himself is the direct speaker of what is quoted. God's revelation of Himself in Christ Jesus therefore is personal revelation: "In the beginning was the Word . . . and the Word became flesh and dwelt among us" (John 1:1,14). In Paul's final charge to Timothy, he said, "Preach the Word!" (2 Tim 4:2). The biblical and theological foundation for text-driven preaching is the fact that God has spoken in Christ and in Scripture, and the nature of this revelation itself demands a text-driven approach to preaching. The authority, inerrancy, and sufficiency of Scripture serve as the theological grounds for text-driven preaching.

TEXT-DRIVEN PREACHING
AND SERMON FORM

All preaching rests on certain convictions about the nature of God, the Scriptures, and the gospel. James Barr said he doubted whether the Bible itself, regardless of one's view of inspiration, can furnish the preacher with a model for sermon form and content that could be conceived as normative.[3] Such a statement is clearly informed by a less than evangelical view of biblical authority. Contrast this with Haddon Robinson's statement: "Expository preaching, therefore, emerges not merely as a type of sermon—one among many—but as the theological outgrowth of a high view of inspiration. Expository preaching then originates as a philosophy rather than a method."[4]

Are all sermon methods equally valid or desirable? Many today would consider expository preaching on an equal plane with virtually any other method of preaching, and perhaps just as many consider it less serviceable for preaching today than other methods such as topical or narrative. The renowned Spurgeon did not think so:

> A sermon, moreover, comes with far greater power to the consciences of the hearers when it is plainly the very word of God—not a lecture about the Scripture, but Scripture itself opened up and enforced. . . . I will further recommend you to hold to the *ipsissima verba*, the very words of the Holy Ghost; for, although in many cases topical sermons are not only allowable, but very proper, those sermons which expound the exact words of the Holy Spirit are the most useful and the most agreeable to the major part of our congregations.[5]

What form should a text-driven sermon take? Today, sermon form is frequently dictated by one or more of the following considerations: tradition, the prevailing paradigm in homiletics, culture, or literary form. Not all sermon forms are created equal, and some are based on a faulty understanding of biblical revelation and/or the human sciences. For example, the New

3. J. Barr, *The Bible in the Modern World* (London: SCM Press, 1973), 139.
4. H. Robinson, "Homiletics and Hermeneutics," in *Hermeneutics, Inerrancy, and the Bible*, ed. E. Radmacher and R. Preus (Grand Rapids: Zondervan, 1984), 803.
5. C. H. Spurgeon, *Lectures to My Students* (Grand Rapids: Zondervan, 1972), 73.

Homiletic, with its disdain for "propositional, deductive" preaching, its elevation of the audience over the text, and its privileging of experience over knowledge, substitutes a narrative sermon form that often leaves the meaning of the text blurred or undeveloped. This is not to say that the New Homiletic has nothing to teach us about preaching, for indeed it does. However, due to the truncated view of biblical authority of many of its practitioners, it does not take seriously enough the text of Scripture itself as God's word to us.[6]

Ultimately, sermon form should be dictated by theology. What one believes about the nature and sufficiency of Scripture will largely determine how sermons are structured. Text-driven preaching does not entail enslavement to a deductive sermonic form nor artificial outlining techniques such as a three-point structure and alliteration. A good text-driven sermon that explains the meaning of the text can be couched in a variety of forms. Scripture uses various genres including narrative, poetry, prophecy, and epistles. Good text-driven preaching will reflect this variety as well. There is a broad umbrella of sermon styles and structures that can rightfully be called "expository" or "text driven."[7]

Therefore, with respect to sermon form, anything less than real exposition that explains, illustrates, and applies the text to the people does not reflect a proper view of biblical authority. Text-driven preaching is built on the solid foundation of the inerrancy and sufficiency of Scripture.

---

6. Narrative preaching has come under significant critique in recent years, even by those who were once its ardent supporters. See, for example, T. Long, "What Happened to Narrative Preaching?" *JP* 28 (2005): 9–14. In 1997, C. Campbell's bombshell *Preaching Jesus: New Directions for Homiletics in Hans Frei's Postliberal Theology* (Grand Rapids: Eerdmans, 1997), and J. Thompson's *Preaching Like Paul: Homiletical Wisdom for Today* (Louisville/John Knox: Westminster, 2001), both leveled broadsides against the New Homiletic. See also D. L. Allen, "A Tale of Two Roads: Homiletics and Biblical Authority," *JETS* 43 (2000): 508–13.

7. For a helpful discussion of this subject, see D. Cahill, *The Shape of Preaching: Theory and Practice in Sermon Design* (Grand Rapids: Baker, 2007).

TEXT-DRIVEN PREACHING:
TOWARD A DESCRIPTION

The Jewish rabbis during the Second Temple period considered the Torah to be the unchanging Word of God. Their first
task in preaching was to make plain the meaning of the passage
(Peshat). This involved defining the words of the text correctly
and understanding their meaning. Once this was accomplished,
the rabbis sought for ways to connect textual relevance to new
situations via interpretation (midrash). For the rabbis, one key
aspect of the midrash of the Tannaim was its text centeredness.[8]
Broadus pointed out that the history of the word "text" points
back to the fact that preaching was originally expository in nature. Preachers during the Patristic era of the church commonly
spoke on texts of some length and "occupied themselves largely
with exposition."[9] The Protestant Reformation saw a revival in
preaching, in biblical preaching, and in expository preaching.
Reformation and post-Reformation preachers returned to the
text of Scripture as the foundation for the sermon. Such a revival
of preaching is what we desperately need today.

"Expository preaching" and "text-driven preaching" are essentially synonymous terms. Authentic biblical preaching must,
by definition, be text driven and hence expository in nature. All
preaching, regardless of the form it takes, should be expositional in nature. The word "homiletics" etymologically derives from
the Greek words *homo,* meaning "same," and *legō*, meaning "to
speak." Homiletics is the art and science of sermon construction and delivery that says the same thing the text of Scripture
says.[10]

What is the role of the text in preaching? The word "text"
comes from a Latin word meaning "to weave" and refers to the

---

8. G. Osborne, *Folly of God: The Rise of Christian Preaching,* in *A History of Christian Preaching,* vol. 1 (St. Louis: Chalice, 1999), 145–46.
9. J. Broadus, *A Treatise on the Preparation and Delivery of Sermons,* rev. ed., ed. E. C. Dargan (Birmingham, AL: Solid Ground Christian Books, 2005/1897), 20.
10. J. Daane, *Preaching with Confidence* (Grand Rapids: Eerdmans, 1980), 49.

product of weaving, hence "composition." The word is used figuratively to express structured meaning in speech or writing. Stenger provided a good definition of "text" when he describes it as "a cohesive and structured expression of language that, while at least relatively self contained, intends a specific effect."[11] Textual structure is therefore a network of relations and the sum of those relations that functions between the elements of the text.[12]

Not only should sermons be based on a text of Scripture; they also should actually expound the meaning of that text. The biblical text is not merely a *resource* for the sermon; it is the *source* of the sermon. A sermon not only *uses* a text of Scripture but also should be *derived* from a text of Scripture and should *develop* a text of Scripture. As a development of a text of Scripture, the sermon should explain, illustrate, and apply the text. There are always two potential problems with all texts: incomprehension or misunderstanding. As Broadus stated, "The only thing worse than a text not being understood is it being misunderstood. We must strive to render it possible that people understand and impossible they should misunderstand."[13] Text-driven preachers must grapple with the actual structure of the text itself in sermon preparation.

A text-driven sermon develops a text by explaining, illustrating, and applying its meaning. Although explanation of the text is the foundation of everything else, there is no set formula as to how these three must be woven together in the sermon or how

11. W. Stenger, *Introduction to New Testament Exegesis* (Grand Rapids: Eerdmans, 1993), 23.
12. Ibid., 23–24. From a semantic standpoint, there is a finite set of communication relations that exists for all languages and functions as something of a "natural metaphysic of the human mind." See R. Longacre, *The Grammar of Discourse*, Topics in Language and Linguistics (New York: Plenum, 1983), xix. These relations are catalogued, explained, and illustrated by Longacre and in a more "pastor friendly" way by J. Beekman, J. Callow, and M. Kopesec, *The Semantic Structure of Written Communication* (Dallas, TX: Summer Institute of Linguistics, 1981), 77–113.
13. Broadus, *Preparation*, 96.

much time should be devoted to each. Indeed, there is room for considerable latitude and creativity in this area. However, when all is said and done, text-driven preaching stays true to the substance of the text, the structure of the text, and the spirit of the text. For the preacher committed to this kind of preaching, Christ is Lord and His written Word, the text of Scripture, is "King."

The kind of preaching that will best engender biblical knowledge and spiritual growth is preaching that works paragraph by paragraph through books of the Bible in a systematic fashion and not just verse by verse. Linguists now point out that meaning is structured beyond the sentence level. When the preacher restricts the focus to the sentence level and to clauses and phrases in verses, there is much that is missed in the paragraph or larger discourse that contributes to the overall meaning and interpretation. Broadus correctly remarked, "There are few sentences in Hebrews or the first eleven chapters of Romans which can be fully understood without having in mind the entire argument of the Epistle."[14] The paragraph unit is best used as the basic unit of meaning in expounding the text of Scripture. Expositional preaching should at minimum deal with a paragraph (as in the Epistles), whereas, in the narrative portions of Scripture, several paragraphs that combine to form the story should be treated in a single sermon since the meaning and purpose of the story itself cannot be discerned when it is broken up and presented piecemeal.

The advantages to this approach are many. Over the long haul, it exposes scripture in context to the people of your church.[15] When the preacher skips back and forth from a

---

14. Ibid., 70–71.
15. Three sterling examples of this kind of preaching are Jerry Vines, pastor emeritus of First Baptist Church, Jacksonville, Florida, who preached through the entire Bible book by book during his 25-year pastorate; Kent Hughes, who likewise preached through books of the Bible during his pastorate at the College Church in Wheaton and whose expository sermons are published in the "Preaching the Word" series of commentaries; and Mark Dever, whose two

passage in Genesis one week to a passage in Psalms the next and then to something out of Romans after that, he may accurately preach the meaning of these individual passages, but the people never see the big picture of each book of the Bible or how Scripture as a whole fits together in the overarching development of God's plan of salvation. Another advantage is the preacher knows exactly what his text will be next week: the next paragraph or two (or narrative unit). This method avoids hobbyhorse preaching and virtually eliminates the accusation against the preacher that he is preaching against any church member's problem or sin. Of course, the wise preacher will vary this method by interspersing shorter series (sermons on marriage, the family, Christmas, etc.) or doctrinal preaching (sermons on Scripture, God, sin, Christ, etc.) intermittently along the way. But even here, these sermons should be examples of "topical exposition."[16]

The text-driven preacher will use proper hermeneutical principles when interpreting and expounding Scripture. He eschews faulty hermeneutical methods such as spiritualizing or allegorizing. Text-driven preachers also believe in creativity in preaching. The first place to look for creativity to use in preaching is often the last place that many preachers look: the text. Ultimately, creativity resides in the text itself. All the creativity in the world is of no value if the text itself is neglected, obscured, or ignored in preaching. Unfortunately, in much contemporary preaching that touts itself as creative, this is the case.[17]

---

volumes, *The Message of the Old Testament: Promises Made* and *The Message of the New Testament: Promises Kept*, contain 66 sermons preached on each book of the Bible to his congregation in Washington, D.C. See also the work of G. Goldsworthy, *Preaching the Whole Bible as Christian Scripture* (Grand Rapids: Eerdmans, 2000).

16. For a definition and illustration of "topical exposition," see T. Warren, "Can Topical Preaching Also Be Expository?" in *The Art and Craft of Biblical Preaching: A Comprehensive Resource for Today's Communicators*, ed. H. Robinson and C. Larson (Grand Rapids: Zondervan, 2005), 418–21.

17. The use of props, dramas, video clips, etc. may have a place in preaching as long as they do not become the main attraction and are used judiciously. If you

TEXT-DRIVEN PREACHING AND LINGUISTICS: WHAT THE PREACHER MUST KNOW TO BE A GOOD EXEGETE

The painstaking work of exegesis is the foundation for text-driven preaching.[18] Exegesis precedes theology and theology is derived from carefully exegesis. To preach well, it is vital that one understand certain basics about the nature of language and meaning.

The hierarchy of language is such that words are combined into larger units of meaning. Words combine to form phrases, phrases combine to form clauses, clauses combine to form sentences, sentences combine to form paragraphs, and paragraphs combine to form discourse. When it comes to a text of scripture, however long or short, the whole is more than just the sum of its parts. Take the sentence "He preached to the people." Here we have five words combined in a sentence. Each word conveys meaning, but the five words construed in this particular order convey something more than just the sum of the individual words. This illustrates the important principle that meaning is more than just the sum of the words construed in a particular

---

cannot preach without such media aids, you will never be able to preach with them. Without exposition of Scripture, congregations will never be taught biblical truth by the use of movie clips, dramas, or props such as beds, boats, and blenders. Every preacher should read and heed Arthur Hunt's warning that the current de-emphasis on and devaluation of "text" and its "hostile supplanting by the image" is nothing less than "a direct assault upon 'the religion of the Book'" (*The Vanishing Word: The Veneration of Visual Imagery in the Postmodern World* [Wheaton, IL: Crossway, 2003], 25). Hunt cogently reminds us that the Renaissance was image based, attempting a revival of pagan Rome, whereas the Reformation was Word-based, seeking "to rekindle the spirit of the first-century church" (78). The line that haunts me the most in the entire book is, "Pagan idolatry is biblicism's chief competitor because one thrives in the absence of the written word and the other cannot exist without it" (71).

18. "No man will succeed in expository preaching unless he delights in exegetical study of the Bible, unless he loves to search out the exact meaning of its sentences, phrases, words. In order to do this, knowledge of the original languages of Scripture is desirable" (Broadus, *Preparation*, 326).

sentence. This is especially evident at the paragraph level when two or more sentences are in play.

Units of meaning as expressed in language cluster together to form other units of meaning. Take, for example, Philemon 13. Paul writes, "I would have preferred that I keep Onesimus here with me in order that he might serve me while I am in prison because I preached the gospel." Notice that the first two propositions combine to form a single unit of meaning: "I would have preferred" (expresses Paul's desire) and "that I keep Onesimus here with me" (expresses the content of that desire). Notice that the latter two propositions, "while I am here in prison" (a temporal clause) and "because I preached the gospel" (a purpose clause), likewise combine to form a unit of meaning. Notice also that this unit of meaning, "while I am here in prison because I preached the gospel," is combined with the proposition "in order that he might serve me" (a larger purpose clause explaining the reason for Paul's desire to keep Onesimus with him). Together these three propositions form a single unit of meaning: "in order that he might serve me while I am here in prison because I preached the gospel." When propositions 1–2 are combined with 3–5, the full meaning of Philemon 13 results.[19]

Philemon 13 also illustrates the linguistic concept of "embedding," where a clause can embed several phrases or another clause and a sentence may embed with it several clauses or sentences. Consider the sentence "I went downtown but Mary stayed home." This sentence actually embeds two sentences: "I went downtown," and "Mary stayed home." These two sentences are coordinated in an adversative fashion by the conjunction "but." In 1 John 1:5, the dependent clause "that God is light and in him is no darkness at all" embeds two sentences: "God is light," and "In him is no darkness at all." The second sentence

---

19. See the discussion of this verse in Beekman, Callow, and Kopesec, *Semantic Structure*, 18. See also J. Beekman and J. Callow, *Translating the Word of God* (Grand Rapids: Zondervan, 1974), 365.

is connected to the first sentence with the coordinating conjunction "and," but semantically, the actual meaning conveyed could be construed in a cause-effect fashion: "because God is light there is no darkness in him at all." Finally, notice that this clause (introduced by the Greek conjunction *hoti*, "that") serves to identify the content of the message that the apostles declared: "God is light. . . ."

Another principle worth noting is that language makes use of content words and function words. Content words are such parts of speech as nouns, verbs, adjectives, and adverbs. Function words are articles, prepositions, and conjunctions. For example, take these first two lines from the poem "Jabberwocky," which Alice read in Lewis Carroll's *Through the Looking Glass and What Alice Found There*: "The slithy toves did gire and gimble in the wabe."[20] We have no clue what "toves" are or what the "wabe" is, but we can tell by their placement in the sentence that they are content nouns. Likewise, we do not know what "gire" and "gimble" mean, but by their placement in the sentence we can deduce that they are verbs expressing some action. The "y" on the end of "slithy" and its placement before what looks to be a noun identifies it as an adjective, even if we do not yet know what it means. On the other hand, the double use of the article "the," the conjunction "and," and the preposition "in" does not convey meaning as content but rather express function. The conjunction "and" serves to combine the two verbs in a coordinated fashion, while "in" identifies where the toves "gire[d] and gimble[d]" are located (when the object "wabe" is supplied). Content words derive their basic meaning from the lexicon of the language. Function words derive their functional meaning from the grammar and syntax of the language. Of course, lexicon, grammar, and syntax combine to give content words and function words their meaning in a given text. It is especially

---

20. L. Carroll, *Through the Looking Glass and What Alice Found There* (Philadelphia: Henry Altemus, 1897), 31.

important in text-driven preaching to pay close attention to the function words in a text. For example, the Greek conjunction *gar* always introduces a sentence or a paragraph that is subordinate to the one preceding it[21] and usually signals that what follows will give the grounds or reason for what precedes it. This is immensely important in exegesis and sermon preparation.

Proper exegesis of a text in preparation to preach also requires knowledge of the verbal structure of the passage. If you are remodeling your home and you desire to convert two small rooms into one larger room, you must remove the wall that separates the two rooms. As long as that wall is a non-load-bearing wall, it can be removed with no problem. However, if the wall is a load-bearing wall, removing it would cause the roof to cave in. Verbs are the load-bearing walls of language. Understanding their function within the text is vital to identifying the correct meaning that the author wants to convey. Hence, I recommend the discipline of "verb charting" during the exegesis phase of sermon preparation. In Greek, for example, so much information is encoded in the verb (tense, voice, mood, person, and number + lexical meaning). The backbone of any text will be identified by means of the verb structure. If a New Testament text has a string of verbs in the aorist tense and then suddenly a perfect verb pops up, there usually is significance to this tense shift. See, for example, Rom 6:1–5, where this very point is illustrated by the use of the perfect tense "have been united" in v. 5. In the Abraham and Isaac narrative of Genesis 22, at the climax of the story, there is a sudden onslaught of verbs placed one after another in staccato fashion in the Hebrew text in Gen 22:9–10. This has the effect of heightening the emotional tone of the story and causes the reader/listener to sit on the edge of his seat as it were, waiting to find out what happens. In the exegetical process, one should pay close attention to verbals

---

21. T. Friberg and B. Friberg, *The Analytical Greek New Testament* (Grand Rapids: Baker, 1981), 834.

as well (participles and infinitives), as these often play crucial modification roles.

The text-driven preacher must also recognize that there are four basic types of meaning conveyed in every text and context. They are referential, situational, structural, and semantic. Referential meaning is what is being talked about—the subject matter of a text. Situational meaning is information that pertains to the participants in a communication act—matters of environment, social status, and so on. Structural meaning has to do with the arrangement of the information in the text itself—the grammar and syntax of a text. Semantics has to do with the structure of meaning and is, in some sense, the confluence of referential, situational, and structural meaning.[22]

Most of us are trained to observe structural meaning, we are intuitively aware of referential meaning and situational meaning, but we often fail to observe the semantic structure of a text. The text-driven preacher will want to analyze carefully each one of these aspects of meaning for a given text. For example, it is important to observe the situational (social) meaning expressed in Genesis 18 in the dialogue between God and Abraham regarding the destruction of the city of Sodom. One must pay attention to the way the Hebrew text references God and Abraham. Notice at the end of the scene we are told by the narrator, "So the Lord went His way as soon as He had finished speaking with Abraham" (Gen 18:33 NKJV). We are not told the LORD went His way when Abraham finished speaking to the Lord but the other way around, because God is the most important figure in the dialogue. The narrator here and throughout Genesis carefully conveys the social status of the various interlocutors in a given dialogue or narrative by means of linguistic clues.

John 1:1 furnishes an example of the importance of lexical meaning at the semantic level. Notice the threefold use of *eimi*,

---

22. See Beekman, Callow, and Kopesec, *Semantic Structure*, 8–13.

"was," in this verse. Here a single verb in its three occurrences actually conveys three different meanings: (1) "In the beginning *was* the Word" (where *eimi*, "was," means "to exist"); (2) "and the Word *was* with God" (where *eimi* followed by the preposition "with" conveys the meaning "to be in a place"); and (3) "and the Word *was* God" (where *eimi* conveys the meaning "membership in a class: Godhood").[23] Notice also in John 1:1 that *logos*, "word," occurs in the predicate position in the first clause but is in the subject position in the second clause. In the third clause, there is again a reversal of the order creating a chiasm: *theos*, "God," is placed before the verb putting emphasis on the deity of the "Word."[24] Lexical meaning not only is inherent in words themselves but also is determined by their relationship to other words in context.

Knowledge of a text's situational meaning is vital for the preacher because meaning does not simply reside in the words of a text themselves and their structural relations but also in the total context in which an author uses them. Take, for example, the words of Tom Sawyer in the episode where Tom was told by his aunt Polly to whitewash a fence on a Saturday, a day Tom would much rather spend in play.[25] On the surface, his statements appear to be descriptive of his genuine feelings about whitewashing the fence. In reality, Tom is engaging in a bit of trickery to persuade his friends to want to do the job for him so he himself can get out of the chore. The surface structure meaning in this text is actually just the opposite of the intent of Tom. The purpose of his statements in the text is not to communicate how wonderful it is to be able to whitewash a fence. Rather, his purpose is to extricate himself from work by means of verbal trickery and reverse psychology in an attempt

---

23. See J. de Waard and E. A. Nida, *From One Language to Another: Functional Equivalence in Bible Translating* (Nashville: Thomas Nelson, 1986), 72.
24. Ibid.
25. M. Twain, *The Adventures of Tom Sawyer* (New York: Harper & Row, 1922), 16–18.

to persuade others to want to do the job themselves so he will not have to do it.[26] Commenting on Tom Sawyer's verbal ruse, Boers pointed out,

> The meaning of each of Tom's statements has to be taken in the context in which he uses them. For example, "Does a boy get a chance to whitewash a fence every day?" expresses an obvious truth in rhetorical form, but that is not its meaning for Tom. Its meaning does not reside in the words themselves, but in the meaning effect to which it contributes in the total context of the situation.[27]

This brings up another important aspect of textual analysis called "pragmatic analysis." Pragmatic analysis asks the questions, "What is the author's purpose of a text?" and "What does an author desire to accomplish with his text?" It is important that the text-driven preacher understand this also, because he is attempting to accomplish some specific objective with each sermon. He should therefore comprehend that verbal or written communication has at least one of three purposes: (1) to affect the ideas of people, (2) to affect the emotions of people, or (3) to affect the behavior of people. We who preach, however, should have all three of these purposes in mind. We should attempt to affect the mind with the truth of Scripture (doctrine). We should attempt to affect the emotions of people because emotions are often (some would say always) the gateway to the mind. Finally, we should attempt to affect the behavior of people by moving their will to obey the Word of God.

Other important linguistic features of texts include unity, coherence, prominence, and parallelism. A text will have thematic

---

26. See R. de Beaugrande and W. Dressler, *Introduction to Text Linguistics*, in Longman's Linguistic Library, no. 26 (London/New York: Longman, 1981), 171–79, where the authors analyze linguistically this discourse pericope in a chapter titled "Situationality."
27. H. Boers, introduction to *How to Read the New Testament: An Introduction to Linguistic and Historical-Critical Methodology*, by W. Egger (Peabody, MA: Hendrickson, 1996), xxxix–xl.

unity. A shift from one theme to another usually occurs at the paragraph level or beyond. Textual cohesion can be signaled by such things as lexical repetition and a string of verbs in the same tense. Prominence can be shown by placing words, phrases, or clauses at the front or the back of a sentence to denote emphasis. As an illustration of marked prominence in a text, consider the nine times in Hebrews the name "Jesus" appears alone. In each case in the Greek text the name occurs last in its clause for emphasis (e.g., Heb 3:1 reads literally in Greek, "Consider the apostle and high priest of our confession, Jesus"). This marked prominence in the Greek text is seldom brought out in English translations of Hebrews. The importance of parallelism in a text can be seen in the tense structure of the verbs in the Beatitudes of Matt 5:3–10. Preachers often overlook the fact that the first and last beatitudes are placed in the present tense, whereas all the intervening beatitudes are in the future tense. This conveys the present reality of the kingdom of heaven and not simply a future intent or fulfillment. This fact has immense repercussions for the theological interpretation of the Beatitudes as well as the Sermon on the Mount as a whole. The parallelism of the verb tenses precludes the interpretation that the Beatitudes or the Sermon on the Mount is intended only for the future millennial kingdom and not for the present dispensation. The text-driven preacher will want to observe all these linguistic features of the text that provide unity, cohesion, prominence, and parallelism.

From a linguistic perspective, text-driven preaching should correctly identify the genre of the text.[28] Longacre identified four basic discourse genres that are language-universal: narrative, procedural, hortatory, and expository.[29] All four of these genres, along with subgenres, occur in Scripture. Significant

---

28. See D. Allen, "Fundamentals of Genre: How Literary Form Affects the Interpretation of Scripture," in *The Art and Craft of Biblical Preaching: A Comprehensive Resource for Today's Communicators*, ed. H. Robinson and C. Larson (Grand Rapids: Zondervan, 2005), 264–67.
29. Longacre, *Grammar of Discourse*, 3. See also Beekman, Callow, and Kopesec, *Semantic Structure*, 35–40.

portions of the Old Testament are narrative. The Gospels and Acts are primarily narrative in genre. Procedural discourse can be found in Exodus 25–40, where God gives explicit instructions on how to build the tabernacle. Hortatory genre is found in the prophetic sections of the Old Testament as well as in the epistolary literature of the New Testament, though it is by no means confined to these alone in the Scriptures. Expository genre is clearly seen in the New Testament epistles, which are actually all combinations of expository and hortatory genre.

The point of what has been said is that text-driven preachers must strive to examine not only the form but also the meaning of all levels of a text with the goal of understanding the whole.[30] Text-driven preaching looks beyond words and sentences to the whole text (paragraph level and beyond). Every biblical text is an aggregate of relations between the four elements of meaning that it conveys: structural, referential, situational, and semantic. The superior value to this approach to textual analysis in preparation for preaching is that it allows one to see the communication relationships within a text in their full extent. Restricting exegesis to a verse-by-verse process alone often results in the details of the text violating the overall message. It becomes hard to see the forest for the trees. Here the chapter and versification of the Bible can hinder as much as help.

In summary, text-driven preachers will do their exegetical homework to determine what the text means. Text-driven

---

30. B. Olsson, "A Decade of Text-linguistic Analyses of Biblical Texts at Upsalla," *ST* 39 (1985): 107, underlined the vital importance of discourse analysis for exegesis when he noted, "A text-linguistic analysis is a basic component of all exegesis. A main task, or the main task of all Biblical scholarship has always been to interpret individual texts or passages of the Bible. . . . To the *words* and to the *sentences* a textual exegesis now adds *texts*. The text is seen as the primary object of inquiry. To handle texts is as basic for our discipline as to handle words and sentences. Therefore, text-linguistic analyses belong to the fundamental part of Biblical scholarship." See also the excellent chapter by G. Guthrie, "Discourse Analysis," in *Interpreting the New Testament: Essays on Methods and Issues*, ed. D. A. Black and D. Dockery (Nashville: Broadman & Holman, 2001), 253–71.

preachers will engage in creative exposition to explain the meaning of the text to a contemporary audience. Although not the focus of this chapter, text-driven preachers will seek to become master communicators with an understanding of their audience and communication techniques that will make for the most effective preaching of Scripture with the goal of life transformation effected by the Holy Spirit.

TEXT-DRIVEN PREACHING: A 12-STEP METHOD[31]

Although there is no one procedural manual for sermon preparation, I have found a particular method to be helpful across the years that is informed by the aforementioned principles. There is little in my approach that cannot be found elsewhere in works on preaching or exegetical method. I have taught this method in introductory preaching courses now for more than 20 years. The following is a step-by-step summary of the

---

31. The following kinds of tools are essential for solid exegetical work: lexicons, grammars, theological dictionaries, exegetical works, and commentaries, especially those that are exegetical in nature. As Old Testament (OT) lexicons go, L. Koehler and W. Baumgartner, *The Hebrew and Aramaic Lexicon of the Old Testament*, vol. 1 (Boston: Brill, 2001), is unsurpassed. The top of the line New Testament (NT) lexicon is W. Bauer, *A Greek-English Lexicon of the New Testament*, ed. and trans. W. F. Arndt, F. W. Gingrich, and F. W. Danker; BDAG, 3rd ed. (Chicago: University of Chicago Press, 2000). Helpful OT grammars are G. Pratico and M. Van Pelt, *Basics of Biblical Hebrew Grammar* (Grand Rapids: Zondervan, 2001), and B. K. Waltke and M. O'Connor, *An Introduction to Biblical Hebrew Syntax* (Winona Lake: Eisenbrauns, 1990). Helpful NT grammars include D. B. Wallace, *Greek Grammar Beyond the Basics: An Exegetical Syntax of the New Testament with Scripture, Subject, and Greek Word Indexes* (Grand Rapids: Zondervan, 1996), and R. A. Young, *Intermediate New Testament Greek: A Linguistic and Exegetical Approach* (Nashville: Broadman & Holman, 1994). One of the finest OT theological dictionaries is W. A. VanGemeren, ed., *New International Dictionary of Old Testament Theology & Exegesis*, 5 vols. (Grand Rapids: Zondervan, 1997). Two excellent NT theological dictionaries are C. Brown, ed., *The New International Dictionary of New Testament Theology*, 3 vols. (Grand Rapids: Zondervan, 1975), and H. Balz and G. Schneider, eds., *Exegetical Dictionary of the New Testament*, vol. 1 (Grand

methodology I use. For purposes of example, we shall use 1 John 2:15–17 as a test case for preparing a text-driven sermon.

The 12 Steps in Preparing a Text-Driven Sermon

I. Begin at the paragraph level, and then move to the sentence, clause, phrase, and word level.

   A. Determine to preach on at least a paragraph unit of meaning.
   B. Determine the boundary of the paragraph(s).
   C. Read the paragraph(s) several times in Greek and in English.
   D. Determine the genre of the paragraph.
   E. Prepare a rough translation from the Greek text.
   F. Analyze how the paragraph is joined to the previous paragraph.

II. Analyze the sentences and clauses within the paragraph.

   A. Identify the verbs and verbals (participles and infinitives).
   B. Parse all verbs (note especially their tense, voice, and mood).
   C. Identify the sentences in the paragraph of the Greek text.
   D. Identify independent clauses and subordinate clauses.

Rapids: Eerdmans, 1990). Among the more helpful guides on OT and NT exegesis, consult D. A. Black and D. Dockery, *Interpreting the New Testament: Essays on Methods and Issues* (Nashville: Broadman & Holman, 2001); D. Bock and B. Fanning, eds., *Interpreting the New Testament Text: Introduction to the Art and Science of Exegesis* (Wheaton, IL: Crossway, 2006); C. Broyles, ed., *Interpreting the Old Testament: A Guide for Exegesis* (Grand Rapids: Baker, 2001); D. A. Carson, *Exegetical Fallacies*, 2nd ed. (Carlisle, U.K.: Paternoster, 1996); R. Chisholm, *From Exegesis to Exposition: A Practical Guide to Using Biblical Hebrew* (Grand Rapids: Baker, 1998); W. Egger, *How to Read the New Testament: An Introduction to Linguistic and Historical-Critical Methodology*, ed. Harry Boers, 1st ed. (Peabody, MA: Hendrickson, 1996); G. Fee, *New Testament Exegesis: A Handbook for Students and Pastors*, rev. ed. (Leominster, England: Gracewing, 1993); M. Gorman, *Elements of Biblical Exegesis: A Basic Guide for Students and Ministers* (Peabody, MA: Hendrickson, 2001); and D. Stuart, *Old Testament Exegesis: A Handbook for Students and Pastors*, 3rd ed. (Louisville: Westminster John Knox, 2001). The two best overall guides to all resources needed for biblical interpretation are D. Bauer, *An Annotated Guide to Biblical Resources for Ministry* (Peabody, MA: Hendrickson, 2003) and F. W. Danker, *Multipurpose Tools for Bible Study*, rev. and expanded ed. (Minneapolis: Fortress, 1993).

    E. Determine the grammatical relationships of clauses to one another (subordinate, etc.).

    F. Identify how the sentences relate to one another. Which of these convey primary information, and which convey secondary (subordinate) information? This step allows you to determine the nuclear part of the paragraph along with its supportive (subordinate) material.

III. Analyze the key phrases in the paragraph.

    A. Identify phrases in the paragraph, especially prepositional phrases.

    B. Determine the syntax and proper translation of the phrases (genitive use, etc.).

IV. Do word studies of significant words in the text. Note things like lexical repetition and words in the same semantic domain (different words that have similar meanings, antonyms, etc.).

V. Do comparative translation work. Look at several translations to see how they handle the text.

VI. Consult commentaries.

VII. Diagram the paragraph (syntactical or block diagram?).

VIII. Develop an exegetical outline from the previous data.

IX. Develop the sermon (homiletical/communication) outline from the exegetical outline.

X. Write the sermon body with a focus on exposition, illustration, and application.

XI. Write the introduction and conclusion.

XII. Think through delivery issues: *how* will you say it so that it reflects the spirit of the text?

A Test Case Using 1 John 2:15–17

First John 2:15–17 is the seventh paragraph unit in John's epistle (based on the Greek text), and the passage is clearly demarcated as a paragraph unit both structurally and thematically. The previous paragraph, 1 John 2:12–14, has a unique structure and theme that clearly identifies it is a paragraph unit.[32] First John

---

32. Note the unusual use of γραφω six times, each followed by a vocative, which demarcates it as a clear paragraph unit. Note also 2:18 begins with a vocative, followed by a new subject, which is again diagnostic of new paragraph onset.

2:18 begins with the use of a vocative, followed by the introduction of a new subject, which often marks new paragraph onset, as it does here. Thus, 1 John 2:15–17 is a paragraph unit.

When reading this paragraph in English and Greek, we are struck by the fact that there is one imperatival verb in the paragraph and it occurs at the very beginning. If we have been preaching through 1 John, we might have noticed that this is the first imperative to appear in the epistle. This turns out to be of some significance for the meaning and structure of the paragraph, as we shall see later. This is the kind of thing to look for when reading through the paragraph several times. It is important to jot down things you notice such as the topic or topics and what is being said about them and words or phrases that are repeated.

With this information before you, you will be able to determine the genre of the paragraph. As noted previously, there are four major genres of discourse that are linguistically universal. Our text is clearly not a narrative, nor is it procedural. We might conclude it is expository since it is a part of a letter. However, the use of the imperative by which John is commanding his readers not to do something clearly identifies this paragraph as hortatory in genre. This paragraph is actually something of a hybrid, containing expository and hortatory aspects to it. However, since linguistically an imperative outweighs other indicative verbs on the prominence scale, when an imperative occurs in a paragraph, it is almost always diagnostic of a hortatory genre.[33]

---

33. Greek, as English, has many ways of expressing hortation: imperatives, hortatory subjunctives, and additionally mitigated ways of commanding or requesting an action. For example, in the communication context of a classroom where I am the professor and it is increasingly warm in the room, I may say, "Open the door!" (imperative), or I might say, "Please open the door" (imperative mitigated by "please"). I might also say, "I wish someone would open the door" (mitigated command expressed as a wish). Finally, I might say, "It sure is hot in here" (a declarative statement with no overt command whatsoever but in context functioning as a mitigated request for someone to open the door). This latter example especially reveals how language works on the semantic level.

At this point you are ready to prepare a rough translation of the passage from the Greek text if you have knowledge of that biblical language. If not, you may study the passage in more than one translation (a step that will be explained later in the process). Your rough translation will be refined throughout the exegetical process.

Since context is vital to interpretation, you should observe how the paragraph under consideration is connected to the previous paragraph. There are various ways this is done in the Greek New Testament. The primary way is by the use of conjunctions. Traditional Greek grammar posits two types of conjunctions: coordinate and subordinate. A paragraph can be related to its previous paragraph in a coordinate fashion or in a subordinate fashion. One of the common ways of beginning a new paragraph that is subordinate to the previous paragraph is through the conjunction *gar*, commonly translated "for." Sometimes paragraphs are not connected by conjunctions, and such is the case with our paragraph. When that is the situation, one must determine what the relationship is more on semantic grounds. Since 1 John 2:15–17 appears to introduce a new theme (love for the world) from what was stated in 2:12–14, it is not related in a subordinate way. The fact that there is no conjunction connecting v. 14 with v. 15 is John's way of signaling not only a new paragraph but also a new theme.

After having analyzed the paragraph as a whole, you are now prepared to move to the sentences and clauses within the paragraph. Work from the Greek text if you can, but if not, work from an English translation at this point. The first step here is to identify all the verbs and verbals in the paragraph and parse them. This chart shows the verbs and verbals with their parsings:

GREEK	PARSING	TRANSLATION	VERSE
mē agapate	Present Imperative	Do not love	v. 15
agapa	Present Subjunctive	loves	v. 15
estin	Present Indicative	is	v. 15
estin[34]	Present Indicative	is	v. 16
estin	Present Indicative	is	v. 16
estin	Present Indicative	is	v. 16
paragetai	Present Mid./Pass.	is passing away	v. 17
ho poiōn	Present Participle	The one who does	v. 17
menei	Present Indicative	remains	v. 17

How many sentences are there in the Greek text of 1 John 2:15–17? According to the UBS fourth edition Greek New Testament, there are three: sentence one is v. 15a, sentence two is vv. 15b–16, and sentence three is v. 17. If you are working from an English translation, most have four sentences: sentence one is v. 15a, sentence two is v. 15b, sentence three is v. 16, and sentence four is v. 17.[35]

Now we are prepared to identify the independent (main) clauses and the dependent (subordinate) clauses and analyze their relationship grammatically and semantically to one another.[36] Sentence one is clearly an independent clause composed

---

34. The verb is not expressed overtly in the text but is understood, as Greek grammar permits.
35. As, for example, KJV, NASB, and NIV.
36. A clause is a part of a sentence that expresses a proposition. It typically consists of at least a subject and a verb and is joined to the rest of the sentence by a conjunction. An independent clause is a complete sentence; it contains a subject and verb and expresses a complete thought in both context and meaning. A dependent (subordinate) clause is part of a sentence. It contains a subject and verb but does not express a complete thought. This type of clause is dependent on the rest of the sentence for both context and meaning. One of the best resources in clause analysis is J. Smith, "Sentence Diagramming, Clausal Layouts, and Exegetical Outlining," in *Interpreting the New Testament Text: Introduction to the Art and Science of Exegesis*, ed. D. Bock and B. Fanning (Wheaton, IL: Crossway, 2006), 73–134. Smith explains the traditional Kellogg/Reid method of syntactical diagramming and explains how to use it for maximum benefit in biblical interpretation.

of a present imperative followed by a compound direct object. Sentence two (vv. 15b–16) is introduced by a conditional clause "If anyone loves the world. . . ." Verse 16 continues sentence two since it is introduced with the conjunction *gar* in Greek, which is usually translated "for" and which always introduces a clause, sentence, or even paragraph that is subordinate to the previous clause, sentence, or paragraph. Verse 17 constitutes sentence three and is introduced by the coordinating conjunction *kai* in Greek, which is normally translated "and," although it can be left untranslated in certain circumstances when it begins a new sentence or paragraph. Note that this sentence is a compound sentence joining two clauses with the adversative conjunction *de* in Greek translated "but." "The world is passing away" conjoins "he who does the will of God abides forever" with the adversative conjunction "but" expressing semantically the notion of contrast. The first clause in this sentence has a compound subject: "the world and everything in it," which is "passing away." The second clause in the sentence has an articular participial clause, "he who does," followed by the direct object "the will of God." This entire clause "He who does the will of God" functions as the subject of the verb "abides."

Sentence one (v. 15a) contains a single compound independent clause: "Love not the world, neither the things in the world." Sentence two (vv. 15b–16) contains a dependent conditional clause "if anyone loves the world" followed by a contrasting independent clause "the love of the Father is not in him." This is followed by a third dependent clause introduced in Greek by *hoti*, "because." This third clause is rather lengthy; however, a little reflection will bring out the syntax clearly. The subject of this clause is "all that is in the world." This subject is followed by what is called an "appositive"[37] phrase in grammar: "the lust of the flesh and the lust of the eyes and the pride of life." This

---

37. In English as well as in Greek grammar, an appositive is a word or phrase that identifies or renames another word or phrase.

triple-compound phrase further defines the meaning of "all that is in the world" and functions as an equivalent phrase, which is the meaning of "appositive" in grammar. Sentence three (v. 17) contains two independent clauses conjoined by "but."

How are these three sentences related to each other syntactically and semantically? Which of the three sentences contains the most prominent information? What is the main theme expressed in the paragraph? Sentence one is the most dominant sentence semantically for two reasons. First, sentence two (vv. 15b–16) is related to sentence one (v. 15a) in a subordinate fashion since it is introduced grammatically by a conditional clause. Sentence three (v. 17) is coordinated to sentence two by the conjunction "and." Thus, John places sentences two and three on the same level syntactically. Second, sentence one (v. 15a) contains the overt imperative "do not love." Imperatives always outweigh indicatives on the semantic scale. Consequently, sentence one (v. 15a) conveys the theme of the entire paragraph: do not love the world. Sentence two (vv. 15b–16) conveys the semantic ground[38] for sentence one: it is impossible to love God and the world simultaneously. In other words, the ground for not loving the world, the command in sentence one, is found in sentence two: you cannot love God and the world at the same time. The *hoti* clause (v. 16) functions as a subordinate clause modifying the conditional clause stated in v. 15b: if anyone loves the world, the love of the father is not in him. In other words, on the semantic level, the meaning John is communicating in sentence two (vv. 15b–16) is that "if you are loving the world you cannot be loving God at the same time. This is true because

---

38. Semantically, Beekman, Callow, and Kopesec define "grounds" as the communication relation that refers to an observation or a known fact given as the basis for a stated, commanded, or questioned state or event (*Semantic Structure*, 106). For example, in the sentence "Dr. Allen is clumsy because he tripped on Dr. Akin's foot," notice that the clause "because . . . foot" is not the *cause* or *reason* of Dr. Allen's clumsiness but rather the *evidence* for the claim that Dr. Allen is clumsy. Thus, the semantic category of "grounds" is distinguished from its near kin "reason."

[*hoti*, "for"] everything in the world, the lust of the flesh, the lust of the eyes and the pride of life, does not have its source in the Father but rather has its source in the world." Sentence three (v. 17) is coordinated to sentence two (vv. 15b–16) by the use of *kai*, "and." It functions to provide two additional grounds for the command in v. 15a: the impermanence of the world ("the world is passing away with its lusts") and the permanence of those who do the will of God ("the one who does the will of God abides forever"). Contextually, the meaning of "the will of God" in the final clause is "do not love the world," as was expressed in the first clause (sentence) in v. 15a. To do the will of God, one must not love the world.

Thus, from a semantic standpoint, the structure of 1 John 2:15–17 can be diagrammed this way:

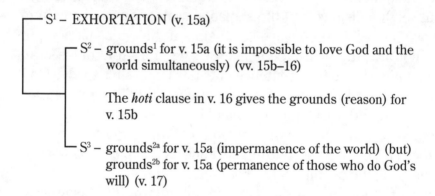

S¹ – EXHORTATION (v. 15a)

S² – grounds¹ for v. 15a (it is impossible to love God and the world simultaneously) (vv. 15b–16)

The *hoti* clause in v. 16 gives the grounds (reason) for v. 15b

S³ – grounds²ᵃ for v. 15a (impermanence of the world) (but) grounds²ᵇ for v. 15a (permanence of those who do God's will) (v. 17)

Having looked at the sentence and clause level, and having determined the semantic relationships expressed by them, we are now prepared to move to the phrase level of analysis. Here one will want to analyze the meaning and structure of key prepositional phrases. In our text, the phrase "love of the father" in v. 15b is crucial. The key question is, what kind of genitive is used here—subjective or objective? If the phrase is construed subjectively, then the meaning would be the Father's love for us, where "God" is the subject of the understood action conveyed by the noun "love." If the phrase is construed objectively, the meaning would be our love for the Father. Note that the usual English translation of this phrase as "the love of the Father" does not clearly disambiguate the meaning. Left alone, the phrase could mean one or the other. Almost all commentators and translators rightly understand the phrase as an objective genitive, meaning "our love for the Father." There are two reasons for this. First, it sustains the parallel structure of the subject in the previous three statements. "You" is the understood subject of the imperative "Do not love the world." "You" is also the understood subject of the second part of the compound direct object: "[You] [do not love] the things in the world." The third statement expressed in the conditional of v. 15b: "if anyone loves the world" expresses the fact that "you" is one of the "anyone." It would be contextually logical to complete this trilogy of subjects with a fourth: "your love for the Father." Second, there is a theological reason for taking this phrase as an objective genitive. If it is a subjective genitive with the meaning "the Father does not love you," then the clear implication is that if you love the world, the Father does not love you. If that is the case, then the person loving the world is not considered to be a Christian by John since it cannot be said that God does not love those who are Christians. On the other hand, clearly it is possible for Christians to love the world at times, contrary to God's will, and when they do, they cannot be loving God at the same time. This is the meaning John is conveying. A further indication supporting this interpretation is the fact that John is writing to Christians as has been established from the preceding paragraphs and especially in 1 John 2:12–14.

In v. 16, there are three other prepositional phrases that one would need to study in this passage: "the lust of the flesh, and the lust of the eyes, and the pride of life." Notice that these three phrases are coordinated in the text by the use of "and." These three phrases are in apposition to the phrase "all that is in the world" and serve to delineate and specify further what "all that is in the world" means. The entire phrase "all that is in the world, the lust of the flesh, and the lust of the eyes, and the pride of life" functions as the subject of the verb "is" followed by the compound predicate complement "not from the Father but is from the world."[39] Notice also that these three phrases are embedded within a dependent clause, which itself modifies a dependent clause in the text. The point for preaching here is that John is not highlighting or focusing on these prepositional phrases as the main point of his text. Yet how many sermons are preached from this passage of Scripture that take as the main thrust of the sermon the exposition of these three phrases? How many three-point sermon outlines are constructed for this passage on the basis of these three prepositional phrases? When the preacher does this, he is not focusing on the main point of the text; rather, he is elevating a subordinate point to the level of a main point. This is what text-driven preaching should avoid. If not, then preachers wind up preaching on secondary or even tertiary things in the text and thus miss the main point. The main point of the text is "do not love the world," not the description of the three categories of things that are in the world.

At this point in our exegetical procedure, you are ready to do word studies on key words in the passage. You will need a good lexicon and concordance, along with at least one good theological dictionary. What are the key words in 1 John 2:15–17 that need to be studied? The list probably would include the following: "love" (three times), "world" (six times), "lust" (two times), "pride" (one time), and the verb translated "passing away" (one time). What John means by "love" and what he means by "world" are crucial to a correct understanding of the passage. For example, by "world," the lexicons indicate John is not referring to the world of people, the world as planet earth, or the world as the universe. Rather he intends a special usage of the word meaning the world as a system of principles opposed to God and dominated by Satan. John is especially fond of using the term in this way,

---

39. The latter two genitive phrases, "from the Father" and "from the world," are both genitives expressing source.

and the immediate and broader context indicates this is John's meaning here. For the sake of time, we will not walk through each of the words listed previously, but the preacher will want to study them carefully to make sure that he understands the meaning as this is crucial when he constructs his sermon.

One step in the preparation of a text-driven sermon I highly recommend is comparative translation work. This can be of great value to the preacher for several reasons. First, it serves to validate one's own exegesis and translation of the passage from the Greek. For example, in v. 15, we have seen how the phrase often rendered in English as "the love of the Father" is semantically ambiguous in translation. KJV, NKJV, NIV, NASB, NLT, ESV, and NCV all have this translation. Does the phrase mean God's love for us or our love for God? As we have seen, most commentators interpret this phrase in Greek to mean our love for God. The following translations disambiguate the meaning and make it clear that it is people who do not love the Father: TNIV—"love for the Father is not in you"; HCSB—"love for the Father is not in him." The message then is "Love of the world squeezes out love for the Father."

A second value in comparative translation work is that it provides ideas on how to say the same thing in different ways, which is vital to creative preaching. If one repeats the phrase "the love of the Father" over and over in one's sermon, not only do the listeners not know what it means, but they also become weary of the rote repetition. However, if one finds synonymous words and phrases to convey the same meaning, then communication is aesthetically pleasing to the ear and the listener pays better attention. There are several good parallel translations now on the market that would be of immense help in this area.[40]

You may have noticed that we have not yet mentioned the use of commentaries. Now we are prepared to bring them into

---

40. For example, J. R. Kohlenberger III, gen. ed., *The Evangelical Parallel New Testament* (New York: Oxford University Press, 2003). The translations in this volume are NKJV, NIV, TNIV, NLT, ESV, HCSB, NCV, and the Message.

the process. A common mistake often made in sermon preparation is to move first, right out of the box, to the commentators to see what they say. I maintain that commentaries should be reserved for the end of the exegetical process. However, they are important to use for many reasons, not the least of which is to check your own exegetical work to this point. I read as many commentaries as time will permit at this stage in the process. I would recommend you consult at least three and major on the expository or exegetical commentaries.[41]

We are now prepared to construct a diagram of the passage. At least two options are available here: a syntactical diagram from the Greek text (or the English text), or a block diagram from the Greek text (or the English text). Building from our semantic diagram, a block diagram of 1 John 2:15–17 in English would look like this:

LOVE NOT THE WORLD, NEITHER THE THINGS IN THE WORLD.
If anyone loves the world, the love of the Father is not in him;
    because all that is in the world:
        the lust of the flesh,
        the lust of the eyes,
        and the pride of life
    is not from the Father,
    but
    is from the world.
And the world is passing away with the lust of it
but
he who does the will of God abides forever.

Notice the first line (sentence one) is in all caps. This shows that it is the dominant statement in the paragraph in terms

---

41. Two excellent commentary surveys are D. A. Carson, *New Testament Commentary Survey*, 6th ed. (Grand Rapids: Baker, 2007), and T. Longman III, *Old Testament Commentary Survey*, 4th ed. (Grand Rapids: Baker, 2007).

of meaning. The rest of the diagram is indented to the right reflecting further levels of subordination. Notice the first part of sentence two (v. 15b) is indented one level, whereas the second part (v. 16) is indented two levels. Sentence three likewise is indented one level but is placed on the same level as sentence one since it is coordinated to it by the conjunction "and."

This block diagram serves as an exegetical outline of the structure of the passage. From the exegetical outline, one can construct the homiletical (sermon) outline. The difference between the two is that an exegetical outline usually makes use of the language of the text itself, whereas the homiletical outline is an attempt to construct more of a communication outline using language that will "get the meaning across" to the listeners. Contemporary language, not necessarily biblical language, is the order of the day here.

Based on the structure of the text itself, how many main points does 1 John 2:15–17 have? It has one main point, expressed in the imperative in v. 15. How many subpoints does the text have? It has two; each one expressed by the grounds of sentence 2 and sentence 3, with sentence three divided into two halves, one negative and one positive, on the basis of the compound structure of the last sentence (v. 17). Here are the points of the text in outline form:

I. Don't love the world . . . because

    A. It is impossible to love God and the world simultaneously.
    B. The world is impermanent . . . but
        The one doing the will of God (i.e., who does not love the world) is eternally permanent.

Based on the structure of the text, how many main and subpoints should a text-driven sermon on this passage have? The answer is one main point and two subpoints. If you preach on this text omitting one or more of these subpoints, then you have not preached the text fully. If you preach this text adding additional main or subpoints beyond these, then you are adding to the meaning of the text. If you make one of the subpoints a main point parallel to v. 15a, then you have mispreached the text in terms of its focus. If you major on the three parallel prepositional phrases in v. 16 and spend most of your time explaining and illustrating them, then you will mispreach the focus of this text. To omit points, to add points, or to major in terms of focus on what the text minors is to fail to preach the text accurately. What you say may be biblical, but it will not be what this text says in the way the text says it. *If we believe in text-driven preaching, then somehow the main and subordinate information that John himself placed in his text must be reflected in the sermon.* There may be many creative ways to do this in expository preaching, but these elements must be there or the sermon will be less than truly text driven.

From this exegetical data, you are prepared to write out the sermon body, keeping in mind the three necessary ingredients in good biblical preaching: exposition, illustration, and application. Here the creativity of the preacher comes into play. The meaning of the text must be explained in a clear way that connects the audience with the author's flow of argument. Avoid pedantry and strive for clarity. Remember, clarity must be constructed. It does not happen accidentally in a sermon. Scintillating and well-placed illustrations will help the audience "get the picture" of the passage. Good expository preaching seeks to turn the ear into an eye. Paint the picture with words so people can see it in their minds and feel it with their emotions. Application should be textually grounded, clear, and pertinent to the audience.

Finally, write the conclusion and introduction to the sermon. The conclusion should summarize the main point(s) the text is trying to convey and should urge the audience to action. Remember, you are always preaching for a verdict. The introduction should connect the text with the contemporary audience and should present clearly what this text is about and why the audience should listen to your sermon. Both introduction and conclusion should be short—somewhere in the three-minute range. If either of these elements makes use of an illustration, four to five minutes might be needed.

Time should be given to thinking through not only what you will say in the sermon but also how you will say it. Delivery issues are critical to great preaching. Remember, it is not a song until it is sung, it is not a bell until it is rung, and it is not a sermon until it is preached. The distance between the pitcher's mound and home plate is identical in high school baseball and the major leagues: 60 feet and 6 inches. What separates the high school pitcher from the professional is delivery. A mere 10 to 15 miles per hour makes all the difference between an average high school pitcher and a multimillion-dollar contract in the major leagues. What separates preaching from great preaching is often delivery. Certainly content is more important than delivery in the long run. Better to have something to say and not say it well than to say nothing well. Better still to have something to say and to say it well. Content coupled with great delivery will make for great preaching. As my friend Danny Akin is fond of saying, "*What* you say is more important than *how* you say it. But, *how* you say it has never been more important!"

CONCLUSION

A text-driven sermon is a sermon that expresses the main and subordinate information of a given text so that modern-day hearers understand the meaning that the original audience would have understood. One does not necessarily have to package this information in a traditional deductive outline in order to accomplish this. However, the preacher must undertake careful exegetical work in grammatical, syntactical, and semantic structure of the text in order to determine what the author has encoded as main and subordinate information in the text. The sermon should stay true to the substance, structure, sense, and spirit of the text. Only when this is done right and done well can valid application be given in a sermon. Application without exposition is groundless. Exposition without application is pedantic. Both must be coupled together with illustration.

The method of text-driven preaching proposed in this chapter will take blood, sweat, toil, and tears, but the payoff is immense. Once you get the hang of it, you can conflate many of the steps and shorten the process. It is not as daunting as it may seem at the moment. God has spoken. His written Word is His speech. May we preachers pay the price to be His accurate spokesmen, rightly dividing the Word of truth. I know of no one who has said it any better than Wayne Grudem:

> Throughout the history of the church the greatest preachers have been those who have recognized that they have no authority in themselves and have seen their task as being to explain the words of Scripture and apply them clearly to the lives of their hearers. Their preaching has drawn its power not from the proclamation of their own Christian experiences or the experiences of others, nor from their own opinions, creative ideas, or rhetorical skills, but from God's powerful words. Essentially they stood in the pulpit, pointed to the biblical texts, and said in effect to the congregation, "This is what this verse means. Do you see the meaning here as well? Then you must believe it and obey it with all your heart, for God himself is saying this to you today!" Only the written words of Scripture can give this kind of authority to preaching.[42]

And only text-driven preaching can adequately communicate God's meaning to His people.

---

42. W. Grudem, *Systematic Theology: An Introduction to Biblical Doctrine* (Grand Rapids: Zondervan, 1994), 82.

6

EXEGESIS FOR THE TEXT-DRIVEN SERMON

David Alan Black[1]

hat is the place of exegesis in teaching and preaching? That is the question I wish to ask—and answer—in this chapter.

We may think of exegesis as a hearing aid. We live in a deafening age. A cacophony of voices seeks to distract us. Spiritually, we have become hard of hearing. But we cannot exposit a text until we have first listened to it.

The Bible says much about listening. We make a grave mistake if we think that we can speak without first being spoken to. At churches on any given Sunday, many men "play preacher,"

---

1. The following people read an earlier draft of this chapter and offered helpful criticisms: Bryan Barley, Jong Hyun Kwon, Alan Knox, Nathan Black, and David Beck. My heartfelt appreciation to each one. I especially wish to thank my colleague Robert Cole for the Old Testament exegesis bibliography at the end of this chapter. Of course, all views and errors are my own.

go through the motions, and think they are teaching truth, unaware that they are only pretending. What would happen if pastor-teachers could wear a hearing aid that would enable them to listen to the text, not as a muffled sound but as a clear-sounding trumpet? In fact, those of us who teach and preach do have such a hearing aid in the Word of God, which is "alive and powerful" (Heb 4:12).[2] Christianity is both vocal and articulate. It is based on life-changing truth, truth that requires a most respectful and careful hearing.

So, then, what should we be alert to when we listen to the text of Scripture? There are as many answers to this question as there are Bible scholars. A flood of books on this subject has appeared in the last 30 years. My own *Using New Testament Greek in Ministry* is one of them.[3] In it, I seek to offer a step-by-step approach to exegesis. My book does not represent a brand-new approach but rather a repristination of Reformation principles of interpretation and a recovery of the doctrine of inspiration that sees "every word, everywhere" not only as God-breathed but also as profitable for teaching (2 Tim 3:16–17). I am convinced that sound exegesis involves 10 important steps, and it is my hope that by reviewing them in this chapter you will be both challenged and encouraged to become the best Bible expositor you can possibly be.

THREE QUESTIONS

Let's begin, however, by concentrating on three broader questions of exegesis. I believe we need to pose these three questions every time we sit down to prepare a message from Scripture:

---

2. All translations in this chapter are my own.
3. D. A. Black, *Using New Testament Greek in Ministry: A Practical Guide for Students and Pastors* (Grand Rapids: Baker, 1993).

1. Do I understand what the context of my passage is?
2. Do I understand what my passage means?
3. Do I understand how to apply my passage?

Switching for a moment to geometric terms, we might say that exegesis involves looking at a text from three different angles. First, we must stand *above* the text, getting a bird's-eye view of the whole. Then we must look *inside* the text, standing within it and discerning its meaning by using all of the exegetical tools at our disposal. And finally, we must stand *under* the text, ready and willing to obey it and to teach it in a way that applies its message to others.

These three basic areas of discovery—"above" the text, "inside" the text, and "under" the text—may now be called *context, meaning,* and *significance.* As I see it, the questions of *context* are both historical and literary. *Historical analysis* deals with the cultural, political, and religious situation facing the author and his original audience. *Literary analysis* deals with the way in which the text fits in with its immediate surroundings in the book under study.

The questions of *meaning* take us into the text itself. Here we find a sixfold emphasis: *textual analysis* (dealing with the original wording of the text), *lexical analysis* (dealing with the meaning of the words), *syntactical analysis* (dealing with the relationships that exist between words), *structural analysis* (dealing with the way the author has arranged the text), *rhetorical analysis* (dealing with the rhetorical devices the author may have used in the text), and *tradition-critical analysis* (dealing with any traditional or preexisting materials).

Finally, the questions of significance are twofold, involving both *theological analysis* (what biblical truth is apparent in the text?) and *homiletical analysis* (how do I best communicate this truth to others?).

I do not for a moment wish to suggest that the exegetical process previously described is a mechanical succession of steps or that all of the steps apply equally to every passage of Scripture.

In practice, we will often find ourselves moving back and forth between questions of context, meaning, and significance. I simply wish to emphasize that unless we go through each of these steps—and ask each of these questions—we run the very great risk of overlooking an important aspect of exegesis. In reality, exegesis is as much an art as it is a science, and we will do well to safeguard the Scriptures, and ourselves, from any "method" that promises an inerrant interpretation.

Now let me try to expand on each of these steps, and then illustrate them by applying them to a passage taken from the letter to the Hebrews. In expanding these steps, my examples will be taken from the New Testament, since this is my field of study. Still, I believe that the principles of exegesis that are discussed here are just as applicable to work in the Old Testament.

QUESTIONS OF CONTEXT

It should come as no great surprise that I begin with questions of context. It is obvious that a text had no meaning—or may assume *any* meaning—outside the parameters set by context. So we must begin our work in the text by examining both its historical context and its literary context.

Historical Analysis

The key question here is, what are the significant historical factors that lie behind the writing of the book under study? We may, of course, derive much of this information from the book itself. But this does not mean that we can overlook or ignore extrabiblical information in our quest to understand better the background of our text. Whenever I study the historical background of a book that I am teaching, I always try to ask and answer at least six questions:

1. Who wrote the book?
2. To whom was it sent?
3. What was the relationship that existed between author and readers?
4. What was the historical situation that occasioned the writing of the book?
5. Where was the author when writing?
6. Where did the readers live?

Although these kinds of questions may appear dull or irrelevant, they are, I believe, indispensable if a text is to be heard in terms of its original setting.

Incidentally, what drives these questions is the fact that the writings of the Bible are to be understood as *occasional documents*—that is, they were occasioned by some special circumstance either from the author's or the readers' perspective. Hence the more we understand about these circumstances, the better prepared we will be to understand the text and then to apply its message to modern life.

Many helpful tools exist today to help us discover the historical background of the Bible. In New Testament studies, the most helpful of these works include F. F. Bruce, *New Testament History* (Garden City: Doubleday, 1971); C. K. Barrett, *The New Testament Background: Selected Documents* (San Francisco: Harper/ London: SPCK, 1987); Everett Ferguson, *Backgrounds of Early Christianity* (Grand Rapids: Eerdmans, 1987); Ben Witherington, *New Testament History* (Grand Rapids: Baker, 2001); Craig S. Keener, *The IVP Biblical Background Commentary: New Testament* (Downers Grove: InterVarsity, 1993); and Paul Norman Jackson, "Background Studies and New Testament Interpretation," in *Interpreting the New Testament*, edited by David Alan Black and David S. Dockery (Nashville: B&H, 2001), 188–208.

Literary Analysis

Not only must we be able to understand something about the historical background of the text under consideration; the literary context also demands our attention. In his classic textbook *Biblical Preaching*, Haddon W. Robinson reminds us that "seeing the passage within its wider framework simply gives the Bible the same character we give the author of a paperback."[4] An example I like to use in my classes is Heb 13:5. Most of my students can easily quote the second part of that verse: "I will never leave you nor forsake you." But very few can quote the first part of the same verse: "Keep your lives free from the love of money, and be content with what you have." Odd, isn't it, how we remember the promise but forget the command? My students are always shocked when I tell them that the Bible had no verses until the mid-sixteenth century. Verses were first introduced in the Greek New Testament by Robert Estienne (also known as Stephanus) in the year 1551. Although this may have made looking up certain passages in the New Testament easier, it also left the erroneous impression that every verse stands on its own. The use of versification in the King James Version in 1611 may have unwittingly perpetuated this distortion. Too often this has led to what I call a bumper sticker or wall motto approach to the New Testament, in which we take verses out of their context, kicking, screaming, and bleeding. But the New Testament (and the Old, for that matter) is not a miscellaneous junk pile of unrelated elements. It is more like a jigsaw puzzle. Remove an isolated piece of the puzzle from its context, and that piece makes no sense whatsoever.

As I see it, asking questions about the literary context of the passage has a threefold benefit:

1. It helps us to think in terms not of verses but of paragraphs, which is the basic thought unit in language.
2. It helps us to outline the book under study by dividing it into its proper subsections. Then, as we teach through the book passage by passage (i.e., paragraph by paragraph), our teaching units are more likely to

---

4. H. W. Robinson, *Biblical Preaching: The Development and Delivery of Expository Messages* (Grand Rapids: Baker, 1980), 58.

reflect what the writer was emphasizing in that book. I once studied Philippians this way, and it made all the difference in the world in how I taught the book. Many people think that Philippians is about joy in the Christian life. But my study of the structure of Philippians led me to conclude that joy was at best a by-product of unity, the main theme of this important letter.[5]

3. Finally, by studying the literary context of a book of the Bible, we are better able to establish its genre. In the New Testament, we find four basic genres (Gospel, acts, epistle, and apocalypse), along with subtypes such as narrative, parables, question, beatitude, hymn, saying, and so forth. The genre of a book, as well as its literary subtypes, affect our understanding of the text in much the same way as differences between feature stories, editorials, and cartoons influence our reading of a newspaper.[6]

Of course, tracing the argument of a New Testament writing is never easy. We must work top-down and bottom-up at the same time. We must try to determine our teaching text by observing both the syntax and the subject matter of the book under consideration. To do this, I have found it especially helpful to look for words and phrases such as "therefore," "so then," "for this reason," and the like. Many times these expressions indicate the beginning of a paragraph, as do linguistic markers such as vocatives ("brothers") and disclosure formulas ("I don't want you to be ignorant").

As you study the literary context of your passage, you should take the time to consult both exegetical commentaries and New Testament survey books. One such work written on a very basic level is *The New Testament: Its Background and Message*, edited by Thomas D. Lea and David Alan Black, revised edition

5. See D. A. Black, "The Discourse Structure of Philippians: A Study in Textlinguistics," *NovT* 37 (1995): 16–49. See also my "The Literary Structure of 1 and 2 Thessalonians," *SBJT* 3 (1999): 46–57, and my "The Problem of the Literary Structure of Hebrews: An Evaluation and a Proposal," *GTJ* 7 (1986): 163–77. I specifically wrote these essays to serve as "ponies" (i.e., guides) for my Greek students.

6. See C. L. Blomberg, "The Diversity of Literary Genres in the New Testament," in *Interpreting the New Testament*, ed. D. A. Black and D. S. Dockery (Nashville: B&H, 2001), 272–95.

Nashville: B&H, 2003). In addition, the attempt to discover the internal unity and structure of a writing is called discourse analysis. For an introduction to this important field of study, see Peter Cotterell and Max Turner, *Linguistics and Biblical Interpretation* (Downers Grove: InterVarsity, 1989) and David Alan Black, editor, *Linguistics and New Testament Interpretation: Essays on Discourse Analysis* (Nashville: B&H, 1993).[7]

QUESTIONS OF MEANING

As we have seen, the questions of meaning have to do with these six steps.

Textual Analysis

Textual analysis is sometimes overlooked in New Testament exegesis. Often we simply assume that the text we are preaching from is the original text without first examining it in any detail. This, I believe, is a grave mistake. New Testament textual analysis (also called "textual criticism") is a necessary step in the exegetical process if for no other reason than that the existing Greek manuscripts vary among themselves considerably. These differences in the Greek manuscripts are reflected frequently enough in our modern English versions (especially in the footnotes) that the expositor will invariably be called upon to make an informed judgment. In Matt 5:22, for example, the words "without a cause" are absent in the majority of English versions, though they are found in the KJV and the NKJV. The question here is a vitally important one for anyone teaching from this passage: does Jesus forbid *all* anger or only *unjustified* anger?[8]

---

7. See also the chapter in this volume on discourse analysis by George Guthrie.
8. For a detailed discussion of this problem, see D. A. Black, "Jesus on Anger: The Text of Matthew 5:22 Revisited," *NovT* 30 (1988): 1–8.

Obviously, an informed understanding of this textual problem is necessary before one preaches from this portion of the Sermon on the Mount. Yet another example is found in John 3:12–13: did Jesus claim to be "in heaven" while talking to Nicodemus? The answer to this question depends on how one resolves the textual problem in this verse.[9]

There are approximately 2,000 significant textual variants in the Greek New Testament. (A "significant" variant is one that affects both translation and interpretation.) Perhaps the most famous of these is Mark 16:9–20.[10] If there are any important variants that appear in your passage, you will need to examine the evidence in support of the competing readings. Traditionally, text critics take into account both external and internal evidence. These usually are the questions of external evidence:

1. Which reading is the oldest?
2. Which reading is the most geographically widespread?
3. Which reading is supported by the majority of text types?

These, on the other hand, are the questions of internal evidence:

1. Which reading best explains the origin of the other?
2. Which reading can be attributed to scribal error?
3. Which reading best conforms to the author's style and thought?

In order to do your own textual criticism, you will need a working knowledge of the subject. In particular, you will need to become familiar with the materials of New Testament textual criticism (i.e., the Greek manuscripts, ancient versions, and citations by early church fathers) and with the textual apparatus

---

9. See D. A. Black, "The Text of John 3:13," *GTJ* 6 (1985): 49–66.
10. For a recent discussion of this passage, see D. A. Black, ed., *Perspectives on the Ending of Mark* (Nashville: B&H, 2009).

of your Greek New Testament. It will also be necessary to know how textual decisions are made. For an overview of the subject, perhaps the simplest introduction available today is David Alan Black, *New Testament Textual Criticism: A Concise Guide* (Grand Rapids: Baker, 1994). Eventually, however, you will want to read the standard text in the field by Bruce M. Metzger, *The Text of the New Testament*, 3rd ed. (Oxford: Oxford University Press, 1992).[11]

Lexical Analysis

Once you have determined the original wording of your passage, you will want to determine the meaning of the words within it. This step is called lexical analysis, or "word study." Words are important because they are the basic building blocks of language. As a rule, a word in Greek has several meanings, only one of which is its "meaning" in any passage in which it occurs. So our responsibility is to discern the meaning that the author intended without reading into the word our own preconceived notions.

When I do a word study, I often ask myself several questions:

1. What are the word's possible meanings?
2. Which meaning best fits the context?
3. How does the author use the same word in other places?
4. Does the word have any synonyms or antonyms that help to define its meaning?

At the same time, I try to avoid fallacies:

1. Etymologizing (determining meaning solely on the basis of a word's etymology)

---

11. For an up-to-date survey of current thinking about the subject, see D. A. Black, ed., *Rethinking New Testament Textual Criticism* (Grand Rapids: Baker, 2002).

2. Illegitimate totality transfer (reading the full range of meanings that a word may have into each passage in which it occurs)
3. Confusing word with concept (failing to recognize that ideas are rarely, if ever, expressed at the word level alone)
4. Overanalysis (performing word studies at the expense of other areas of exegesis)

Most of these fallacies are easy to commit. They are also very "preachable." How often have we been told that the Greek word ἐκκλησία means "called out ones"? The word actually has nothing to do with its etymology (ἐκ, "out of," and καλέω, "call"). You do not have to have been born and raised in Hawaii, like I was, to know that a pineapple is not an apple that grows on a pine tree. As we have seen, the key to lexical analysis is remembering that a word in Greek can have several different meanings, only one of which is likely to be its semantic contribution to any particular sentence in which it occurs.

In doing a word study, I recommend these steps:

1. First, consult the major lexicons (especially BDAG) to get an idea of the range of meaning of the word you are studying.
2. Next, check a concordance to get a feel for your author's distinctive use of the word.
3. Finally, look the word up in a theological dictionary (such as the *NIDNTT*).

Remember that dictionaries of New Testament words do not always give full and sufficient attention to the context. To a great degree, the meaning of any particular word in the New Testament is bound with the structure of the passage in which it occurs. As an example, I like to tell my beginning Greek students that the first five words of the Gospel of John (ἐν ἀρχῇ ἦν ὁ λόγος) can, in an appropriate context, be rendered, "The treasurer was in the middle of a body of troops." *I cannot stress too much the importance of context in exegesis.* This point is neatly summed up in the story about the sheik who wanted to give an employee a present. The intended beneficiary suggested "a few golf clubs." Later the recipient received an e-mail saying, "Have bought you Pebble Beach and am negotiating for the Riviera."

So remember, lexical analysis is not the "Open Sesame" or "Abracadabra" of exegesis. It is a handmaiden and not the queen. Still, it is an indispensable step in the process and one that we ignore to our own injury. These books will help you develop your skill in doing lexical analysis:

Moisés Silva, *Biblical Words and Their Meaning: An Introduction to Lexical Semantics* (Grand Rapids: Zondervan, 1983).

D. A. Carson, *Exegetical Fallacies*, 2nd ed. (Grand Rapids: Baker, 1996).

David Alan Black, *Linguistics for Students of New Testament Greek: A Survey of Basic Concepts and Applications*, 2nd ed. (Grand Rapids: Baker, 1995).

The standard New Testament Greek lexicon is *A Greek-English Lexicon of the New Testament and Other Early Christian Literature*, 3rd ed., rev. and ed. Frederick William Danker (Chicago: University of Chicago Press, 2000). This work is often abbreviated as BDAG. Also helpful is the four-volume *New International Dictionary of New Testament Theology*, trans. and ed. Colin Brown (Grand Rapids: Zondervan, 1975–86), often abbreviated as *NIDNTT*.

Syntactical Analysis

Syntax is an extremely important part of the exegetical task. Unfortunately, its importance is often overlooked. Too often the exegete stops with lexical analysis. It is always a great joy for me to see my students move beyond "word bound" exegesis and begin to explore the rich dimension of syntactical analysis.

Simply defined, syntax involves the grammatical and semantic relationships between words. It focuses on clauses and other sense units that are larger than individual words. It also includes such matters as tense, voice, mood, person, number, and case of individual words. The study of syntax always takes us back to the original text of Scripture, because syntactical features are frequently masked in even our most literal English versions. If you are a bit rusty on your syntax, I would suggest that you take a moment to review your introductory Greek grammar.

Our primary concern in syntactical analysis is determining any grammatical feature that might affect our interpretation and eventual application of a passage. Ephesians 5:18 offers us an example of the importance of syntactical analysis. Here the main verb is πληροῦσθε ("be filled"). W. A. Criswell, in his sermon on this passage,[12] begins with a word study of the verb πληρόω ("fill") and then evolves the body of his sermon directly from the grammatical nuances of the verb's syntactical features:

1. God commands us to be filled with the Spirit (the verb is in the imperative mood).
2. This filling is a repeated experience (the verb is in the present tense).
3. We must yield ourselves to the influence of the Spirit in our lives (the verb is in the passive voice).

As you can see, in this sermon syntax has played a key role. Greek syntax is also an important factor in the exegesis of problem texts. In Heb 6:4–6, for example, the shift from the five aorist-tense participles to the two present-tense participles suggests that apostates can be reclaimed unless they *persist* in "crucifying" and "ridiculing" the Son of God.

These works will help you with questions of syntax:

James A. Brooks and Carlton L. Winbery, *Syntax of New Testament Greek* (Lanham, MD: University Press of America, 1979).

J. Harold Greenlee, *A Concise Exegetical Grammar of New Testament Greek* (Grand Rapids: Eerdmans, 1986).

David Alan Black, *It's Still Greek to Me: A Easy-to-Understand Guide to Intermediate Greek* (Grand Rapids: Baker, 1998).

---

12. W. A. Criswell, *The Holy Spirit in Today's World* (Grand Rapids: Zondervan, 1966), 132–36.

David Alan Black, *Learn to Read New Testament Greek*, 3rd ed. (Nashville: B&H, 2009).

Daniel B. Wallace, *Greek Grammar Beyond the Basics* (Grand Rapids: Zondervan, 1997).

Structural Analysis

Once you have reached a decision about the wording and syntax of your passage, you will want to look at the passage's larger composition. Structural analysis is concerned with the relationships that exist between larger units of meaning such as clauses and sentences.

For complex passages, I have found it helpful to make a full structural analysis at this point. The purpose of a structural analysis is to rearrange the words of a passage in such a way that the central theme of the passage becomes evident. In Greek, the main clause of the passage will normally indicate the main proposition (idea) of the text, whereas the dependent clauses generally represent expansions of the main idea. I emphasize the phrase "in Greek," because what appears as the main clause in an English version is often a dependent clause in Greek. It is always necessary to work in the Greek text as much as possible when doing structural analysis.

The procedure that I prefer to follow in doing a structural diagram consists of three steps:

1. Place all of the independent clauses at the left-hand margin of the page.
2. Place all of the dependent clauses or phrases on the next line under the word(s) they modify.
3. Restate the author's argument in my own words.

Once again, the object in making a structural analysis is to reconstruct as clearly as possible the original thought of the author. This type of analysis maximizes your opportunity to be truly inductive in your study of a passage. Personally, I find that the study of structure is one of the most enjoyable and rewarding aspects of my work in the Greek text.[13] As an example, let us look at Phil 1:9–11, Paul's prayer for the Philippians. Here the main clause may be set forth as follows, with the subordinate clauses indented to the right:

And this is my prayer:
    that your love may abound yet more and more in knowledge and
    full discernment
        so that you may approve what is excellent
        [and] so that you may be pure and blameless in the day of Christ
            having been filled with the fruit of righteousness that
            comes through Jesus Christ to the glory and praise of God

Paul's logic appears as follows. First he states that he is praying for the readers. Then he states the content of his prayer. Next he gives the twofold purpose for his prayer (the immediate purpose is that they may approve what is excellent, and the ultimate purpose is that they might be pure and blameless when Christ returns). Finally, he states the reason he can pray this way (i.e., God has already filled them with righteousness). A teaching outline might look something like this:

Title: Paul's Prayer for the Philippians
Outline:

I.   The **petition** (prayer for abounding love)

---

13. Several of my analyses have been published. See, for example, D. A. Black, "On the Style and Significance of John 17," *CTR* 3 (1988): 141–59; D. A. Black, "The Pauline Love Command: Structure, Style, and Ethics in Romans 12:9–21," *FN* 2 (1989): 3–22; D. A. Black, "Paul and Christian Unity: A Formal Analysis of Philippians 2:1–4," *JETS* 28 (1985): 299–308; D. A. Black, "Hebrews 1:1–4: A Study in Discourse Analysis," *WTJ* 49 (1987): 175–94; D. A. Black, "A Note on the Structure of Hebrews 12, 1–2," *Biblica* 68 (1987): 543–51. I believe that even beginning students of Greek will find these essays to be accessible models of how to do structural analysis.

II. The **purpose** (approving what is excellent and being pure and blameless)
III. The **provision** (the righteousness that God supplies)

If diagramming a paragraph in this fashion is new to you, I recommend these resources to help you get started in making a structural analysis of a passage from the New Testament:

Johannes P. Louw, *Semantics of New Testament Greek* (Philadelphia: Fortress, 1982).

Gordon D. Fee, *New Testament Exegesis: A Handbook for Students and Pastors*, 3rd ed. (Philadelphia: Westminster, 2002).

Walter L. Liefeld, *New Testament Exposition: From Text to Sermon* (Grand Rapids: Zondervan, 1984).

Rhetorical Analysis

When we turn from structural analysis and begin to look at the literary dimensions of our passage, we encounter a relatively new field in New Testament studies called rhetorical analysis. The fundamental basis for rhetorical analysis is the belief that the text's design is part of its meaning and that to neglect this design is to overlook an important part of the inspired text. In other words, *how* something is said is often as important as *what* is said. Ancient authors often used literary techniques in order to assist readers to understand the message of the text or to persuade them of the truth of the presentation.

Rhetorical analysis is as much an art as it is a science. It involves close attention to the contours of a text (its beginning and end), the use of figures of speech in the text (e.g., simile and metaphor), the observation of compositional techniques (such as parallelism and chiasm), and judgments about the relationship of form to meaning. These are some things you should look for as you analyze the rhetoric of a passage:

1. Alliteration (the repetition of words beginning or ending with the same letter or sound)

2. Asyndeton (the omission of conjunctions that would normally be present)
3. Chiasm (the rhetorical inversion of words or thoughts)
4. Paronomasia (an intentional play on two similar-sounding words)
5. Polysyndeton (the superfluous repetition of conjunctions)

Do not become discouraged if at first you find it difficult to discover the use of such literary techniques in the text. With practice, your observations will increase in both number and depth. Thankfully, more and more exegetical commentaries on the New Testament are paying attention to the use of such devices. In addition to consulting these commentaries, you may also wish to secure and read Eugene A. Nida et al., *Style and Discourse, with Special Reference to the Text of the Greek New Testament* (Cape Town: Bible Society of South Africa, 1983).

Tradition Analysis

Thus far under the heading "Questions of Meaning," we have looked at five areas of analysis: textual, lexical, syntactical, structural, and rhetorical. To these we may now add a sixth, namely, tradition analysis. Tradition analysis is concerned with such matters as the identity and extent of sources that may lie behind a given work. In the New Testament Gospels, for example, source critics claim to have identified several layers of tradition that the Gospel writers have used in composing their accounts of the life of Christ. The dominant hypothesis today concerning these traditions is called the "Two-Document Hypothesis" because it posits the priority of the Gospel of Mark with its subsequent use by Matthew and Luke, plus the existence of a sayings source (called "Q"), also used by Matthew and Luke. Alternative theories argue for the priority of Matthew or Luke.[14]

---

14. On the possible literary interdependence between the Gospels, see D. A. Black and D. R. Beck, eds., *Rethinking the Synoptic Problem* (Grand Rapids: Baker, 2001). For an argument in favor of the order Matthew–Luke–Mark, see D. A.

Preexisting traditions are sometimes found in the New Testament letters, a classic example being the simple confession "Jesus is Lord" (1 Cor 12:3). Moreover, New Testament scholars sometimes feel they can identify sources behind the hymns that we find in the New Testament, including the famous Christ-hymn in Phil 2:6–11.[15] Also of importance are the frequent Old Testament quotations that are found in the New Testament.[16] The value of tradition analysis is seen clearly in Gospel studies in that it helps us to determine how a Gospel writer may have selected, arranged, and presented his material to his audience.[17]

QUESTIONS OF SIGNIFICANCE

The two steps involved here—*theological analysis* and *homiletical analysis*—may be discussed briefly, as both of these topics are treated in greater detail elsewhere in this book. Basically, the questions of significance are the logical consequence of all that has preceded them. Exegesis is not complete until we seek to apply the text first to ourselves and then to the people we are teaching. This involves determining the key thought of the passage and discerning the real-life issues in it that have relevance to the believing community and then putting the results of your exegesis into a workable outline that sets forth the text's claims in ways that are timeless and relevant.

It remains only to say that what I have offered thus far in this chapter is nothing more than the reflections of one who is more

---

Black, *Why Four Gospels? The Historical Origins of the Gospels* (Grand Rapids: Kregel, 2001).

15. See D. A. Black, "The Authorship of Philippians 2:6–11: Some Literary-Critical Observations," *CTR* 2 (1988): 269–89.
16. See K. Snodgrass, "The Use of the Old Testament in the New," in *Interpreting the New Testament*, ed. D. A. Black and D. S. Dockery (Nashville: B&H, 2001), 209–29.
17. This is called redaction criticism. For a helpful overview, see G. R. Osborne, "Redaction Criticism," in *Interpreting the New Testament*, ed. D. A. Black and D. S. Dockery (Nashville: B&H, 2001), 128–49.

anxious to learn from his fellow teachers than to teach them. My own habit is to go through each of these steps somewhat mechanically, which, for me, means about 8 to 10 hours of concentrated study. And even though not every question is equally important in the final analysis, I try at least to ask each question lest I leave out something of importance.

EXEMPLAR: HEBREWS 12:1–2

If you feel conformable in doing so, you might want to study this passage on your own before comparing the results of your exegesis with mine. My point in offering this example is not to imply that there is only one way of analyzing this text. Instead, by tracing the steps of exegesis, I hope to highlight the practicability of the method I previously presented. It is my hope and prayer that something of the loveliness of this passage might shine through the analysis offered here.

Step 1: Historical Analysis

Here we must be content with a general sketch of the historical background. In the east, Hebrews was always included among the Pauline epistles, though the eastern church was aware that Pauline authorship was not universally accepted. Today the consensus of New Testament scholarship is that Paul could not have written the epistle. I disagree.[18] But the important thing to note here is that the epistle has always been defended as canonical, even if its authorship has been (and still is) hotly debated.

Due to the letter's emphasis on the superiority of Christ's sacrifice over the Old Testament sacrifices, it seems to me that the original title—"To the Hebrews"—is best taken as a reference

---

18. See D. A. Black, "Who Wrote Hebrews? The Internal and External Evidence Reexamined," *FM* 18 (2001): 3–26. One of the editors of this volume, David Allen, argues for direct Lukan authorship of Hebrews. See D. L. Allen, *Lukan Authorship of Hebrews*, NAC Studies in Bible and Theology (Nashville: B&H, 2010).

to a Jewish Christian audience. Most scholars assume that the letter was sent to Rome, either to the entire Christian community there or to a house church. This, at least, seems to be the natural way of taking 13:24 ("The brothers and sisters from Italy greet you"). If the letter was Paul's, it had to be written before the year 67. The absence of any reference to the destruction of Jerusalem and the temple also argues for a date prior to AD 70.

Step 2: Literary Analysis

The theme of Hebrews is that Jesus is the true high priest. This theme has been carefully developed by a series of concentric arguments.[19] We may outline the epistle like this:

		1:1–4	Introduction
I.		1:5–2:18	The Name of Jesus
II.	A.	3:1–4:14	Jesus, Trustworthy High Priest
	B.	4:15–5:10	Jesus, Compassionate High Priest
		5:11–6:20	(Preliminary Exhortation)
	A.	7:1–28	According to the Order of Melchizedek
III.	B.	8:1–9:28	Perfection Achieved
	C.	10:1–18	Source of Eternal Salvation
		10:19–39	(Closing Exhortation)
IV.	A.	11:1–40	The Faith of the Men of Old
	B.	12:1–13	The Necessity of Endurance
V.		12:14–13:18	Make Straight Paths
		13:20–21	Conclusion

Hebrews 12:1–2 can be considered a typical exhortation based on the author's previous comments in chapter 11. James Swetnam has shown that 12:1–2 is "the consummation of all the

---

19. See D. A. Black, "The Problem of the Literary Structure of Hebrews: An Evaluation and a Proposal," *GTJ* 7 (1986): 163–77.

faith-witnessed heroes of the past."[20] At the beginning of chapter 12, however, the readers are now invited to run with endurance the race that is set before *them*, following the example of Christ, "who endured the cross" (12:1–2).

Step 3: Textual Analysis

A significant textual variant occurs in v. 1. Instead of εὐπερίστατον ("easily besetting"), εὐπερίσπαστον ("easily distracting") occurs. The latter reading is weakly attested and is probably an attempt to clarify the meaning of εὐπερίστατον, which is found only here in ancient Greek literature.

Step 4: Lexical Analysis

In Heb 12:1–2, the pivotal words include "cloud," "witness," "race," "burden," "easily besetting," "Pioneer," and "Perfecter." The term "cloud" is obviously a metaphor for a large mass of people. A "witness" is one who testifies to what he or she personally knows to be true. The idea here is not that the "cloud of witnesses" is a cheering audience as much as they are testifying to the importance of steadfast faith. The "race" spoken of pictures an athletic contest in which each believer is considered a foot runner. To run the race successfully, the runner must lay aside every "burden," a possible reference to anything that might hamper progress (such as loose clothing). The Greek word translated "easily besetting" implies that sin easily gets hold of the runners, who must therefore be continually aware of temptation. Jesus is called here both the "Pioneer" and the "Perfecter" of faith. The former term probably implies that He has blazed the trail for the runners, whereas the latter indicates that He made their salvation "complete" through His death, resurrection, and exaltation.

---

20. J. Swetnam, "Form and Content in Hebrews 7–13," *Biblica* 55 (1974): 340.

Step 5: Syntactical Analysis

During syntactical analysis, several ideas become prominent:

1. The verbal aspect of the main verb τρέχωμεν implies that the race is a process and not a single step ("Let us keep on running").
2. The arthrous construction "the faith" (τῆς πίστεως) infers that the author is speaking about the *facts* of the Christian faith (on which one's subjective faith rests).
3. The perfect tense of κεκάθικεν ("has taken His seat") emphasizes the definitive and lasting results of Christ's session at the right hand of God in heaven.

Step 6: Structural Analysis

The structure of Heb 12:1–2 may be displayed like this:

τοιγαροῦν καὶ ἡμεῖς δι᾽ ὑπομονῆς **τρέχωμεν** τὸν προκείμενον ἡμῖν ἀγῶνα

    τοσοῦτον **ἔχοντες** περικείμενον ἡμῖν νέφος μαρτύρων

    ὄγκον **ἀποθέμενοι** πάντα καὶ τὴν εὐπερίστατον ἁμαρτίαν

    ἀφορῶντες εἰς τὸν τῆς πίστεως ἀρχηγὸν καὶ τελειωτὴν Ἰησοῦν

        ὃς ἀντὶ τῆς προκειμένης αὐτῷ χαρᾶς ὑπέμεινεν σταυρὸν
        αἰσχύνης καταφρονήσας ἐν δεξιᾷ τε τοῦ θρόνου τοῦ θεοῦ
        κεκάθικεν

Therefore with endurance **let us run** the race that is set before us

    having so great a cloud of witnesses surrounding us

    laying aside every weight and the easily besetting sin

    fixing our eyes on Jesus, the Pioneer and Perfecter of the faith

        who for the joy set before Him endured the cross and
        despising the shame has taken His seat at the right hand
        of the throne of God

Here the basic thought units jump off the page like the white lines of a football field. The main theme of the paragraph is brought out to the left, whereas the subordinate elements cluster to the right. From the first line of the analysis, which alone contains an independent finite verb (τρέχωμεν), we are immediately introduced to the author's main point: running the race with endurance. Thereafter come three participial clauses that qualify the "race":

1. It is by the knowledge that others have completed the race that the present generation of runners can hope to finish it.
2. No runner, however, can hope to attain the goal without an abhorrence of personal sin.
3. The runner must look to Jesus, the "Pioneer and Perfecter of the faith."

The remaining items in the paragraph are a description of Jesus, showing how the main theme of "running the race" climaxes in "Jesus and who He is."

Step 7: Rhetorical Analysis

What features of ancient rhetoric can be detected in this passage? There are several:

1. The use of "cloud" as a metaphor.
2. The play on words using the prepositional prefix ἀπό/ἀφ᾽ in **ἀποθέμενοι** ("putting **off**") and **ἀφορῶντες** ("looking **off**").
3. The metaphor of an athletic competition ("race").
4. The vivid images of Jesus as "Pioneer and Perfecter."
5. The use of chiasm. Indeed, the entire text can be seen as chiastically structured:

A. having so great a cloud of witnesses **surrounding** [i.e., **seated around**] us
  B. **laying aside** every weight and the easily besetting sin
    C. therefore with **endurance**
      D. let us run the race that is **set before** us
        X. **fixing our eyes on Jesus**, the Pioneer and Perfecter of the faith
      D'. who for the joy **set before** Him
    C'. **endured** the cross
  B'. and **despising** the shame
A'. has **taken His seat** at the right hand of the throne of God.

Step 8: Tradition Analysis

As in 1:3; 8:1; and 10:12, here the author uses Ps 110:1 to refer to the event of Christ's session at the right hand of God. Jesus Himself referred to this verse during His last week of public teaching (Matt 22:43–44).

Step 9: Theological Analysis

We noted previously that the theme of the paragraph is the need for the readers to run the race (of the Christian life) with endurance. Jesus Himself is the ultimate paradigm of faithful endurance. The readers are to "go the distance" in their commitment to Jesus.

Step 10: Homiletical Analysis

Our structural analysis clearly demonstrates how, by analyzing the Greek text, we can move from theory to practice. In shaping one's outline by the contours of the text's internal structure, one can emphasize the dominant thoughts of the author without majoring on the minors. By reducing these elements to an outline, we can move directly from interpretation to application:

Text: Hebrews 12:1–2
Title: Run with Endurance!
Theme: The Christian is called upon to follow the example of Christ into a life of submission and obedience ("with endurance let us run").
Outline:

I.   Our **Encouragement** ("having so great a cloud of witnesses surrounding us")
II. Our **Entanglements** ("laying aside every weight and the easily besetting sin")
III. Our **Example** ("fixing our eyes on Jesus, the Pioneer and Perfecter of the faith")

CONCLUSION

We have seen that the aim of biblical exegesis is to explain what the text meant to its original audience and what it means to hearers today. The primary exegetical principle is that the meaning of the text is the author's intended meaning and not "what it means to me." It is within these parameters of authorial intent and grammatical form that faithful biblical interpretation takes place.

In short, the basic goal of exegesis must always be to determine as exactly as possible just what the writer meant by the words he wrote. This task calls for a good deal of technical learning. It will force us to bring to the text all of the exegetical tools at our disposal—historical, cultural, linguistic, and theological. When we move to the further task of applying the text to our modern situation, we will seek to be as true to the text as possible in how we present its timeless truths. Our guiding principle will be that the best homiletical outlines of a passage are those that are derived from the text itself.

It is obvious that the questions we ask of the text—about its context, its meaning, and its application—will require us to become good listeners of the text. Of course, we cannot go about our task without prayer and the guidance of the Holy Spirit. There is nothing magical—or easy—about exegesis. But if we are diligent, we may expect to reap results. The psalmist sensed this truth three millennia ago (Ps 126:6): "Those who go out weeping, bearing the seed for sowing, will come home with shouts of joy, bringing in their sheaves."

APPENDIX: OLD TESTAMENT
EXEGESIS BIBLIOGRAPHY

by Prof. Robert Cole (SEBTS)

Historical Analysis

Pritchard, James, ed. *Ancient Near Eastern Texts Relating to the Old Testament*. Princeton, NJ: Princeton University Press, 1969.
Sasson, Jack M. *Civilizations of the Ancient Near East*. 2 vols. Peabody, MA: Hendrickson, 1996.

Literary Analysis

Alter, Robert. *The Art of Biblical Narrative*. New York: Basic Books, 1981.
Bar-Efrat, Shimon. *Narrative Art in the Bible*. Edinburgh: T&T Clark, 2004.

Textual Analysis

Tov, Emanuel. *Textual Criticism of the Hebrew Bible*. 2nd rev. ed. Minneapolis: Fortress and Assen, Royal Van Gorcum, 2001.
Würthwein, Ernst. *The Text of the Old Testament: An Introduction to the Biblia Hebraica*. 2nd ed. Grand Rapids: Eerdmans, 1994.

Lexical Analysis

Brown, F., S. R. Driver, and C. A. Briggs. *A Hebrew and English Lexicon of the Old Testament*. Oxford: Clarendon, 1953. Also published by Hendrickson, 1996.
Even-Shoshan, Abraham. *Konkordantsyah hadashah: Le-Torah, Neviim u-Khetuvim*. (New Concordance of the Torah, Prophets, and Writings). Jerusalem: Kiryat Sefer, 1996.

Syntactical Analysis

van der Merwe, Christo H. J., Jackie A. Naudé, and Jan H. Kroeze. *A Biblical Hebrew Reference Grammar*. Sheffield: Sheffield Academic Press, 2000.
Williams, Ronald J. *Williams' Hebrew Syntax*. Revised by John C. Beckman. 3rd ed. Toronto: University of Toronto Press, 2007.

Structural Analysis

Berlin, Adele. *The Dynamics of Biblical Parallelism*. Rev. ed. Grand Rapids: Eerdmans, 2008.
Walsh, Jerome T. *Style & Structure in Biblical Hebrew Narrative*. Collegeville, MN: The Liturgical Press, 2001.

Rhetorical Analysis

Muilenburg, James. "A Study in Hebrew Rhetoric: Repetition and Style," VTSup 1 (1953), 97–11.
Trible, Phyllis. *Rhetorical Criticism: Context, Method, and the Book of Jonah*. Minneapolis: Fortress, 1994.

Tradition Analysis

Rendsburg, Gary A. *The Redaction of Genesis*. Winona Lake, IN: Eisenbrauns, 1986.
Wilson, Gerald H. "Shaping the Psalter: A Consideration of Editorial Linkage in the Book of Psalms." Pages 72–82 in *The Shape and Shaping of the Psalter*. Edited by J. Clinton McCann. JSOTSup 159. Sheffield: Sheffield Academic Press, 1993.

Theological Analysis

Rendtorff, Rolf. *The Canonical Hebrew Bible: A Theology of the Old Testament*. Leiden: Deo, 2005.
Vanhoozer, Kevin J., ed. *Dictionary for Theological Interpretation of the Bible*. Grand Rapids: Baker, 2005.

7

BIBLICAL GENRES AND
THE TEXT-DRIVEN SERMON

Robert Vogel

One of the glorious features of the Scriptures is their literary diversity. Stories, poetry, proverbial sayings, law, discourse, letters, and apocalyptic symbolism are among the major forms to be found in the Bible. In addition, some of these types may be divided further, reflecting additional nuances. Stories, for example, may be historical narrative or parables (fictional and symbolic in character). Their plots may be comic, tragic, or punitive, to mention just a few of the possible patterns.[1] The psalms (poetic genre) may express laments, or consist of descriptive or declarative praise, or they may be wisdom or royal psalms. Prophetic texts may, in form, be poetry or

---

1. L. Ryken, *How to Read the Bible as Literature* (Grand Rapids: Zondervan 1984), 53. See this source for helpful descriptions of these narrative variables.

narrative; some contain apocalyptic symbolism, in contrast to more natural imagery. Gospels are a genre in their own right, consisting of historical narrative primarily but including other genres such as discourse, parable, song, and the like.

AN EXAMPLE OF VARIETY IN GENRE

Biblical truths are given varied character as they appear in various genres. As Thomas Long puts it, "Two biblical texts may share the same theological theme but by virtue of different literary dynamics, do quite different things with that common conceptual core."[2] For example, the faithfulness of God is a prominent theme throughout the Scriptures. A lexical study of the term (*aman* and its derivatives and synonyms in the OT; *alētheia* and *pistos* in the NT) discloses that this trait, when used with reference to God, is among His attributes, and its basic sense is that He is totally dependable or reliable; He is true to His word. This basic sense is elaborated in various contexts in which the term is used, and the literary genre regularly gives nuance to the sense conveyed.

In the covenant, legal formulations of the Pentateuch are found primarily in Exodus 20 through Deuteronomy 33.[3] Although covenant faithfulness is clearly evident in Genesis as well, God's faithfulness is declared to be the ground of His covenant making and keeping (see Exod 6:4–5; Deut 4:31; 7:7–9; 32:4).

---

2. T. G. Long, *Preaching and the Literary Forms of the Bible* (Philadelphia: Fortress, 1989), 13.
3. G. D. Fee and D. Stuart, *How to Read the Bible for All Its Worth* (Grand Rapids: Zondervan, 1982), 137. The ancient suzerainty treaty form followed in the Mosaic Covenant established provisions of benefit and obligation involving the parties to the covenant. Obedience to the commandments was the obligation of Israel; God's obligation was to be Israel's God and to provide for and protect His people. R. H. Stein, *Playing by the Rules* (Grand Rapids: Baker, 1994), 188–89, notes the component parts of this treaty form: preamble, historical prologue, stipulations, provision for continual reading, list of witnesses, blessings and cursings, and oath. Although all of these elements may not be included in the biblical covenants, Stein observes that they are patterned along similar lines.

The Exodus itself was an act of God. As reported in a narrative account, it fulfills the promise made to Abraham and his descendants by delivering the nation from bondage and taking them to the promised land. His faithful providence from Abraham through the Exodus established the pattern of faithfulness He would continue as Israel's suzerain. Among the literary forms expressing this faithfulness are the Suzerain-vassal treaty form (established in those terms at Mt. Sinai), various legal formulations (the ethical, ceremonial, and civil laws), blessing/cursing provisions for keeping or violating the covenant, and so on.

In narrative texts, which tend to be less direct than some other genres, God's faithfulness may be evident in His words and actions, though the term "faithful" may not appear. For example, after Jacob was sent away from his family, God appeared to him in a dream, confirming to him the Abrahamic Covenant and assuring the wandering patriarch of His providential care: "Behold, I am with you and will keep you wherever you go, and will bring you back to this land; for I will not leave you until I have done what I have promised you" (Gen 28:15 NASB; the full narrative episode is Gen 28:10–17).[4] The only reason Jacob (or anyone) would believe these promises is that the One making them is reliable or faithful. In the broader narrative, God's faithfulness to keep His word is reported in Jacob's return to his homeland (Genesis 33) after many years of service to Laban. Among others, one impact of the narrative setting for this truth is that in the difficult situations of life, Jacob (and by application the contemporary believer) may be confident that God remembers His own and faithfully sustains them in life.

In poetry, featuring the literary traits of imagery, figure, and parallelism, the glory of God's faithfulness is amplified, built up, and given magnificence. Superlatives are used to declare His faithfulness as great (Lam 3:23), unshakably established (Ps 89:2), infinite, reaching to the heavens (Ps 36:5), and never

---

4. For additional examples, see Gen 21:1; Josh 21:45; 23:14; 1 Kgs 8:14,20,23,24,56.

ending (Ps 119:90). The effect created through the literary features is to elevate and beautify what otherwise might be a true but prosaic expression.

In the wisdom literature, which is concerned with the fear of the Lord as the grounding point for the practical matters of living life wisely, as God intends us to live it (Prov 1:1–7), the faithfulness of God is seen as the standard of righteous human conduct. In one particular way, the believer's speech and dealings with others is to reflect his or her fear of the Lord in the imitation of divine faithfulness. Using the poetic devices of antithetic parallelism and imagery, the sage establishes the priority of human faithfulness (reliable dealing and truth speaking) by contrasting the trait with lying lips: "Lying lips are an abomination to the LORD, but those who deal faithfully are His delight" (Prov 12:22 NASB).

The faithfulness of God is asserted in the logical patterns of discourse and epistolary literature. In such settings it may be presented matter-of-factly rather than with the glorious attributions of poetry. But the theological proposition of God's faithfulness in such instances usefully serves to ground an argument or a logical inference in doctrinal texts or to provide the basis for a practical directive for the Christian life. God's faithfulness is the ground for our calling into fellowship with Christ (1 Cor 1:9). It is also the basis of the promise that God will strengthen us to bear temptation (1 Cor 10:13). It is moreover the ground of our assurance that, upon confessing our sins, God will forgive and cleanse us (1 John 1:9), and the assurance that His faithfulness to His promises is the basis upon which we are urged to draw near to Him and to hold fast the profession of our faith (Heb 10:22–23).

Defining Genre

Literary criticism is a discipline concerned with the composition of texts. Its interests include words and their uses (lexical study), their form and function (grammar), syntax, and patterns or structures of thought. The study of genre is another of the subsets of literary analysis, recognizing that texts take varying literary forms (i.e., one text may be a story, another a poem, etc.) and that these texts must be interpreted in consideration of the distinctive features of their form.

What is literary genre? Jonathan Culler explains, "Literary genre is nothing less than 'a norm or expectation to guide the reader in his encounter with the text.'"[5] This norm consists of a set of rules or characteristics of writings belonging to the particular genre in which a text is presented. Reyburn and Fry specify the distinguishing characteristics of varying genres as "communicative function (goal of speaking), content, and particular stylistic features."[6]

These distinguishing rules and characteristics help the interpreter/expositor know how to approach a text of that genre (i.e., what to look for as interpretive keys to the passage) and, consequently, how to interpret and explain what is written. So working with a poetic passage, one knows that parallelism is a structural feature of this particular genre and that both exegesis and exposition should take account of the parallels used. Are two lines saying virtually the same thing (synonymous parallelism)? Are they putting a point across by contrasting two ideas (antithetic parallelism)? Are the lines building upon one another to enlarge the idea (synthetic parallelism)? Observations of this sort help the preacher understand more the "how" of the passage than the "what" of the passage,[7] but these two dimensions interact to establish the meaning of the passage and to put it across to the hearer.

Leland Ryken contends that all writing is not literature,[8] and therefore all writing is not to be analyzed according to the

---

5. J. Culler, *Structuralist Poetics* (Ithaca: Cornell University Press, 1975), 135. Cited in Ryken, *How to Read the Bible as Literature*, 25.
6. W. D. Reyburn and E. McG. Fry, *A Handbook on Proverbs*, UBS Handbook Series; Helps for Translators (New York: United Bible Societies, 2000), 677.
7. Ryken, *How to Read the Bible as Literature*, 28, 29.
8. Ibid., 12.

criteria of genre. However, the restricted sense in which he uses the term, limiting literature to creative or imaginative writing, may be better understood as a matter of degree than kind.[9] That is, some genres may involve a more elaborate scheme of literary features or may incline toward greater literary effect than others, but all biblical writings reflect some measure of unique characteristic and rule that must be taken into account when interpreting and preaching the text. A genealogy may not rise to the artistic level of a psalm, but it is, nonetheless, a form of writing that possesses distinct characteristics, intentions, and substance.

Genre consists in a number of major forms and a multitude of smaller ones. Forms may consist of whole books of the Bible (e.g., Psalms), major forms found within a larger textual unit (e.g., parables, riddles, etc. in a larger book), and figures of speech (e.g., metaphor, simile, or hyperbole). Holladay provides another taxonomy: "In some instances, entire books belong to a single genre, such as historical narrative (1 Samuel), poetry (Psalms), wisdom (Job), prophetic oracle (Amos), Gospel (Matthew), letter (Romans), or apocalypse (Revelation)." In the category of smaller literary forms to be found in various Bible books, he includes such forms as genealogies, narratives that relate the stories of individual figures (such as Abraham or Joseph), legal codes, testaments, prophetic oracles, prayers, hymns, exhortations, and warnings. He acknowledges that his list is not comprehensive but that it indicates that the Bible, "rather than being a single literary genre, contains many genres and subgenres."[10] Unlike Ryken, who is inclined to limit the scope to imaginative writing, Holladay sees a wide range of forms present in Scripture, each with its particular distinguishing characteristics.

---

9. Ibid. After asserting that not everything that is written is literature, Ryken qualifies his idea, noting that biblical writings exist on a continuum, on which some textual forms are more literary and others are less so.
10. C. R. Holladay, "Biblical Criticism," in *Harper's Bible Dictionary*, ed. P. J. Achtemeier (San Francisco: Harper & Row, 1985), 129–33.

Objections to Literary Study

Whereas the literary variety of the Scriptures contributes to the richness of their meaning, some conservative expositors have been reluctant fully to embrace literary exegesis, with its resultant effects in their preaching. Objections to literary approaches are, most likely, a reaction to the excesses of the higher critics, who regularly engage in forms of literary criticism. Some literary critics, through comparative literary studies, diminish biblical texts by claiming that they are merely Jewish or Christian adaptations of common cultural myths and traditions. So, for example, some higher critics contend that the biblical accounts of creation and the flood draw upon ancient creation and flood stories that are found in ancient religious traditions, and therefore they are not to be taken as historical accounts in any sense. Certainly higher critical scholarship has produced notions that Genesis 1–11 (or parts thereof) and Jonah are myth rather than history, that the Pentateuch is a redaction of documents from four literary traditions rather than the work of Moses, and that the Gospels are midrash consisting of stories created to provide settings for the sayings of Jesus. But these excesses are not necessarily endemic to literary analysis. One may, for example, acknowledge the literary features of a biblical story without denying its historicity.[11] Or one may appreciate the richness of expression through poetic imagery without claiming, as an interpretive principle, that the meaning of a poem is in what it "means to me" rather than what an author intended to express.

Indeed, although there are possible excesses involved in genre studies, conservative interpreters and expositors recognize that, rightly wed to a high view of biblical inspiration, such studies are valid and fruitful. Hirsch provided a generally accepted theoretic basis for the indispensability of genre study, stating, "All understanding of verbal meaning is necessarily genre-bound."[12]

---

11. For a brief discussion of this matter, see Stein, *Playing by the Rules*, 153–57.
12. E. D. Hirsch, *Validity in Interpretation* (New Haven: Yale University, 1967), 76.

Literary perspective is not endemically antithetic to grammatical-historical interpretive methods. Rather, it is a necessary complement in order to assure that the composition is understood as the author intended it to be, both in fullness of effect and with a rightful understanding of the way in which he used words. Moreover, literary genre study does not diminish the truth character of biblical texts. As Carl F. H. Henry notes, propositional truths may readily be inferred from literary figures and images, thus combining the emphatic and beautifying qualities of literature with the straightforward sense conveyed in propositions.[13]

Genre in Haddon Robinson's Definition of Expository Preaching

Haddon Robinson's well-known definition of expository preaching underscores the importance of literary consideration, both in the hermeneutical/exegetical realm and in the expository sermon resulting from such a study of a passage. This is Robinson's definition:

> Expository preaching is the communication of a biblical concept, *derived from* and *transmitted through* a historical, grammatical, *and literary* study of a passage in its context, which the Holy Spirit first applies to the personality and experience of the preacher, then through the preacher, applies to the hearers.[14]

Two observations pertaining to Robinson's definition are in order. First, literary study of a passage is an essential part of the hermeneutic Robinson endorses. Thus, an exegetical method

---

13. C. F. H. Henry, *God, Revelation, and Authority* (Wheaton, IL: Crossway, 1999), 4:108–9.
14. H. Robinson, *Biblical Preaching*, 2nd ed. (Grand Rapids: Baker, 2001), 21, emphasis added.

applying this hermeneutic must take account of literary genres and features. Second, not only is the hermeneutic used to guide the interpretation of the text by the preacher in his study, but it also controls the explanation of the text by the preacher in his pulpit. Hence, a text-driven preacher should expect to explain in his sermon the interpretive significance of literary forms and devices found in the passage under consideration. As Robinson puts it in his own exposition of his definition, "This deals first with how expositors come to their message and, second, with how they communicate it. Both involve the examination of grammar, history, and literary forms."[15]

Expository preaching, then, to be true to the biblical text, must take account of the literary features in both the exegesis and the preaching. The weight of both textual content and form should be explained to do full justice to the passage preached. One might rightly derive and preach a set of theological principles on divine providence from Psalm 23, but unless he also describes the images of a pastoral setting and explains something of the care of sheep, he has not done justice to the passage. The emphases and effects created by the literary features must be included in the sermon.

ADVANTAGES OF LITERARY STUDY FOR INTERPRETATION AND PREACHING

Perhaps the most evident reason for attending to literary genre is exegetical; the literary form yields essential clues for rightly interpreting the author's intended meaning of a passage.[16] Or to put it another way, the literary form governs the meaning of sentences. For example, Ps 91:4 reads, "He will cover you with His pinions, and under His wings you may seek refuge." Taken

---

15. Ibid., 24.
16. Holladay, "Biblical Criticism."

literally, the statement would be understood to describe God as existing in the material form of a bird. However, realizing that the text is poetic genre, with heavy reliance on imagery and figures to express ideas (in this case, the figure of zoomorphism), one interprets the text not to teach something of God's material form but rather to express the fact of His providential care. Matthew 5:29–30, literally construed, might lead one to physical dismemberment (cutting off a hand or putting out an eye) as the remedy for lust. However, Jesus intended the statement to be taken figuratively (hyperbole), an exaggerated directive to be understood as emphasizing the importance of avoiding lust.

Attending to literary features also serves the practical purpose of engaging the listener in the sermon preached. Genre, well presented, fires the imagination of the listener and increases the likelihood of active, rather than passive, listening. Ryken explains the role of human imagination: "Because literature *presents* an experience instead of telling us *about* that experience, it constantly appeals to our imagination (the image-making and image-perceiving capacity within us). Literature *images forth* some aspect of reality."[17] An interpretive reading of Ps 119:105, for example, will lay vocal stress upon the key words and phrases of a literary metaphor: "Thy Word," "lamp to feet," and "light to path." Accompanied by a descriptive explanation of the form and function of an ancient oil lamp, the word picture is both appreciated and understood; the listener forms a mental picture of a person on a dark street or rural path finding his way home, aided by the light cast from this small clay vessel, and understands by it the guiding, illumining role and function that God's Word has in the believer's life.

Proper attention to textual literary form lends appropriate variety to sermonic form. This is not to imply that a sermon preached from a poetic text must be a poem, but it does mean that poetic structure (indicated in parallelism) will guide the

---

17. Ryken, *How to Read the Bible as Literature*, 14.

preacher's sermon structure. So, if three lines of synonymous parallelism assert a single idea, in the sermon the single idea would become a main sermon point, and the particular expressions of each line would constitute a developmental subpoint. For example, in three parallel lines Ps 1:1 asserts that the blessed person shuns the influence of the wicked. The three parallel lines, in turn, become subpoints detailing the workings of sinful influence the believer must avoid. In a narrative text, the structure could be expected to trace the plot or the development of a character (the protagonist).

Literary study of a text exposes its subject matter with concrete and experiential force.[18] The literary features of a passage embellish its explicit or embedded propositions tangibly. The interplay of proposition and literary features is evident in Hebrews 11. In that well-known chapter on faith, the subject is first described as the ground upon which one apprehends spiritual reality (v. 1). The context, both near (v. 6) and broader (the entire book), makes clear that this faith is not one of an undefined object, but rather it is directed toward God, who redeems us through Christ. Moreover, by this God-directed faith, saints of previous generations gained approval (v. 2). These two statements, as abstract propositions, describe the character of faith and assert its importance. The next movement in the chapter is a sequence of narrative examples, some little more than the mention of names, others briefly elaborated, but all calling to mind Old Testament narrative accounts in which faith is displayed in day-to-day living. In this fashion, the chapter joins direct statements of divine truth with literary forms to enrich and emphasize its expression.[19]

---

18. Ibid., 13, 17.
19. Indeed, Hebrews is generally understood to be a sermonic epistle. As such, it models well the manner in which the preacher can project the eloquence of the text in his preaching. The propositions of Heb 11:1–2 are developed with narrative illustrations, each presented with the patterned formula, "by faith . . . ," emphasizing the subject through repetition and providing structural markers for the chapter.

The experiential characteristic of biblical literature is particularly pertinent to the applicational and transformational goals of expository preaching. The explanatory function seeks to show the truth claims and teaching points of the text and how they are developed; the applicational function seeks to relate those teaching points to the life of the hearers at all levels—cognitive, affective, and behavioral. Sermons use stories for illustration in order to clarify ideas and suggest application of them by analogy or through transferrable concepts. Stories in Scripture do the same.

Appealing to the experiential character of literature, Ryken discourages the tendency to "turn every biblical passage into a theological proposition."[20] However, the transformational intent of Scripture is expressed as their profitability for "doctrine, reproof, correction, and training in righteousness" (2 Tim 3:16), all characteristics that require that truth be propositionally stated and applied. Accordingly, expository sermons must express the teaching propositions of a passage under consideration, whether they are stated directly (as in epistolary literature) or more indirectly (as in poetry).

The preacher may be thankful that he is not required to choose between directly proclaiming textual truth and respecting literary form. Indeed, the two readily work together. For example, in preaching Psalm 23, the preacher can express theological propositions of divine providence, inferred from the metaphor of the shepherd's care for the sheep, such as the Lord providing for all the needs of His own (vv. 2–3) and protecting them from harm (v. 4). At the same time, the preacher would expect to develop those principles by reading, describing, and explaining the care of sheep, the metaphor (image) used to express the doctrine of providence.

Another practical advantage of genre study is found in the parallels between biblical literature as art and preaching as

---

20. Ryken, *How to Read the Bible as Literature*, 18, 21.

an art form. Ryken notes that literature (and all art), in form, consists in pattern or design, theme or central focus, organic unity, coherence, balance, contrast, symmetry, repetition or recurrence, variation, and unified progression.[21] Although all of these traits may not be required in the expository sermon and although some critics may object to sermons that slavishly incorporate them (e.g., a rigid and forced alliteration, assonance, or syntactic parallelism as forms of symmetry), most texts on homiletic method espouse these kinds of features among other essentials of sermon form. By general consensus, textbooks on expository preaching advocate a pattern of design in such terms as structure, outline, moves, plots, and the like. Theme or central focus is expressed in terms of a big idea, a central idea, a central proposition, a theme, a title, or a unifying idea. Unity and coherence require that the development of the sermon clearly and directly pertain to the theme rather than encouraging tangents or parenthetic asides that are off the point. Unified progression in art finds its homiletic counterpart in the move to decision or in the progression from a spiritual need to its resolution in the text and the resultant application to life. Although some differences may exist between the characteristics of literary and rhetorical art, with resultant distinctions in the form of the text and the sermon, the parallels between the two are many, and in those points of likeness, the text should be expected to exert control over the sermon.

Another beneficial parallel between the art of the text and that of the sermon is the emphatic force of artistic or literary features. The figurative language in Scripture is particularly potent in this regard. E. W. Bullinger notes how figures work:

> Applied to words, a figure denotes some form which a word or a sentence takes, different from its ordinary and natural form. This is always for the purpose of giving additional force, more life, intensified feeling, and greater emphasis.... For an

---

21. Ibid., 23–24.

unusual form (*figura*) is never used except to *add* force to the truth conveyed, emphasis to the statement of it, and depth to the meaning of it.[22]

Captured in preaching, this sort of emphasis lends textual force and energy so that, although the message may be resisted, it cannot be ignored or avoided.

Because literary features regularly tap the affective domain of the human being, attending to these in preaching can serve to inspire, motivate, and foster delight and enjoyment of the truth of the biblical text preached. Expository preaching, by nature, is concerned with cognitive apprehension of biblical truth. But that truth is intended by God to do more than expand the mind. Rather, the cognitive understanding is the first step in the process of internalizing the truth so that it transforms the whole person—our thoughts, motives, attitudes, beliefs, passions, loyalties, commitments, devotion to God, convictions, decisions, behaviors—anything that is part of our being. The variety of literary forms in which God chose to reveal Himself in Scripture enables the preacher to craft sermons aimed at balanced, holistic transformation. The purpose (or intended rhetorical effect) of the text at hand may govern the intended outcome the preacher expects to see as the result of the preached sermon.

In short, the literary features of the Bible magnify its eloquence for the reader/interpreter, and the preacher's sermon is also strengthened by the projection of that eloquence into his sermons. As Ryken summarizes the advantages of the literary medium in general, the benefits to the preacher are readily apparent: "They [the advantages of literature] include memorability, ability to capture a reader's attention, affective power, and ability to do justice to the complexity and multiplicity of human life as we actually experience it."[23] The preacher must gain and

---

22. E. W. Bullinger, *Figures of Speech Used in the Bible*, repr. ed. (Grand Rapids: Baker, 1968), v–vi.
23. Ryken, *How to Read the Bible as Literature*, 23.

hold attention, his message must be remembered if it is to be effective, it must touch the heart as well as the mind, and it must be brought home with practical application.

GENRE RELATED TO PREACHING

Much more has been written concerning particular genres in Scripture.[24] The remainder of this discussion, however, is devoted to the application of the principles of literary genre to the preaching task. The process for preparing a sermon is treated in three stages: (1) exegesis, in which the author's intended meaning for the text is determined; (2) principle development, in which the timeless truths of the text and their significance are derived from the exegetical analysis; and (3) homiletics, in which the exegetical evidences and the principles are crafted into a sermon structure featuring explanation and application of the text.

Each stage of this process is described and illustrated through an example of one of the predominant literary genres of the Bible, narrative. More specifically, the account of King Amaziah, found in 2 Chronicles 25, will be used to show how genre may be featured in the preaching task.

Genre and Exegesis

Genre analysis is not a full program for textual exegesis, but it is an essential part of the interpretive process. Accordingly,

---

24. A number of helpful works have been written that treat genre in greater, more particular detail than is possible in the limited scope of this treatment. Among such works are W. W. Klein, C. L. Blomberg, and R. L. Hubbard, *Introduction to Biblical Interpretation*, rev. ed. (Nashville: Thomas Nelson, 2004); part 4 is devoted to various biblical genres. See also Fee and Stuart, *How to Read the Bible for All Its Worth*; G. R. Osborne, *The Hermeneutical Spiral*, rev. ed. (Downers Grove: InterVarsity, 2006), part 2; and L. Ryken, *Words that Delight*, 2nd ed. (Grand Rapids: Baker, 1993).

the preacher/exegete must understand the interpretive keys involved with the various genres and apply them in the exegetical work involved with a Scripture text. Long describes the process: "An experienced reader comes to a text with a storehouse of skills and aptitudes and a repertoire of reading strategies acquired through previous encounters with various forms of literature."[25]

Long suggests a set of exegetical questions that can be used to probe the literary features of a text, which is helpful in discerning its meaning and intended impact upon its readers:

1. What is the genre of the text?
2. What is the rhetorical function of this genre?
3. What literary devices does this genre employ to achieve its rhetorical effect?
4. How in particular does the text under consideration, in its own literary setting, embody the characteristics and dynamics described in questions 1–3?[26]

Considering 2 Chronicles 25, it is clear that the genre is historical narrative (Long's first question). The chapter begins with historic reference points concerning the family lineage of Amaziah, his age, and the span of his reign as king in Judah. Historic events that occurred during his reign are described throughout the account, and the chapter ends with reference to Amaziah's death and burial. Moreover, the narrative may be defined as a tragedy, for the character and fortune of the protagonist in the story (Amaziah) go from good to bad.

---

25. Long, *Preaching*, 21. It should be noted that Long appears to favor a form of reader-response hermeneutic. However, one may follow the presuppositions of an authorial-intent hermeneutic and still find Long's process useful. To place the locus of control of meaning with the author does not nullify the role of the reader/interpreter, but it does require the reader to seek to discern the author's intended meaning rather than assigning his own.
26. Ibid., 24.

The rhetorical function (or purpose) of biblical historical narrative is to provide a record of salvation history, demonstrating the ways of God with His people and to instruct them in their walk with Him (cf. 1 Cor 10:6–11). Accordingly, this text functions to account for a king in the Davidic line, an unstable king who began his reign as a faithful theocratic monarch but who ended up betraying his stewardship as king in rebellion against God due to a particular spiritual flaw common in the fallen human condition. Further, the text functions rhetorically to warn against tolerance of this flaw, lest one become a rebel like Amaziah.

This particular account develops naturally along the typical lines of narrative literature (Long's third and fourth questions). Among the primary literary keys for interpreting narrative literature are setting or scene, characters, plot, and narrator's comments. These keys interact with one another throughout the story, and one of them may be more prominent than others at a particular point in a narrative text. For example, the progression of a plot, which is constructed from the actions and dialogue of the characters, may disclose the development or change in the character. The narrator may at times interrupt the flow of the plot he is narrating to describe a character or to interpret a character's actions.

Attending to the setting (or scenes) of the narrative enables the exegete to see the seams in the broader context and define the boundaries of the text to be preached. Scenes are marked by changes of time or place. With the change of scene comes a new thought that is built into the logic and structure of the story.[27] The preacher may preach a single scene, or the broader narrative may be better served if he preaches a sequence of scenes that make up the whole story. In either case, each scene will incorporate characters and plot that move the narrative forward.

In 2 Chronicles 25, there are six scenes. Verses 3–4 compose the first, in which Amaziah assumes the throne of Judah and

---

27. W. C. Kaiser Jr., *Preaching and Teaching from the Old Testament* (Grand Rapids: Baker, 2003), 65.

establishes his kingdom. The second is in vv. 5–10, in which he prepares for battle against the Edomites, hiring (and then firing) mercenary soldiers from the northern kingdom to assist him. The scene changes in vv. 11–13, where Amaziah defeats the Edomites, while the mercenary soldiers he had hired from Israel plundered the cities of northern Judah while returning home. The next scene is found in vv. 14–16. Here Amaziah worships the false gods of the Edomites, incurring the wrath of God and a rebuke by God's prophet. Tragically, Amaziah spurns the word of the prophet. In the next scene (vv. 17–24), Amaziah foolishly challenges Joash, the king of Israel, to a battle in retaliation for the plundering the northern army had inflicted upon the cities of northern Judah. Reluctantly Joash agrees to the battle, in which Amaziah and his army are soundly defeated. In the final scene (vv. 25–28), Amaziah's death at the hands of conspirators is reported, and the account ends with his burial. Each of these scenes occurs in a particular place and in a sequence of events in time.

In addition to the setting, analysis of the characters is essential to interpreting narrative texts. Characters are the actors and speakers in the narrative, and one of the primary variables in the account. They will vary in role (some are main characters, others have support roles), and their relationships with God and their faith may differ. They may be static or dynamic; the former type remains the same through the story, whereas the latter changes as the events unfold. The prominent or lead character of the story, and the one with whom the reader identifies, is the protagonist. This character is of particular importance, for his or her development may be the unifying force in the account. Most importantly, God Himself is regularly represented among the characters. Sometimes He is personally present; at other times, His viewpoint and interests are portrayed in a prophet or another human character closely associated with Him.

In this 2 Chronicles account, the protagonist is King Amaziah. Other characters such as King Joash of Israel are named, but most of the characters (soldiers, assassins, etc.) are static characters, briefly mentioned rather than named and developed in full dimension. God is prominent in the story, for the regulative force of His law is emphasized in the first scene; He speaks through His prophet in the second and fourth scenes; His providential hand is evident in Amaziah's victory over the Edomites in the third scene; the narrator informs us that His wrath burned against Amaziah in the fourth scene; and in the fifth scene, the narrator further informs us that Amaziah's defeat at the hand of Joash was the work of God in judgment upon Amaziah's rebellion, as His prophet had foretold. Note that Amaziah put himself at variance with God early in the story, and the antagonism between the two leads the interpreter to see Amaziah as a foolish man.

The plot (yet another interpretive key in narrative) traces the movement in the story, relating the events and episodes as they emerge. Plot usually moves toward a climax and some type of resolution and generally follows the chronological sequence of events and dialogue. In this way, the plot creates a "chronologic" of the story and can be a useful indicator of the structure (and outline) of the narrative. Disruptions of the order of the plot, introducing parallel events or sidebars, call attention to the author's emphasis. Building to its climax, the plot will include elements of testing and choice, and the choices made often account for changes in the situation of the characters in the narrative.

In the narrative of Amaziah, the scenes flow in chronological sequence. Obviously, they do not recount every detail of Amaziah's life and reign in Judah, but the scenes included give emphasis to the "make or break" events, particularly as they expose Amaziah's progressive rebellion against God. The turning point in the narrative is in the fourth scene, when Amaziah refuses the prophet's rebuke for his idolatry—a scene in which he, in effect, told God to "shut up." In this act of defiance his destiny was confirmed, and thereafter he lived and died in disgrace, the consequence of his rebellion. His words and actions, as the protagonist, drive the plot and reveal the inner workings of his heart.

Finally, the intention of the narrator/author of the text is paramount in understanding the meaning and the teaching of the passage, and his influences pervade the account. The ways in which he shapes the account create a point of view from which his story is told. He may express his viewpoint by direct comment, stepping into the flow and adding a word of description, explanation, or interpretation. Or his viewpoint may be represented by a character or characters, particularly in instances in which God or His spokesman acts or speaks.

Superintended by the Holy Spirit, the author/narrator selected the events and dialogue that constitute the story. We might reasonably conjecture that much more was said and done in most situations recorded in the Bible than what the author conveys, implying that the author wrote with careful intention. This does not mean that every detail is of equal importance; some details may be included for the sake of clarity or so that the story "works," whereas others will get at the teaching intended in the account.

The narrator's hand in 2 Chronicles 25 is evident throughout the chapter. His primary comment, and the one that provides the interpretive key to the whole account, is found in v. 2: "He did right in the sight of the Lord, yet not with a whole heart." With this comment, the narrator exposes the fatal spiritual flaw in Amaziah's character, the reality that accounts for the dismal decline in his behavior throughout the story. In the opening scene he did what was right in God's sight, obeying the divine law. But in subsequent scenes, the rebel heart emerges, culminating in the open defiance of God and His prophet (vv. 14–16) and the political folly in the following scene.

Not only does the narrator interpret the story in light of Amaziah's failed heart, but he also pointedly reveals God's view of Amaziah's actions, noting that God was not pleased when Amaziah sought strength for the battle with Edom in the armies of Israel rather than in His providence. Moreover, he reports that God's wrath burned against Amaziah's worship of the false gods of Edom, precipitating the prophetic rebuke of v. 15. The narrator also explains that Amaziah's foolish insistence on going to war with Israel and his defeat at the hand of Joash were God's punitive judgment for Amaziah's sin (v. 20).

Incorporating the exegetical analysis of the setting/scenes, characters, plot, and narrator's comments, one can create an exegetical outline of the account. The exegetical main idea is suggested by the narrator's explanatory introductory comment (v. 2): the tragic failure of Amaziah's life and kingdom were due to his lack of full devotion to the Lord; he began well but did not persevere. The outline follows the chronologic sequence of the account, with each successive scene disclosing another step on the path to ruin. The exegetical structure might be expressed in the following main idea, followed by an outline consisting of descriptive scene titles:

> Main Idea: The tragic failure of Amaziah's life and kingdom were due to his lack of full devotion to the Lord (v. 2).

Scene 1 (vv. 3–4)	Amaziah faithfully obeys God's Word.
Scene 2 (vv. 5–10)	Amaziah grudgingly obeys the word of God's prophet.
Scene 3 (vv. 11–13)	Amaziah defeats the Edomites by the power of the Lord.
Scene 4 (vv. 14–16)	Amaziah embraces the gods of the Edomites, rebels against God, and refuses His reproof.
Scene 5 (vv. 17–24)	Amaziah experiences the devastating consequences of his rebellion.
Scene 6 (vv. 25–28)	Amaziah dies in disgrace.

The logical progression of the chronological scenes traces a course of failure, which began with apparently faithful obedience but ended in his rebellion, defeat in battle, and assassination.

Genre and Textual Principles

The exegetical treatment of a passage of Scripture is intended to determine the author's intended meaning of the text. That meaning certainly addressed a body of original recipients, in their historical situation. The meaning of the author, in its particularity, may or may not directly apply to readers in other times and places. However, the Scriptures are God's written revelation of Himself, and He "still speaks through what he has spoken."[28] The difficulty with some texts, however, is discerning correctly what God is saying today—that is, what the contemporary significance of the meaning of a biblical passage (and its resultant legitimate application) is.

Although the way of describing the solution to this difficulty varies among authors of homiletic textbooks, the general consensus is that legitimate application involves "principlizing,"[29] which Kaiser defines as follows: "To 'principlize' is to state the author's propositions, arguments, narrations, and illustrations in timeless abiding truths with special focus on the application of those truths to the current needs of the Church."[30] A principle, as used here, is a timeless truth taught in a biblical passage. It may be a generalization abstracted from a textual particular,[31] or it may be a fixed statement that, on its face, transcends time and place.[32] In the case of textual truths already expressed in transcendent form, the significance and application are more readily determined. In the case of abstractions, care must be taken to make valid inductions and subsequent deductions.

---

28. J. R. W. Stott, *Between Two Worlds* (Grand Rapids: Eerdmans, 1982), 100.
29. Klein, Blomberg, and Hubbard, *Introduction to Biblical Interpretation*, 498.
30. W. C. Kaiser Jr., *Toward an Exegetical Theology* (Grand Rapids: Baker, 1981), 152.
31. For example, in Matt 12:9–14 (the record of an event in the Sabbath controversy), Jesus enters a synagogue and encounters a man with a withered hand. Jesus is asked by the Pharisees if it is lawful to heal on the Sabbath. Jesus replies by citing the law permitting one to rescue an animal in distress on the Sabbath, though it would entail working on that sacred day (cf. Exod 23:4–5; Deut 22:4). From that law, Jesus abstracts a general inference that "it is lawful to do good on the Sabbath." Then he implicitly deduces that it is lawful to heal (i.e., a particular way of doing good), and he restores the afflicted man's hand.
32. Gal 6:7 expresses one of the immutable ways of God's working in human affairs: "Do not be deceived, God is not mocked; for whatever a man sows, this he will also reap." The principle here is evident.

It is at this stage of the homiletical process that some genres are more susceptible to abuse than others. Didactic texts, such as those found in the New Testament epistles, are more consistently direct in their applicability. Narratives, however, are often stretched when minute details of an account are made to yield spiritual lessons that cannot be validated on other than speculative grounds.[33] Understanding the workings of a particular genre may help the preacher attend to the textual particulars that yield valid principles rather than forcing timeless spiritual lessons from texts that do not teach them.

With regard to narrative in particular, Ryken notes that history tells us what *happened*; literature tells us what *happens*.[34] Whether the narrative is historical record or fiction (such as a parable), scriptural narrative is included to convey the timeless and typical to teach us what *happens*. The intention of biblical stories is to teach us about God and His ways. They capture and express timeless truth concerning God and the human condition in relation to Him.

The teaching intentions of historical narratives are expressed by Paul in 1 Cor 10:6–11. Verses 6–10 refer to five episodes in the wilderness wanderings (Numbers), each episode providing the basis for a warning against a sin (craving evil things, idolatry, immorality, testing the Lord, and grumbling). Before and after this series of warnings (see vv. 6,10) is the assertion that these situations are typical; that is, they happened as examples for us and were written for our instruction. The interpretation of

---

33. For example, the parable of the Good Samaritan (Luke 10:30–37) begins, "A certain man was going down from Jerusalem to Jericho. . . ." Some preachers have seen this as a statement of spiritual decline in the life of the man, for he was "going *down*" and away from Jerusalem, the Holy City. However, this detail in the narrative serves only for narrative consistency. The road mentioned was notoriously dangerous, creating the situation in which the man would be mugged and thus in need of help; and in elevation, one would necessarily go "down" from Jerusalem (built on a mountain) to Jericho (a city in the valley). The context in Luke 10 makes it abundantly clear that the parable has nothing to do with the spiritual condition of the wounded man but rather the neighborly conduct of the Samaritan.

34. Ryken, *How to Read the Bible as Literature*, 44.

the cited accounts shows the cause-and-effect relationship between sins in Israel and judgment that came upon them as they
wandered. But Paul understands these accounts to represent
human tendencies to sin against God and notes that God does
not view such misconduct lightly. Accordingly, these typical accounts serve to instruct and warn readers later in time and in
other places; Paul's readers were living nearly 1,500 years after
the events to which he referred had occurred. This notion of the
typical character and teaching intention of narratives is an assumption that provides a basis for drawing principles from them.

Principles derived from a passage should be governed be the
authorial intent discerned in the exegetical phase of sermon
preparation. Clues of authorial intent and purpose may be found
in surrounding context, as well as embedded in the narrative
account itself.

Characters, as we noted, are among the exegetical keys to
interpreting narrative, and God is the primary character to
which one should attend in narrative. The way He is understood
from the narrative should readily yield timeless principles,
since He does not change. As He was in the situations narrated
in Scripture, He remains today. His viewpoint presented or His
person disclosed will, by nature, express truths about the God
who does not change and whose purposes, person, plans, and
ways transcend the limits of time and place.

When the timeless teachings of the text concerning God
and His ways have been duly noted, the preacher should pay
careful attention to the protagonist in the narrative as representative, exemplary, or typical of a whole segment of humanity interacting with God's immutable and transcendent ways.
The account will often disclose something of the fallen condition of the main character at points analogous to people in other
times and places. Linking characters to plot, one may see how
a character is tested, and the test may suggest a contemporary
analogy. The test narrated in the Scripture may be directly comparable to the contemporary situation, or it may be comparable
at a more general level of abstraction.

The narrator's role in presenting a divine viewpoint through his own interpretive comments is another key indicator of textual principle and will indicate the primary timeless truth of the story as well as secondary emphases.

Sometimes there is a degree of ambiguity concerning whether something timeless should be made of an aspect of a story, particularly since historical narratives are largely descriptive accounts of single events. Caution is in order in such cases, and it is advisable not to make points about which there is some doubt in the preacher's mind. However, a safeguard in such cases is to interpret narrative details in the context of moral commands and assertions of truth made elsewhere in the Bible. Besides reducing ambiguity, this strategy can help the preacher confirm what otherwise might be understood as a unique situation and, as a result, an exception rather than a rule.

Returning to the account of Amaziah, the exegetical outline identifies key ideas and situations expressed in the story. The narrative genre, featuring people and God in speech and action, provides natural transferable concept and empathy, indicators of the mutual reality of fallen condition between the life presented in the text and our situation today.[35] And so, echoing the exegetical outline, it is possible to see these timeless truths, or principles, emerging from the narrative:

1. A half-hearted spiritual commitment will lead to spiritual failure (v. 2).
2. Apparent obedience may mask a divided heart (vv. 3–4).
3. A divided heart may obey under protest (vv. 5–10).
4. God may bless qualified obedience, despite a divided heart (vv. 11–13).

---

35. B. Chapell, *Christ-Centered Preaching*, 2nd ed. (Grand Rapids: Baker, 2005), 50. Chapell refers to the mutuality between the world of the text and our own as the "fallen condition focus," which he defines as "the mutual human condition that contemporary believers share with those to or about whom the text was written that requires the grace of the passage for God's people to glorify and enjoy him." This mutual condition informs textual and sermon purpose and enables valid application in Chapell's homiletical model, and it is commendable for its theological view of the human condition. See further discussion in Chapell, chapters 2, 10.

5. A divided heart eventually shows itself in rebellion against God and His reproof (vv. 14–16).
6. God will judge one whose heart is disloyal to Him (vv. 17–28).

These principles will serve as the raw materials from which the sermon structure will be constructed. They are derived from the exegetical emphases of the text so that they bear the authority of God's Word, and they are cast to express the significance of the text's meaning for other times and places so that they may rightly be applied in a contemporary setting. The first principle listed is drawn from the main exegetical idea of the passage and will likely be the main idea of the sermon. The remaining principles derive from the action and dialogue in sequential scenes.

Genre and the Sermon

Long suggests that, upon exegeting the literary and rhetorical characteristics of a passage, the overarching homiletical question becomes, "How may the sermon, in a new setting, say and do what the text says and does in its setting?"[36] To answer this question, the preacher must determine the legitimate parallels between the original setting and the contemporary situation. The meaning of the text is fixed by the author in his setting, but its significance across time and place allows the preacher to make legitimate applications of the author's meaning to contemporary situations. The legitimacy of those applications is established by showing that the author's meaning and purpose (what the author intended to be understood and what the author's intended effect was) parallel those of the preacher. Principlizing the text builds the bridge from the text to the contemporary situation so that the remaining task in sermon building is to craft a homiletical structure and develop it.

---

36. Long, *Preaching*, 24.

Genre may helpfully inform the sermon's structural form and outline. A sermon taken from a narrative text might be organized to trace the flow of the plot, for chronology is a form of logic and what generally conveys the movement of a story. Or the narrative might emphasize the development of a character in his or her relationship to God, and so the sermon outline might trace the sequence of changes in the character.

Treating a narrative passage, the primary principle of a passage will become the main preaching point of the passage. This principle follows from the exegetical stage, where it was discerned by first identifying what the story is about (its subject matter or topic) and then how the writer (who emphasizes the divine viewpoint) intends for the reader to view the experience presented.

Tracing the plot conflict is one of the best and most natural ways to organize the body of the message. Elements of the plot that lend homiletic unity and order can be found in the unifying presence of the protagonist, cause-effect order of activity, or some other progression through the events or episodes.

Principles may have emerged at various points in the flow of the text, and these should be considered as they relate to and develop the main idea of the passage. They may be expressed as sermon points and can be introduced, explained, and applied in turn as the plot unfolds.

In 2 Chronicles 25, at the previous stage, six principles were discerned. These timeless truths flow from a combination of narrator's comments, expressions of divine perspective through the narrator and the prophet (a character) in the text, and dialogue and actions in which Amaziah disclosed the state of his heart. Arranging them so that they preserve the rightful emphasis and narrative flow of the passage, with some adjustment to account for emphasis and overlap of ideas, this sermon outline emerges:

Main Idea: A half-hearted spiritual commitment will lead to spiritual failure (v. 2).

Transition: How does this progression of spiritual failure unfold?

I. Spiritual failure may begin with apparently faithful obedience (vv. 3–4).

II. Spiritual failure may appear as grudging obedience (vv. 5–10).

III. Spiritual failure will appear in open rebellion and idolatry (vv. 11–16).

IV. Spiritual failure will result in divine judgment (vv. 17–28).

The main idea is drawn from v. 2, and if one were to preserve the order of the text, this overarching principle would be expressed in the introduction of the message, with the transition bridging from the proposition to its textual development. Applications might be attached to each point, and in the conclusion the primary applicational inference—to guard one's heart—would sum up the message.

Another structural option is inductive in form. In this approach, the introduction raises the question, why is it that people sometimes start their Christian lives with great fervor for God, but over time rebel against Him? Amaziah and his story, then, serve as a case study of the situation posed in the opening question. Each scene is presented and explained (as previously outlined), noting the sequential connections between scenes and noting the character's (Amaziah's) progressive display of a divided heart. After showing the progression of Amaziah's decline, the question is posed once again and then answered from v. 2, with the expression of the main idea. This then leads to the primary purpose and application of the text and the message, namely, to warn the listener of the perils of divided spiritual loyalty and to call for an unqualified loyalty and obedience to Christ. The concluding appeal of the message is to call the listener to guard his or her heart and its loyalties; the proof of one's commitment may not be seen today, but it will be evident 10, 15, or 20 years from today.

CONCLUSION

This discussion has addressed the impact of literary genre in preaching in a limited way. Much more can be said about the many genres to be found in Scripture and the ways to treat them homiletically. The intent of this discussion is to create an appreciation of the necessity and potential of attending to literary genre. This perspective, in turn, will lead the preacher to faithful exposition and rewarding variety in his preaching.

8

BIBLICAL THEOLOGY
AND PREACHING

James M. Hamilton Jr.

INTRODUCTION

The time is short. Redemption draws nigh. Urgent tasks
call. I am eager to linger on a slow walk with my wife.
The children grow fast. Church members are in the hos-
pital. The elderly slip away. Young men need to be raised up
and sent out. I need more time in the Bible and prayer. The
demands are many, the moments scarce. Sunday comes soon.
Time to stand and deliver.

Biblical theology and preaching?

Urgency forces us to ask, do I need this to preach? If so,
what is it? How do I do it? How do I preach it? Can God's people
handle it? How do I get started?

DO I NEED THIS TO PREACH?

If you intend to preach the whole counsel of God (Acts 20:27), you need biblical theology.[1] If you believe that "all Scripture is breathed out by God and profitable for teaching, for reproof, for correction, and for training in righteousness" (2 Tim 3:16),[2] you need biblical theology. Here is a little more on these two points.

Preaching the Whole Counsel of God

Is there one main storyline that runs from Genesis to Revelation? Could you sketch its contours in a paragraph? Here is my attempt.

God made the world as a place where He would be worshiped, served, and known. God is served and worshiped and present in His temple, so this reality, with others, points to God making the world as a cosmic temple.[3] God then charged His image-bearers, whom He put in the garden of Eden, to subdue the earth, which seems to mean they were to expand the borders of the place in which God was served, worshiped, and known until God's glory covered the dry lands as the waters cover the sea. They failed. God judged. But through the judgments He also promised to save.[4] God made promises to Abraham that directly addressed the curses,[5] saved Abraham's descendents through

---

1. See the excellent treatment of the subject of this chapter by my mentor, T. R. Schreiner, "Preaching and Biblical Theology," *SBJT* 10, no. 2 (2006): 20–29.
2. Unless otherwise noted, all Scripture quotations in this chapter come from the ESV.
3. See esp. G. K. Beale, *The Temple and the Church's Mission: A Biblical Theology of the Dwelling Place of God* (Downers Grove: InterVarsity, 2004); and T. D. Alexander, *From Eden to the New Jerusalem: Exploring God's Plan for Life on Earth* (Nottingham England: InterVarsity, 2008).
4. See further J. M. Hamilton, *God's Glory in Salvation through Judgment: A Biblical Theology* (Wheaton, IL: Crossway, 2010); J. M. Hamilton, "The Skull Crushing Seed of the Woman: Inner-Biblical Interpretation of Genesis 3:15," *SBJT* 10, no. 2 (2006): 30–54.
5. See J. M. Hamilton, "The Seed of the Woman and the Blessing of Abraham," *TynBul* 58 (2007): 253–73.

the judgment of Egypt at the exodus, and when he planted them in the new Eden of the promised land, their task was the same as Adam's—to expand the boundaries of the place where God was served, worshiped, and known until God's glory covered the dry lands as the waters cover the sea. Like Adam, Israel failed. As Adam was judged and exiled from Eden, God judged Israel and exiled them from the land.[6] Israel's prophets promised that through the judgment of exile a glorious eschatological future would dawn, but they were really promising a return from two different exiles—Adam's from Eden and Israel's from the land. The return initiated by Cyrus that resulted in the rebuilding of the temple and the city addressed the exile from the land, but it did not address the exile from Eden. To address the exile from Eden, God sent His Son, Jesus, God incarnate, who recapitulated the history of Israel,[7] fulfilled all righteousness, and then became a curse and died on the cross to propitiate God's wrath and make a way for God to show just mercy. The people of Jesus, the church, which is His body, are now carrying forward the task given to Adam and Israel. By making disciples of all nations, the church seeks to cover the dry land with Yahweh's glory as the waters cover the sea. Once all have heard the gospel, there will be a final fulfillment of the exodus, with seven trumpet and seven bowl plagues, and through the judgment of the world God's people will be saved. Jesus will come as a new and greater conquering Joshua, defeat His enemies, and lead His people into a new and better promised land for a thousand years. After the final rebellion, Jesus will lead His people into the new and better Eden, the new heaven and new earth, and the exile will finally be over. God's glory will cover the dry lands as the waters cover the sea.

---

6. See S. G. Dempster, *Dominion and Dynasty: A Biblical Theology of the Hebrew Bible*, New Studies in Biblical Theology (Downers Grove: InterVarsity, 2003).

7. See J. Kennedy, *The Recapitulation of Israel: Use of Israel's History in Matthew 1:1–4:11*, vol. 257, Wissenschaftliche Untersuchungen zum Neuen Testament 2 (Tübingen: Mohr Siebeck, 2008).

Does this storyline have a central theme or main point? I believe it does. God is making Himself known, revealing His character, showing His glory. This is the best thing that God can do for the world, because there is nothing better than God.[8] So at creation God builds a cosmic theater for the display of Himself. And then at every major signpost of the story, God reveals His justice and His mercy, His holiness and His love, His wrath and His kindness. God describes Himself as a just and merciful God when He declares His name to Moses in Exod 34:6–7.[9] Moses asked to see God's glory, and God told Moses He would show him His goodness and proclaim His own name (Exod 33:18–19). This event profoundly shaped the theology of the first biblical author, and every biblical author after Moses learned from him that Yahweh is a saving and judging God. God judges so that mercy will have meaning. He upholds justice to highlight the stunning glory of His mercy. So in my view, the center of biblical theology, the main point of the whole story, is that God will be glorified in salvation through judgment.[10] God saves Noah through the judgment of the flood. He saves Israel through the judgment of Egypt at the exodus and again through the judgment of the exile. God then accomplishes salvation from sin through the judgment of Jesus on the cross, and Revelation portrays God saving His people from this broken world through the judgment of all the enemies of God. In addition to these major moments of the display of God's glory in salvation through judgment, this is the existential experience of those who are born again. People

8. See further J. Piper, *God's Passion for His Glory: Living the Vision of Jonathan Edwards, with the Complete Text of The End for which God Created the World* (Wheaton, IL: Crossway, 1998).
9. For stimulating discussion of Exod 34:6–7, see R. W. L. Moberly, "How May We Speak of God? A Reconsideration of the Nature of Biblical Theology," *TynBul* 53 (2002): 177–202; and H. Spieckermann, "God's Steadfast Love: Towards a New Conception of Old Testament Theology," *Bib* 81 (2000): 305–27.
10. I argue for this in my book, *God's Glory in Salvation through Judgment*, and in J. M. Hamilton, "The Glory of God in Salvation through Judgment: The Centre of Biblical Theology?" *TynBul* 57 (2006): 57–84.

who experience the new birth have realized that they are under God's just wrath. Through that judgment, they feel a need for what Jesus has accomplished on the cross, and when they trust Him they receive the astonishing mercy of God. Believers are saved through judgment—through the judgment that fell on Jesus condemning their sin. Believers see the glory of God's justice and mercy, and they worship God for His goodness, exalting His name. We even boast in affliction in the hope that God's glory will be revealed (Rom 5:3), trusting that all things will work for the greatest good of the display of God's glory. The center of biblical theology is the glory of God in salvation through judgment.

Biblical theology helps us get our arms around the big picture that ties together everything from Leviticus to Esther, and we see how Amos, John, Romans, and Revelation fit, too. Knowing what the forest looks like enables understanding of the individual trees. If we are to preach the whole counsel of God, we need biblical theology.

What sets the agenda in your preaching? Nehemiah really is not about the building program some church wants to initiate, and the Psalms are not in the Bible for amateur psychotherapists to explore their inner depths from the pulpit. Has God communicated His agenda in the Bible's big story—its overarching message? Does the Bible's big story set the agenda for your preaching or does something else drive it? If we are going to understand God's purposes, which are revealed in the Bible, we need biblical theology.

Biblical theology pushes us to understand the contribution individual books of the Bible make to the Bible's big story. We might call the Bible's big story its metanarrative. However we describe it, the point is that the whole Bible fits together to tell us God's revealed story of where the world came from, what is wrong with it, what He is doing to fix it, where we fit in the program, and what we can expect in the near and distant future. But there is a greater end to all this information: God is revealing Himself to us. We need biblical theology to know God. Knowing God fuels worship. Biblical theology is for worship.

Thinking in terms of biblical theology really boils down to reading the Bible in context—not just the near context of the phrase, sentence, paragraph, the wider passage, or the individual book but also the context of the whole canon. If we do not read the Psalms in the context of the canon of Scripture, we can make the Psalter's abstract statements mean almost anything we want (especially if we foolishly ignore the superscriptions of the Psalms). If we do not read Samuel and Kings in light of Deuteronomy, we will not understand the way the narrator of those books is subtly condemning and commending people by the ways he notes what they did. If we know Deuteronomy, we will know whether God's law has been kept or broken. Biblical narrators cast characters as negative, positive, or ambiguous as they rehearse a character's deeds. They relate what the characters did, and they render unspoken judgments, for instance, by showing deeds of disobedience, even if the broken law is not restated as the disobedience is narrated. Moving from the Old Testament to the New, if we do not read the Gospels and the Epistles in light of the Law and the Prophets, we will not understand how what God has accomplished in Jesus is the fulfillment of everything in the Law, Prophets, and Writings (cf. Luke 24:44). We must read each piece of the Scripture in light of the canonical whole, which is to say, we must do biblical theology.

All Scripture Is God Breathed and Profitable

So does your preaching indicate that you believe that *all Scripture* is *profitable*? Or does your preaching indicate that the inspired and profitable parts are the letters of Paul, the four Gospels, Acts, some of the Psalms, maybe some narratives about Joseph, Moses, David, and (when you want to build) Nehemiah?

Be honest: would you preach Ezra? Chronicles? Revelation? Zephaniah? Ezekiel? Ecclesiastes? I am not talking about picking out a favorite verse or passage. I'm talking about preaching the whole book and explaining it from one end to the other, relating the whole book to the rest of the canon.[11] Nor do I have in mind the relegation of these books to the evening Bible study on Sunday or Wednesday night. I am talking about Sunday morning preaching. Answer the question honestly, and you will know whether you agree with Paul that *all Scripture is profitable.*

If we are going to preach the whole counsel of God, and if we are going to preach all Scripture because we believe all of it is inspired and profitable, we need a healthy understanding of biblical theology to do it. After all, we do not want to produce pessimistic fatalists from our exposition of Ecclesiastes. That is not the message of Ecclesiastes, but in order to see what Ecclesiastes does mean, we need to understand the Bible's big story and how this book fits within it.[12] For that, we need a clear understanding of what biblical theology is.

WHAT IS BIBLICAL THEOLOGY?

When we do biblical theology, we are trying to lay hold of the perspective from which the biblical authors have interpreted earlier biblical texts and from which they write. We are looking for the matrix of assumptions and conclusions that necessitate the statements made by the biblical authors. We are trying to get at the worldview that gives rise to the assertions the biblical authors make. The only access we have to their beliefs

---

11. Expository preaching happens when the main point of a biblical text is the main point of a sermon and when the structure of the biblical text determines the structure of the sermon. If your point is not the text's point, you are not preaching the text.

12. See esp. A. G. Wright, "The Riddle of the Sphinx: The Structure of the Book of Qoheleth," *CBQ* 30 (1968): 313–34; A. G. Wright, "The Riddle of the Sphinx Revisited: Numerical Patterns in the Book of Qoheleth," *CBQ* 42 (1980): 38–51; A. G. Wright, "Additional Numerical Patterns in Qoheleth," *CBQ* 45 (1983): 32–43; and N. Perrin, "Messianism in the Narrative Frame of Ecclesiastes?" *RB* 108 (2001): 37–60.

and assumptions is what they actually wrote, so biblical theology seeks to understand the literary features that the biblical authors used to (1) structure their message, (2) connect it to earlier Biblical passages, (3) locate it in the grand story, and thus (4) encourage their audience by showing them God's glory in His displays of justice, all of which highlight His mercy and love for His people. Biblical theology is the attempt to understand the Bible in its own terms.

Biblical theology is a necessary step in the interpretive process. Exegesis of the Bible cannot stop at the clause, paragraph, book, or even collection of letters. That is to say, we must read Rom 5:1 in light of Romans 1–4, Romans as a whole, then all of Paul's letters can shed light on what he says in that one verse. But if we stop there, we have not completed the hermeneutical spiral. We must move on to the next step: reading that text and how it fits in Paul's argument in light of the whole canon. The same can be said of a book like Proverbs. Thinking in terms of biblical theology will point us to the literary cues Solomon has used in Proverbs to show himself as the king who has obeyed Deuteronomy 17's instructions, where the king is commanded to copy out the law and study it (Deut 17:18–20), along with Deuteronomy 6's instructions to parents to teach the law diligently to their children (Deut 6:6–9; cf. esp. Prov 3:1–8). Solomon is the king who knows the Torah, and he is the father to his people. In Proverbs he teaches them the truths of Torah in practical, memorable, colorful ways.

Biblical theology invites us to ask, is the Bible shaping the way we read the world, or has the world shaped the way we read the Bible? In order for us to be able to read the world through the Bible rather than the Bible through the world, we must understand this *book*, the Bible, which is really a collection of books.[13] Books have literary features, and authors of books

---

13. See the discussion of precritical, figural interpretation in J. H. Sailhamer, *The Meaning of the Pentateuch: Revelation, Composition and Interpretation* (Downers Grove: InterVarsity, 2009), 89–91.

deploy literary features to communicate meaning.[14] Earlier, I enumerated four things authors use literary features to accomplish. This is not an exhaustive list, but we can be helped by further consideration of each of these.

Structural Features

The biblical authors have given us carefully constructed presentations of God's truth. John Sailhamer writes, "The most influential, yet subtlest, feature of an author's rendering of historical narrative is the overall framework with which he or she arranges it."[15] Sailhamer goes on to say, "To a large degree, the structure of biblical narratives determines their meaning."[16] The techniques the biblical authors used to mark turning points in their work are different from the printing conventions used by modern authors, such as chapter titles or section headings. The biblical authors have often marked their turning points in the structure of their books through the use of repeated words or phrases.[17] Using these repeated words, phrases, and themes, the biblical authors have signaled their structure and meaning for careful readers. These signals give information about the meaning of the passage at hand, how it fits in the structure of the whole book, and how it relates to earlier parts of Scripture.

The scope of this presentation permits only a few examples from the book of Revelation.[18] John's vision of Jesus in Rev 1:9–20

---

14. For the benefits Bible reading has for understanding literature, see Timothy T. Larsen, "Literacy and Biblical Knowledge: The Victorian Age and Our Own," *JETS* 52 (2009): 519–35.
15. Sailhamer, *The Meaning of the Pentateuch*, 29.
16. Ibid., 30.
17. See, e.g., George H. Guthrie, *The Structure of Hebrews: A Text-Linguistic Analysis* (Grand Rapids: Baker, 1998).
18. For elaboration on the points made here, see J. M. Hamilton Jr., *Revelation*, Preaching the Word, ed. R. Kent Hughes (Wheaton, IL: Crossway, forthcoming), where I rely heavily on the excellent studies of R. Bauckham, *The Theology*

is very similar to the vision Daniel has in Daniel 10. Daniel was overwhelmed by glorious figures from heaven, who then revealed to him the history of the future in Daniel 11–12. So the vision in Daniel 10 is followed by the revelation of the future in Daniel 11–12. This structure is matched by the events in Revelation, where John first sees Jesus (Rev 1:9–18), then Jesus instructs John to write what he has seen, what is, and what will take place after this (1:19).[19]

Table 1. The sequence of events in Daniel 10 and Revelation 1

Daniel 10	Event	Revelation 1
10:5a	Seer looks	1:12a
10:5b–6	Description of: "a man" in Daniel, "one like a son of man" in Revelation	1:13–16
10:8–9 (cf. "deep sleep" in Gen 2:21; 15:12; 1 Sam 26:12; Dan 8:18)	Seer undone: Daniel—no strength, deep sleep John—fell . . . as though dead	1:17a
10:10–14 10:15–21 note 10:16, "one in the likeness of the children of man"	The one revealed touches the seer and explains the vision	1:17–20

Not only is there this match between the order of events in Daniel 10 and Revelation 1, but there are also significant correspondences in the descriptions of the heavenly beings, as can be seen in Table 2.

---

of the Book of Revelation, New Testament Theology (New York: Cambridge University Press, 1993); and R. Bauckham, The Climax of Prophecy: Studies on the Book of Revelation (Edinburgh: T&T Clark, 1993).

19. For further discussion, see G. K. Beale, The Use of Daniel in Jewish Apocalyptic Literature and in the Revelation of St. John (Lanham: University Press of America, 1984).

Table 2. The descriptions of the ones revealed in Daniel 10 and Revelation 1

Daniel 10	Revelation 1
10:5, "clothed in linen, with a belt of gold"	1:13, "clothed with a long robe and with a golden sash around his chest"
[7:9, "the hair of his head like pure wool"]	1:14a, "hairs of his head were white like wool"
10:6c, "his eyes like flaming torches"	1:14b, "His eyes were like a flame of fire" (description also found in 2:18)
10:6d, "his arms and legs like the gleam of burnished bronze"	1:15a, "his feet were like burnished bronze, refined in a furnace" (description also found in 2:18)
10:6e, "and the sound of his words like the sound of a multitude"	1:15b, "and his voice was like the roar of many waters"
10:6b, "his face like the appearance of lightning"	1:16c, "and his face was like the sun shining in full strength"

I am not suggesting that the correspondence between Revelation 1 and Daniel 10 is merely a literary contrivance. Rather, I would suggest that texts such as Daniel and Ezekiel shaped John's perception of what he saw in his vision. The categories for his perceptions were provided by earlier biblical texts, and then when he described what he saw in terms of those earlier biblical texts John was intentionally signaling to his audience that his vision was fulfilling earlier prophecies.

Along these lines, in Revelation 10 John has an experience that matches Ezekiel's. In Revelation 10:8–11 John is told to take a scroll from an angel, eat it, and prophesy, just as Ezekiel was told to take a scroll from a hand stretched out to him, eat it, and speak to Israel (Ezek 2:8–3:4).

Table 3. Ezekiel and John eat the scroll

Ezekiel 2:9–3:4	Revelation 5:1; 10:2,9–10
2:9, "And when I looked, behold, a hand was stretched out to me, and behold, a scroll of a book was in it."	10:2, "He had a little scroll open in his hand . . ."
2:10, "And he spread it before me. And it had writing on the front and on the back, and there were written on it words of lamentation and mourning and woe."	5:1, "Then I saw in the right hand of him who was seated on the throne a scroll written within and on the back, sealed with seven seals."
3:1, "And he said to me, 'Son of man, eat whatever you find here. Eat this scroll, and go, speak to the house of Israel.'"	10:9, "So I went to the angel and told him to give me the little scroll. And he said to me, 'Take and eat it; it will make your stomach bitter, but in your mouth it will be sweet as honey.'"
3:2, "So I opened my mouth, and he gave me this scroll to eat."	10:10a, "And I took the little scroll from the hand of the angel and ate it."
3:3, "And he said to me, 'Son of man, feed your belly with this scroll that I give you and fill your stomach with it.' Then I ate it, and it was in my mouth as sweet as honey."	10:10b, "It was sweet as honey in my mouth, but when I had eaten it my stomach was made bitter."
3:4, "And he said to me, 'Son of man, go to the house of Israel and speak with my words to them.'"	10:11, "And I was told, 'You must again prophesy about many peoples and nations and languages and kings.'"

Ezekiel then prophesies of judgment (Ezek 3–32) followed by salvation (Ezek 33–48). John has an experience like Ezekiel's, which designates him as a true prophet of God, then John prophesies of judgment (Rev 11–19) followed by salvation (Rev 20–22). The matching structure presents John as a true prophet and his vision as the fulfillment and culmination of all the biblical prophecies that preceded his.

That John is presenting his apocalyptic prophecy as the culmination of all preceding prophecy is marked in the way he has structured his book, not only in the two instances just mentioned, but also in wider terms. If we were to summarize the overarching message of Isaiah, Jeremiah, Ezekiel, and the Twelve, it would be this: Israel has broken the covenant, so God will judge her by sending her into exile. Through judgment God will save for His glory: God is preparing a magnificent eschatological salvation that will come through the judgment after exile. Further, that future salvation is often likened to the exodus from Egypt (e.g., Jer 16:13–16). Thus, the prophets speak of a future mighty act of salvation that will be a new exodus and that will open the way to a return from exile, putting the people of God back in the promised land. In part, this will involve God bringing judgment on those He used to judge Israel (see esp. Nahum and Habakkuk).

What does this have to do with Revelation? It is widely recognized that the judgments of the trumpets (Rev 8–9) and the bowls (Rev 15–16) are reminiscent of the plagues on Egypt. I would suggest that John presents these final judgments as the new plagues that will liberate the people at the new and final exodus. Just as Israel was delivered from Egypt through the judgments of the 10 plagues and just as the judgment of Nineveh and Babylon restored the people to the land, so also the people of God will be delivered from the wicked powers of this world through the seven trumpet and seven bowl judgments. Little wonder that the culmination of God's judgment is announced with the cry that Babylon has fallen (e.g., Rev 14:8). It was the fall of Babylon in 539 BC that brought Cyrus into power (cf. Isa 44:28–45:1), and it was this Cyrus who decreed the return to the land (e.g., Ezra 1:1–4). Just as Israel entered the promised land after the exodus from Egypt, so also after the fulfillment of the exodus in Revelation the people of God will enter into the fulfillment of the promised land, the millennial kingdom followed by the new heaven and new earth.

My point in this section is that at the levels of the structure and content of his material, John is alerting his readers to his position as a true prophet who is taking up all the threads of prophecy that preceded him and weaving them together. Moreover, the events prophesied by the earlier prophets will find their fulfillment in the events that John describes.

Intertextual Connections

The previous section highlighted some of the ways that John signals the fulfillment of earlier prophecy in his own book by structuring his vision in ways that draw attention to such connections. These structural features are one way John establishes intertextual connections, but what usually comes to mind when we think of intertextuality is established at the level of individual words and phrases. Similarities in language between the trumpets and bowls in Revelation and the plagues on Egypt in the book of Exodus can be seen in these two tables:

Table 4. The exodus plagues and Revelation's trumpets

Trumpet in Revelation	Plague in Exodus
1. Rev 8:7, hail, fire	7th, Exod 9:23–25, hail, fire
2. Rev 8:8–9, sea to blood, one-third of living creatures die	1st, Exod 7:20–21, Nile to blood, fish died
3. Rev 8:10–11, rivers and springs made bitter	1st, Exod 7:19, rivers, canals
4. Rev 8:12, one-third of sun, moon, and stars darkened	9th, Exod 10:21–29, three days of darkness
5. Rev 9:1–11, darkness, locust-like scorpions	9th and 8th, Exod 10:21–29, darkness; Exod 10:12–20, locusts
6. Rev 9:12–19, angels released, mounted troops, fire, smoke, and sulfur kill one-third of humanity	10th, Exod 11:1–10; 12:29–32, death angel?
Rev 10:1, angel wrapped in a cloud with legs like pillars of fire	Israel led out of Egypt by the pillar of cloud by day and fire by night

Table 5. The exodus plagues and Revelation's bowls

Bowl in Revelation	Plague in Exodus
1. Rev 16:2, sores	6th, Exod 9:10, boils/sores
2. Rev 16:3, sea to blood, all living things die	1st, Exod 7:17–21, Nile to blood, fish die
3. Rev 16:4–7, rivers and springs to blood	1st, Exod 7:17–21, rivers and springs to blood
4. Rev 16:8–9, sun burns people	
5. Rev 16:10–11, darkness	9th, Exod 10:21–29, darkness
6. Rev 16:12–15, Euphrates dried up and the demons prepared for battle	10th, Exod 11:1–10; 12:29–32, death angel? Exod 14, Red Sea parted
7. Rev 16:17–21, air, earthquake, hail	7th, Exod 9:13–35, hail

The Bible is laced with this kind of intertextuality. The biblical authors learned key patterns from earlier texts, noticed repetitions of those patterns, and highlighted the repetition of such patterns in their accounts. I would suggest that John's thinking was profoundly shaped by the account of the plagues on Egypt in the book of Exodus, and this was in turn reinforced and developed by the many references to a new exodus in the Old Testament Prophets. Thus, when John beheld the judgments that accompanied the trumpets and the bowls in his vision, he naturally "read" his vision as the fulfillment of earlier prophecies. He described the judgments of the trumpets and bowls in terms that are reminiscent of the exodus plagues because the past exodus plagues built the framework for his future expectation.

In precisely these ways, the biblical authors have connected later events and accounts to earlier ones by means of the reuse of key terms and phrases, which in turn create strong connections between sequences of events. These connections between words and phrases that highlight similarities in event sequences in turn point to the ways that key figures play similar roles in the outworking of the history of redemption. Often these connections establish points of historical correspondence, and as the story unfolds, the significance of events increases. Where we have *historical correspondence* and *escalation* in significance, we have typology.[20] Typology involves key patterns seen in persons, events, or institutions in the outworking of the salvation historical drama unfolded in the Old and New Testaments. Again, the biblical authors establish these connections by the reuse of key terms and phrases, the repetition of key sequences of events, and the growing significance of these events in the progress of revelation.[21]

Hans Frei has suggested that the discipline of biblical theology only arose once the worldview in which typology made sense had been discarded.[22] Rather than interpreting the world with the categories given by the Bible, conservatives adopted the categories used to undermine the Bible in an attempt to defend it. The business of using the world's categories to defend the Bible has distracted many conservative interpreters of the Bible from the task of discerning the Bible's categories and using them to interpret the world.

---

20. For reasons that are unclear to me, Sailhamer distinguishes between typology and figural interpretation. See Sailhamer, *The Meaning of the Pentateuch*, 91. I use the term typology to refer to what he describes as figural interpretation, and it seems to me that the terms are used as synonyms in the wider discussion. For one example of the term "typology" being used interchangeably with figuration, see H. W. Frei, *The Eclipse of Biblical Narrative: A Study in Eighteenth and Nineteenth Century Hermeneutics* (New Haven: Yale University Press, 1974), 6. Remarkably, Sailhamer summarizes Frei's discussion in his description of figural interpretation.
21. For my explorations in typology, see J. M. Hamilton, "The Virgin Will Conceive: Typological Fulfillment in Matthew 1:18–23," in *Built upon the Rock: Studies in the Gospel of Matthew*, ed. John Nolland and Dan Gurtner (Grand Rapids: Eerdmans, 2008), 228–47; and J. M. Hamilton, "Was Joseph a Type of the Messiah? Tracing the Typological Identification between Joseph, David, and Jesus," *SBJT* 12 (2008): 52–77.
22. Frei, *The Eclipse of Biblical Narrative*, 1–16.

Believers must embrace the worldview in which typology makes sense—a worldview that includes God sovereignly directing the events recorded in the Bible and the way the biblical authors recorded them. Building on this, believers must interpret the world through the Bible rather than the Bible through the world. This involves seeing the web of meaning created by the Bible's own intertextual connections. We learn this web of meaning from the Bible, and then we use what we have learned in the Bible to understand what we see in the world around us.

So when we see Abel murdered by Cain, Isaac mocked by Ishmael, Jacob threatened by Esau, Joseph sold into slavery by his brothers, Moses opposed by Israel, David persecuted by Saul, and the same story repeated in the experience of prophets from Elijah to Jeremiah, we gather that in the Bible the righteous are opposed by the wicked. Then we hear Jesus say that "this generation"[23] will be held accountable for the blood of all the righteous from Abel to Zechariah (Matt 23:35), and we realize that this pattern will be fulfilled in Jesus. Nor are we surprised to see that Jesus promises the same treatment to those who follow Him (John 15:18–20). This is the age-old conflict between the seed of the serpent and the seed of the woman (Gen 3:15; cf. Rom 16:17–20; Rev 12). These intertextual connections in the Bible teach us what to expect if we follow Jesus, and they teach us to trust God through the tribulation that will inevitably come upon us.

Placement in the Big Story

Seeing the big story of the Bible and understanding how it works and where it is going enables us to understand what

---

23. On the typological significance of references to "this generation," see E. Lövestam, *Jesus and "This Generation": A New Testament Study,* trans. M. Linnarud, Coniectanea Biblica (Stockholm: Almqvist and Wiksell, 1995).

might otherwise be obscure parts of the Bible. Once we understand the big scheme of God's desire to cover the dry lands with His glory, the failure of His people that results in exile, and His promise to restore them after exile and accomplish His purpose of filling the earth with the knowledge of His glory,[24] we are in position to understand a text like Deut 4:25–31. There Moses begins by warning Israel about what not to do when they enter the land (Deut 4:25–26) and ends by telling them what will happen when they do exactly that (4:27–31). Israel will go into the land, break the covenant, be exiled, and then God will restore them when they seek Him with all their hearts from exile. We see the evocation of this big story from the way that Jeremiah, for instance, refers explicitly to Deut 4:29 in Jer 29:12–14. Nehemiah quotes the same passage, Deut 4:29–31, after exile (Neh 1:9).

Knowing that this is the big story of Israel also helps us to understand what the prophets, Isaiah through the Twelve, are saying, and they are all talking about the same thing! They are indicting sinful Israel for breaking the covenant, declaring that the exile is coming, and pointing to the glorious eschatological future that God is preparing through judgment. Those who prophesy after the exile (Haggai, Zechariah, Malachi) are applying this message to the survivors of Israel. The eschatological future is going to be like resurrection from the dead (Ezek 37). Yahweh the lion will tear Israel (Hos 5:14), but after three days He will raise them up (6:2). Like Jeremiah, Hosea refers to God's promise that in exile Israel would seek Him and find Him (Hos 5:15–6:3; cf. Deut 4:29). Exiled from God's presence, Israel will be dead as a nation, outside the realm of life, exiled to the realm of death. They will be like a valley of dry bones. But God will breathe life into them, raise them from the dead, and

---

24. On this, see R. E. Ciampa, "The History of Redemption," in *Central Themes in Biblical Theology: Mapping Unity in Diversity,* ed. S. J. Hafemann and P. R. House (Grand Rapids: Baker, 2007), 254–308.

restore them to their land, the realm of life (Ezek 37:1–14, esp. 37:14). This life-giving moment of resurrection, again, will be like a new exodus (cf., e.g., "as at the time when she came out of the land of Egypt" in Hos 2:15).

These are the terms and categories that the New Testament authors use to describe what God has done in Jesus, and they learned this way of interpreting the Bible from Jesus Himself,[25] who in turn interprets the Old Testament the same way later Old Testament authors interpreted earlier Old Testament passages. The death of Jesus is the lowest point of the exile, the moment when the temple is destroyed (John 2:19–21), when the curse of the covenant was poured out in full (Gal 3:13). At the same time, the death of Jesus is the moment when the new exodus begins (Luke 9:31), and He dies as the new and better Passover lamb (John 1:29,36; 19:36; 1 Cor 5:7).

The new exodus has happened in the death of Jesus, and the return from exile has been inaugurated in His resurrection. The final fulfillment of the new exodus and return from exile await the final judgments and the millennial kingdom, giving way to the new heaven and new earth. In the present, the authors of the New Testament deploy the history of Israel as a kind of paradigm through which the present experience of the church is interpreted (cf. 1 Cor 10:1–13).

Thus Peter can address the members of the churches to which he writes as "elect exiles" who are "sojourners" on the way to the promised land (1 Pet 1:1; 2:11). The new exodus has happened in the death of the spotless lamb, Christ (1:19). Therefore, just as Israel was called to holiness at Sinai after the first exodus, so the church is called to holiness after the second (1:15–16). At Sinai, Israel was given instructions for the building of the tabernacle (Exod 25–40), and likewise the church is

---

25. See further E. E. Ellis, "Jesus' Use of the Old Testament and the Genesis of New Testament Theology," in *Christ and the Future in New Testament History* (Boston: Brill, 2000), 20–37.

being built into a dwelling place of God (1 Pet 2:4–5). At Sinai, Israel was called a kingdom of priests and a holy nation (Exod 19:6), and now that the second exodus has taken place, that becomes the church's role (1 Pet 2:9). Sojourning toward the land of promise (2:11; 5:10), the church is to follow Christ's example and suffer for doing good, mistreated by the wicked just as He was (2:19–21).

This is the big story into which believers have been incorporated. The church has been redeemed at the "new exodus" when Jesus the Passover lamb died on the cross, and the church is being built into a new temple, indwelt by the Holy Spirit.[26] As churches indwelt by the Holy Spirit follow in the footsteps of Jesus, God's glory is made known in their proclamation of the great salvation God has accomplished through judgment, in their love for one another, and in their faithfulness to God through all manner of affliction and persecution. The great commission (Matt 28:16–20) is nothing less than the call to cover the dry lands with the glory of God by making disciples of all nations.

Encouragement

It is not difficult to see how the biblical authors mean to encourage their audience by means of the structural features and intertextual connections they use to describe and interpret God's big story, showing their audiences how they fit into that grand metanarrative that stretches from Eden to the new Jerusalem. The biblical authors encourage their audiences with the knowledge of where the world came from, what went wrong, how God is addressing the wrongs justly and at the same time lavishing mercy, and how He will make known His goodness and

---

26. J. M. Hamilton, *God's Indwelling Presence: The Holy Spirit in the Old and New Testaments*, NAC Studies in Bible and Theology (Nashville: Broadman & Holman, 2006).

glory. They show us where we fit in the story and assure us that the plot will be resolved. We need only to endure in faith, not loving our lives even unto death (Rev 12:11).

HOW DO I DO BIBLICAL THEOLOGY?

The kind of biblical theology advocated here has been described as reflection upon the results of the exegesis of particular passages in light of the whole canon.[27] Another way to say it is that biblical theology is exegesis of a particular passage in its canonical context. This means that, in order to do biblical theology, we must know the Bible and meditate on it. The only way to do biblical theology is to read the Bible, a lot, in the original languages. We must know the texts so well—words, phrases, sequences—that we notice when later authors reuse words, phrases, and sequences from earlier texts. There is no substitute for knowing the texts in the original languages, for only this will enable us to see the subtlest of allusions, parallels, echoes, and partial quotations.

If one is handicapped by an inability to access the original languages, the best solution is a literal translation. The major problem with translations that are more interpretive is that dynamic equivalent renderings do not preserve intertextual connections.[28] Even the more literal translations cannot reproduce every intertextual connection and allusion. One must be able to read the texts in Hebrew, Aramaic, and Greek if one wants to do biblical theology.

---

27. G. K. Beale, "Did Jesus and His Followers Preach the Right Doctrine from the Wrong Texts? An Examination of the Presuppositions of Jesus' and the Apostles' Exegetical Method," in *The Right Doctrine from the Wrong Texts? Essays on the Use of the Old Testament in the New*, ed. G. K. Beale (Grand Rapids: Baker, 1994), 401.
28. See also E. E. Ellis, "Dynamic Equivalence Theory, Feminist Ideology and Three Recent Bible Translations," *ExpTim* 115 (2003): 7–12.

So the prescription for doing biblical theology is really simple: know the Bible in the original languages backward and forward. Read it a lot. Ask God for insight. Memorize the Bible and meditate on it day and night. And read books that will help you put the whole Bible together.

HOW DO I PREACH BIBLICAL THEOLOGY?

I was taught that an introduction to a sermon should do five things: (1) grab the audience's attention; (2) raise the audience's awareness of their real need for what the passage being preached provides; (3) state the main point of the passage, which is also the main point of the sermon; (4) preview the structure of the passage, which is also the structure of the sermon; and (5) give the wider context of the passage. In addition to the context of the passage in the placement of the biblical book, we who preach should strive to address the canonical context of the passage we are preaching. Doing this will model biblical theology for the people of God Sunday by Sunday, text by text, book by book.

In addition to placing a passage in its biblical-theological context in the introduction, wider biblical themes are often essential to understanding the particulars of individual passages. Consider, for instance, what Jesus said to Peter and Andrew: "Follow me, and I will make you fishers of men" (Matt 4:19). The meaning of this is clear enough, but if we put it in the broader biblical-theological context, a deeper and richer meaning arises from the text. I have referred to the many pointers to a "new exodus" and "return from exile" in the Old Testament Prophets, and I have alluded to Jer 16:13–16 as an example of a place where that theme can be found. Consider what that text says:

> "Therefore I will hurl you out of this land into a land that nei-
> ther you nor your fathers have known, and there you shall

serve other gods day and night, for I will show you no favor."
[exile; cf. Deut 4:28] "Therefore, behold, the days are coming, declares the LORD, when it shall no longer be said, 'As
the LORD lives who brought up the people of Israel out of
the land of Egypt,' [first exodus] but 'As the LORD lives who
brought up the people of Israel out of the north country and
out of all the countries where he had driven them.' For I will
bring them back to their own land that I gave to their fathers.
[second exodus; cf. Deut 4:29–31] "Behold, I am sending for
many fishers, declares the LORD, and they shall catch them.
And afterward I will send for many hunters, and they shall
hunt them from every mountain and every hill, and out of the
clefts of the rocks." (Jer 16:13–16)

This text promises exile, and then it promises a new act of salvation after exile that will be so definitive that it will eclipse the
exodus from Egypt. That great act of salvation will be followed
by the Lord "sending for many fishers" (Jer 16:16), who will find
the exiles and bring them home. I submit that Jesus is alluding
to this passage and this motif when He tells Peter and Andrew
He will make them "fishers of men" (Matt 4:19). Jesus is telling
them that God's new act of salvation that will eclipse the exodus
from Egypt is about to happen, and Jesus is telling them that
they will be the "fishers" who will bring the exiles home.

The people of Israel may have returned from the exile from
the land in 586 BC, but they had not returned from the exile
from Eden. Jesus will take the people of God all the way home.
The people of God are no longer those whom God brought "out
of the land of Egypt, out of the house of slavery" (Exod 20:2).
The people of God today are those who were bought with the
price of the blood of Jesus. The cross of Christ is God's great act
of salvation by which God redeemed His people and by which
they are identified. Jesus died as the Passover lamb, inaugurat-
ing the new exodus and return from exile. Those whom Jesus
called "fishers of men" (Matt 4:19) are the very "fishers" God
promised to use to fish out His people (Jer 16:16). The more biblical theology we know—which is to say, the more thoroughly

we know the Old and New Testaments (especially in the original languages)—the easier it will be for us to understand and explain the Old and New Testaments.

How do we preach biblical theology? By explaining texts in canonical context. By highlighting the literary structures the authors have built into their texts, through which they make their points. By drawing attention to the reuse of words, phrases, and sequences from earlier biblical texts. By locating particular texts in the context of the Bible's big story. By showing how the biblical authors sought to encourage their audiences and connecting that encouragement to the members of their audience to whom we preach.

CAN GOD'S PEOPLE HANDLE THIS?

Can God's people operate those complicated remote controls that come with everything from their new flat-screen TVs to their new cars? Can God's people use computers; navigate grocery stores; hold down jobs; and acquire homes, cars, toys, and all the stuff they jam into the garage?

Let me be frank: I have no patience for suggestions that preachers need to dumb it down. Preachers need to be clear, and they need to be able to explain things in understandable ways. But human beings do not need the Bible to be dumbed down. If you think that, what you really think is that God the Holy Spirit did not know what He was doing when He inspired the Bible to be the way it is. Not only does the suggestion that the Bible is more than God's people can handle blaspheme God's wisdom; it also blasphemes His image bearers. People are made in the image of God. Human beings are endowed with brains and sensibilities of astonishing capacity.

Do you want people to think that everything that is interesting or artistic or brilliant comes from the world? Dumb down the Bible.

Do you want them to see the complexity and simplicity of God? The sheer genius of the Spirit-inspired biblical authors? The beauty of a world-encompassing metanarrative of cosmic scope? Teach them biblical theology.

Do not discount the capacities of God's people. They may be stupid and uninformed when their hearts are awakened, but do not punish them by leaving them there. Show them literary artistry. Show them the subtle power of carefully constructed narratives. Show them the force of truth in arguments that unfold with inexorable logic. If they are genuine believers, they will want to understand the Bible. Show them the shouts and songs, the clamor and the clarity, the book of books. Let their hearts sing with the psalmist, weep with Lamentations, and ponder Proverbs. Give them the messianic wisdom of the beautiful mind that wrote Ecclesiastes. Preach the word!

Unleash it in all its fullness and fury. Let it go. Tie it together. Show connections that are there in the texts from end to end. Tell them the whole story. Give them the whole picture. Paint the whole landscape for them, not just the blade of grass.

HOW DO I GET STARTED?

Go back to the Bible, and go back to the Lord. Repent of the false theology that called God's wisdom into question and denigrated His image bearers. Ask the Lord for forgiveness, and then ask for insight into the text. Then start reading the Bible. One of my teachers at Dallas Theological Seminary, John Hannah, once recounted a conversation he had with S. Lewis Johnson. Late in his life, Johnson told Hannah that looking back he wished he had spent a lot more time reading the Bible instead of reading so many other things.

When we look back on our lives, we want to have read more of the Bible than of blogs. We want to have spent more time in the text than on Twitter. We do not want to regret that we know so many batting averages, so many Hall of Famers, and so little biblical theology. We do not want to recognize that we wasted our time on politics when we could have been studying the Scriptures.

So let me encourage you to take a guided tour of the Old Testament with Paul House. Get House's *Old Testament Theology*[29] and read through the Old Testament with it. House goes book by book through the Old Testament. Read his discussion of a portion of an Old Testament book, then go read that portion of the book itself. With this I would highly recommend Stephen Dempster's *Dominion and Dynasty* and Thomas Schreiner's *Paul, Apostle of God's Glory in Christ*[30] and his *New Testament Theology*.[31] If you have read this far, you might be interested in my own attempt to go book by book through the whole Bible.[32]

May God bless your study of the Bible, and may He do so for the good of His people, that His glory might cover the dry lands as the waters cover the sea.

29. P. R. House, *Old Testament Theology* (Downers Grove: InterVarsity, 1998).
30. T. R. Schreiner, *Paul, Apostle of God's Glory in Christ: A Pauline Theology* (Downers Grove: InterVarsity, 2001).
31. T. R. Schreiner, *New Testament Theology: Magnifying God in Christ* (Grand Rapids: Baker, 2008).
32. Hamilton, *God's Glory in Salvation through Judgment*.

PART III

PREACHING THE
TEXT-DRIVEN SERMON

9

COMMUNICATION THEORY AND TEXT-DRIVEN PREACHING

Hershael W. York

As a freshman at Michigan State University, I enjoyed the privilege of being in the Honors College, which was a student's academic dream. Although the benefits it afforded were many, the greatest advantage was that all requirements for graduation were waived except the total number of hours. In other words, an Honors College student could take *anything* the university offered in any combination of classes he or she desired. Advisors would weigh in with some guidance, but the student got to make the decision and tailor the studies to meet his or her own needs.

Since I was an English major, my advisors encouraged me to take doctoral seminar work in subjects that interested me, even while I was only a freshman. George Bernard Shaw, Shakespeare, American Poetry, and the Romantics all lay before me, inviting me to raid the literary candy store and engorge myself.

Only months out of high school, I enrolled in a very popular professor's seminar on twentieth-century American drama.

This was a heady environment for a sheltered Baptist teenager from Kentucky whose spiritual development was in small rural churches. Feeling the intimidation, I worked especially hard to prove that I could perform at that level and that I fit, particularly when the professor gave me my first assignment.

He and I quickly became affable adversaries. He had a nose for young Christian students and loved challenging them. To be fair, he made no attempt to destroy my faith or anything quite that direct, but he relished making me defend my views, which were completely at odds with his. Like most of his colleagues, he explicitly labeled himself a "humanist," which I had always heard was barely a step away from devil worship.

So when he assigned me a class period in which to present and explicate Edward Albee's *The American Dream* to my older and more experienced classmates, I spared no effort to understand its murky meaning. I found Albee challenging, to say the least. Best known for his play *Who's Afraid of Virginia Woolf?* this author had gained a reputation for writing bitingly sarcastic and eviscerating dialog between his characters, most often trapped in marital misery. His portrayal of American marriage always unfolds through scenes of slow verbal torture in which the couple brutalize one another. Even as recently as this decade, Albee continued to write and push the limits of decency and tolerance with Broadway plays like *The Goat: or, Who Is Sylvia?*[1] which depicts an affair between a married man and a goat as its main subject matter and even contains a passionate kiss between a father and his son.

An Albee play like *The American Dream* was enough to make any former "Sunbeam" squirm.[2] Undaunted, I spent hours reading and rereading the work, trying to grasp its subversive subtleties and layers of meaning. I doggedly perused scholarly

---

1. *The Goat: or, Who Is Sylvia?* actually won the Tony for best Broadway play, in spite of its perverse subject matter.
2. A "Sunbeam" was a popular missions program for preschoolers in Southern Baptist churches.

criticism that had been previously published lest I miss the mark by much myself. In that phase of research, I discovered that Albee is a homosexual, and most critics surmised that he really intended the play to be about a gay couple, but because of social standards in 1960, when he penned the play, he felt constrained to make his characters heterosexual. Sure enough, when I reread the play after learning this, I could see nuances of biting social commentary and a gay perspective hidden in the dialog that I had not previously noticed.

I felt thoroughly prepared when the day of my presentation finally arrived. Having the benefit of already seeing some of the graduate students present their assigned plays certainly gave me a little confidence, and I knew how hard I had worked. Opening the class, the professor introduced me and then said, "Mr. York, help us 'experience' the truth of *The American Dream*. The next two hours are yours." I was not yet astute enough to know that his brief introduction calling for an "experience" rather than an "explanation" had already laid a trap into which I was innocently about to fall.

After providing a brief overview of the play and its themes, I mentioned some biographical details about Albee's life and other works. Then, with no small degree of pride at what I had uncovered, I announced as matter-of-factly as I could that Albee was a homosexual and that if one read the play carefully, one could see that his real intent was to present a brutal path and trajectory that such relationships typically follow. Thinking that this would clearly demonstrate either the depth of my research or my own incisive thinking, I was shaken when I noticed the professor abruptly turned crimson right before the class. Glaring at me with protruding eyes and veins bulging through the blotches on his neck, he immediately did what he had not done in any previous presentations—he interrupted me.

"What did you say?"

For a number of good reasons, I had suspected that the professor might himself be homosexual, so I had carefully avoided any statement that sounded like a judgment about homosexuality.

I had limited my remarks by only commenting on the *fact* of Albee's sexual orientation, evading any conclusion about its morality—or lack thereof. Still, I found myself like a matador who has dropped his cape in the face of a charging bull. All I knew to do was to answer his question and repeat myself: "Albee was a homosexual, and his intent was to present the emotional brutality and lack of love that often marks a relationship after the initial infatuation is gone."

A second time, but with growing ire and added volume, he asked, "*What* did you say?" Now a third time I offered the offending statement, though I could not discern why it was so troubling to him.

Finally releasing me from his unblinking stare, he looked at my classmates and said with obvious forced restraint, "Class, the rest of you may leave now. I would like to speak privately to Mr. York."

I sat stunned as the graduate students I had desperately wanted to impress silently gathered their books and bags and filed out as quickly as they could as if they had seen this drill before. Five minutes into a two-hour class, my professor had seen fit to send everyone home but me.

I sat there for what must have been only 30 seconds but seemed like an hour as the others all scurried out the door like rats. Bracing myself for a lecture on the virtues of tolerance and a warning about bigotry, I sat under his steady glare that had now returned and fixed on me. Finally, he broke the interminable silence. I was not prepared for the question he asked.

"What makes you think you can ever know what an author intends?"

"Huh?" I responded, now more confused than scared. He repeated himself, this time expanding his question so I could not miss his point. "What makes you think that you can read an author's mind, that you can take the words on the page and know what he was thinking as he wrote? And besides," he continued, "why would you even want to do that? That isn't what literature is about!" With each sentence, his voice grew louder and more animated as he proceeded to explain that reading literature was not about figuring out the author's intention, but rather having an *experience* of the work, an experience that was not the author's but was, instead, authentically *mine*. He made it clear that neither the author's intention nor the words on the page mattered nearly as much as what the work meant *to me*.

His doctrinaire diatribe continued for close to an hour. I sat in silence while he quoted everyone from Shakespeare to e. e. cummings to prove that I should not even ask questions about what the author thought, meant, or intended. I should only seek my own personal meaning, because only then would I truly *experience* passion. Then, saving his most lethal words for his summation, he finally made it very personal. "Mr. York, so long as you read the words of others trying to imagine what they meant, you will remain emotionally stunted, unable to experience life for yourself, always seeing the world through the eyes of others, never through your own."

Pursing his lips and drawing himself as tall in his chair as he could, he inhaled deeply through his nose and closed his eyes, looking as though he had just finished a bravura performance and presented unassailable logic. Finally exhaling he spoke, much more quietly this time, touching my arm with his hand, looking deeply in my eyes, and doing his best to show genuine concern.

"Do you understand what I am telling you?"

I cannot claim that the answer I gave was completely motivated by a humble pursuit of truth, nor can I defend it as a final stand for the faith, but somewhere deep within me I knew that what he was saying just did not make sense, and I knew that his question had exposed the soft underbelly of his logic.

"I thought that wasn't the point," I said.

My response reaped another hour of reprimand and wrath, but I endured it, replete with the knowledge that my single rejoinder had eviscerated his entire line of reasoning. If I could understand his words, why couldn't I, with sufficient context, understand *any* speaker's or author's words? And if it was not possible for me to understand the intent of any other writer or speaker, why would the professor even bother to ask me if I understood *him*?

THE MODEL OF COMMUNICATION

Reflecting on my deliverance from the fiery furnace of that classroom, I now realize that at that moment God confirmed in my heart a conviction that today drives my study of His Word, my preaching, and my teaching. Perhaps I had always intuitively accepted that God has spoken to us through a Word whose meaning and application we can apprehend, but on that day it changed from an inference to a conviction. Only when we believe that God has spoken will we dare to speak in His name, and only when we believe that we can *understand* what He has said will we speak *confidently*.

An acquaintance with the foundational concepts of communication theory is necessary for the Bible student as well as the preacher. Communication theory, in its simplest form, can be illustrated like this:[3]

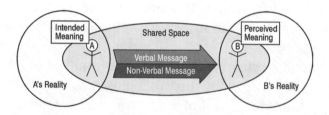

Communication, by definition, involves the intentional transmission of a mutually meaningful concept between at least two individuals. In the diagram, person A has a thought that he must "encode" by putting it into some kind of signal comprised

---

3. This diagram and much of the discussion that follows is adapted from H. W. York and B. Decker, *Preaching with Bold Assurance* (Nashville: Broadman & Holman, 2003), 136–37.

of symbols that will convey his meaning to person B. Those symbols can be *anything* that has *mutual* meaning to the two parties—hieroglyphs, pictograms, words, sign language, moving lips, smoke signals, a raised eyebrow, flashing lights, or anything, so long as both parties agree to its significance. If A encodes his message into symbols that B cannot decode, then they simply do not communicate. In other words, for communication to actually *occur*, person B has to be able to understand those symbols and "decode" them so that he accurately *understands* what person A intended.

If a Native American sends smoke signals from a mountaintop to greet someone, he has not communicated until someone who knows the meaning of those puffs of smoke sees them and accurately decodes their intended meaning. I might see them, but if I am unable to decode them, he and I have not communicated because I did not understand his intended meaning.

We communicate daily in thousands of different ways, even nonverbally, especially with our intimates. When I was a child, if I was a bit distracted or rambunctious in church during one of my father's sermons, my mother had a distinct clearing of her throat that I recognized as a warning to sit up and listen. If one of my church friends was sitting with me and we grew preoccupied and forgot where we were for a moment, my mother, who always made it a point to sit a few rows behind me, would clear her throat in a manner that was distinct and recognizable to me. When I heard that unmistakable signal, immediately I trained my eyes on my father in the pulpit and sat up still and erect. My playmate, however, did not even notice, much less decode my mother's intended meaning. Unwittingly continuing to act as though we had not been corrected, he made me feel like I was still in danger of getting reprimanded further. I would then have to "interpret" my mother's meaning for my friend, encoding her correction into a gesture to my friend or words that told him my mother was on to us.

Believe it or not, preaching is not terribly unlike that scenario in which my mother communicated to me, and I heard it and decoded it properly and then made certain that my friend understood, too. Whether I had to overcome the fact that he did not hear or did not understand, the predicament was the same. I had to encode appropriately the signal that I had just decoded correctly.

To be a bit more precise, the aforementioned model of communication relates to text-driven preaching on three distinct but necessary levels.

Level One: God (Encode) <<<<< SIGNAL >>>>>>> (Decode) Prophets/Authors

First, we have **a conviction about the nature of inspiration**. God is the initial "source," as defined in the model, who encoded His revelation through various means and symbols to the biblical authors. By faith, we accept the internal evidence of the Bible, the witness of the Spirit, and proven experience, and thereby we believe that the biblical authors understood God's meaning and intention. Whether through direct revelation couched in unmediated prophecy, the apostolic office, or through historical events, God ensured that their understanding matched His revelation. He did not allow the biblical writers to record anything different from or contrary to His intended meaning.

Level Two: Biblical Authors (Encode) <<<<< SIGNAL >>>>>>> (Decode) Readers

Second, we hold **a conviction about the nature of Scripture**. These holy men of God *spoke* or *wrote* as the Holy Spirit moved them (2 Pet 1:20–21). After being the receptors on level one as they decoded God's revelation, they then became the sources for transmitting God's Word to their readers, the receptors on level two of the model. We further believe that the Holy Spirit carefully superintended this encoding of God's revelation and protected it from any loss, attrition, or miscommunication. Using the linguistic symbols available to them, they accurately conveyed the exact content of what God had said, and now readers can decode and understand the intended meaning. Believers have the added benefit of the Holy Spirit who is available to help them also understand and *apply* the meaning of the authors (John 16:13).

At the heart of the doctrine of inerrancy of Scripture lies this conviction: though the biblical authors transmitted the revelation they received from God in their own vocabulary and through their own experience, the Holy Spirit enabled them to do so without human error creeping in and marring the message. If, in fact, the biblical authors miscommunicated the signal they received and decoded, then the message the readers discerned could not be the same that God gave the authors. The Bible is trustworthy, therefore, in every way. In a very real sense, we can say, "Thus says the Lord" of biblical history as much as we can of biblical prophecy or of what the Bible says about Christ, because all of the Word of God accurately reflects God's revelation to the authors who then accurately encoded it for their readers.

To be sure, as readers, we must sometimes make a significant effort to decode accurately the meaning that the biblical authors intended. Understanding the signals that they used, whether linguistic, literary, or cultural, may take some effort on our parts, but in every case the basic meaning of the authors is attainable.[4] Thankfully, in the vast majority of texts, that meaning is readily clear. This articulates our belief in the *perspicuity* of Scripture, that the basic meaning of the Bible is clear to the reader. We may not be able to understand *everything* in Scripture because of our own limitations, distance from the vocabulary or context of the text, or even our sinfulness and unwillingness to

---

4. Though slightly beyond the scope of this chapter, another corollary truth is worth noting. If one cannot know the authorial intent of a passage, then accurate translation of the text would be impossible as well as any hermeneutical skill.

believe it, but we can certainly apprehend the *main* things in nearly every text. Using biblical tools, the power of context, the analogy of faith, and other exegetical rules and skills, we can usually arrive at the main thrust of a passage because we can understand the words that the authors used.

Take, for example, a passage often regarded as one of the toughest texts to interpret in the Bible, 1 Pet 3:18–22 (HCSB):

> For Christ also suffered for sins once for all, the righteous for the unrighteous, that He might bring you to God, after being put to death in the fleshly realm but made alive in the spiritual realm. In that state He also went and made a proclamation to the spirits in prison who in the past were disobedient, when God patiently waited in the days of Noah while an ark was being prepared; in it, a few—that is, eight people— were saved through water. Baptism, which corresponds to this, now saves you (not the removal of the filth of the flesh, but the pledge of a good conscience toward God) through the resurrection of Jesus Christ. Now that He has gone into heaven, He is at God's right hand, with angels, authorities, and powers subjected to Him.

Although scholars debate many aspects of meaning *within* this passage, they hardly debate the overall meaning *of* this passage at all. Our ability to decode some of Peter's signals and discover his precise meaning might be limited. Who are the "spirits in prison," fallen angels or lost people of Noah's day? When did Christ preach to them, in the days of Noah or between His death and ascension? What message did He preach, one of judgment or an offer of salvation? One can find no small number of opinions and theories attempting to answer these questions.

On the other hand, however, one should also take note that these questions, though important and interesting, do not at all change the clear and attainable character of the passage's overall meaning. Whatever Christ did with regard to the imprisoned spirits and whenever He did it, it does not negate or call into question that He suffered and died for sins once for all.

Whenever He preached to the "spirits in prison," He did it as part of His redemptive plan to "bring you to God." One's ability to decode certain details might be limited by a lack of vocabulary, cultural knowledge, or related background material, but the main meaning remains clear. By the same token, no doubt many students of this passage have gotten it right and have explained the details of this text correctly. Certainly the ones who agree with me have!

Although my last comment is facetious, my point is very serious indeed. We ought not to be intimidated by certain passages in the Bible that we find difficult to understand and therefore fail to study and determine the big picture that God has clearly painted for us. The main message of the Bible is clear.

God has not, however, called us to be merely readers, always staying on the right side of the communication model. Because God has spoken, we must speak, as reflected in the next level of application of the communication model.

Level Three: **Reader/Preacher (Encode)** <<<<< SIGNAL >>>>>>> (Decode) Audience

Third, we have **a conviction about the nature of preaching**. Just like the second level of the model, those who previously decoded the message then encode it for another audience. In the third level, those who have read the biblical text become the source, and then they encode it into proclamation that must be heard and decoded by the preaching audience. If we have done our jobs correctly, then our audience can hear and understand a message that began with God Himself.

This model of communication definitively shapes our philosophy and methodology of preaching. Our goal, therefore, is not to create, innovate, edit, or improve the message that God gave. We do not apologize for its inconvenient parts or passages that seem out of step with contemporary culture. We do not infuse meaning into details of the text in which the Bible itself has not added that meaning. We do not "add to" or "take away from" the words of God's book. Our task is to proclaim faithfully what God has spoken. In this way, our audience should be able to hear the message proclaimed and to read the written text and see that both emanate from the same ultimate source. They must be able to witness a congruity between the inscripturated truth they read and the truth proclaimed by the preacher whom they hear. When parishioners express amazement to their preacher that they would never have seen a certain thing in the biblical text had he not said it, that preacher may not be getting the compliment that he desires. If a preacher proclaims the truth as it has been written in the Scripture, a member of the congregation using the same tools of decoding should see precisely where that truth comes from in the text.

Our preaching must be lashed to the Scriptures. We are committed to think deeply and clearly about what the text means so we can also show how it applies. Furthermore, we keep an eye on the audience as well so we can craft the sermon in such a way that takes into account the way our audience perceives. Everything we do is orchestrated to serve one goal: communicating what God has spoken in the most accurate and compelling way possible.

THE FIRST CHALLENGE TO TEXT-DRIVEN COMMUNICATION

At first glance this explanation may seem merely like an academic exercise that has little or no bearing on preaching, but in fact, it has *everything* to do with it because preaching sermons derived directly from the text is currently under attack from two very different fronts. Liberals attempt to deny the absolute truth content of the text, whereas some conservatives deny its appropriate emotional content and purpose. Both of these challenges to preaching require an explanation and a response.

On the one hand, those who deny the inerrancy of Scripture or the ability to know an author's intent dismiss this text-driven approach to preaching because they believe that preaching with any authority is beyond the scope and even the possibility for preachers today. Fred Craddock's *As One Without Authority*, one of the best-selling books on preaching in the last 40 years, sums up this view as evidenced by the title. Craddock's contention throughout the book is that the authority of the sermon lies with the audience rather than with the text. In his watershed work *Overhearing the Gospel*, Craddock bluntly states, "The stone the builders rejected was the hearer."[5]

He certainly does not locate the authority with the preacher, either. Commenting on a deductive and propositional preaching methodology (such as expository preaching), Craddock writes,

> There is no democracy here, no dialogue, no listening by the speaker, no contributing by the hearer. If the congregation is on the team, *it is as a javelin catcher*. One may even detect a downward movement, a condescension of thought, in the pattern. Of course, this may or may not appear in the delivery, depending on the minister. Some sensitive and understanding preachers modify the implied authority in a variety of ways: by voice quality, humor, or an overall shepherding spirit that marks all their relationships. But even here, a critical eye may detect a *soft authoritarianism* in the minister's words to those most obviously dependent upon her. Sometimes a term of affection may be a way of reducing another to a child, or a non-personal status. One may recall with what devastating warmth African American men were once called "boy" or "uncle."[6]

Obviously, suggesting that propositional preaching might have something in common with the condescending attitude of racism adds insult to gross misunderstanding if not intentional misrepresentation.

---

5. F. B. Craddock, *Overhearing the Gospel* (St. Louis: Chalice, 2002), 63.
6. F. B. Craddock, *As One Without Authority* (St. Louis: Chalice, 2001), 46–47, emphasis added.

In mainstream preaching, however, Craddock's view has won the day. In fact, no single philosophy of preaching has shaped this generation—perhaps *any* generation—like Craddock's. The pantheon of inductive and narrative preaching proponents genuflects at Craddock's image. Eugene Lowry, David Buttrick, and many others who advocate and practice narrative preaching have been heavily influenced by Craddock, if not molded in his image. For them, as well as for the thousands of preachers in mainstream pulpits whom they have influenced in turn, the text may be evocative, helpful, suggestive, and even powerful, but they do not believe it to be the completely true and inerrant Word of God. They suggest that it may *contain* the Word of God, so the preacher's consequent task is to distill it, not merely to distribute it. They search for the canon within the canon, choosing which sections of the Scriptures are applicable or palatable to contemporary life. They will often call the Bible "authoritative," but as Adrian Rogers used to say, "They're saying our words, but using their own dictionary."

In this view, the preacher hopes to lead listeners to "encounter" God in the text, to experience Him in devotion, but he dare not hope that the text can reveal God in its very words. Buttrick comments,

> The trouble with a lofty concept of biblical authority is that it imposes a "vertical" God-in-Godself model on scripture. Thus, the Bible, forever fixed, becomes a sovereign, unassailable "wisdom from on high," that can be neither contradicted nor disobeyed with impunity. Of course, anyone with psychological acuity knows that a heavy-handed authority usually breeds contempt, particularly a "fixed" authority that is bound to discourage freedom of movement. Because overt sassiness toward scripture has often earned reprisal, a subtle disdain may be encouraged instead.[7]

---

7. D. Buttrick, *Homiletic: Moves and Structures* (Philadelpia: Fortress, 1987), 245. Whereas Buttrick's erudite discussion of the internal components of a sermon and the structural theory of the preaching task are thought-provoking and

If the biblical text cannot be taken literally, historically, or authoritatively, then the preacher is left to search among the gospel story for bones that he attempts to make live by breathing into them the breath of creativity and poignancy. If the preacher cannot find the biblical author's meaning, then he only has two choices: bestow on it his own significance or help the audience experience their own subjective meaning.

These prospects bring me back to the opening story of this chapter. In the same way that my professor accused me of failing to experience the story myself in a vain pursuit of the author's intent, so many contemporary preachers would scoff at the notion of a sermon that is driven by the text. They reject the notion that the preacher's task is to say the same thing as the text as well as the conviction that the text is truly equivalent to God's thought.

The current rejection of textual authority is by no means unique to biblical studies and criticism. Biblical scholars have simply mimicked what transpired first in the worlds of art and literary criticism. Both of those disciplines experienced a sea change in the twentieth century that shook them to their foundations.

In centuries past, for example, an observer would look at a painting in an effort to discern what the painter was trying to say, what message he was attempting to convey. Studying Rembrandt's painting of the crucifixion, for example, one cannot help but note that the master painted himself into his own work of art. He stands at the foot of the cross, a participant in the death of his Savior. Clearly, Rembrandt had a message to convey and viewers of the work tried to decode it.

The contrast with a twenty-first-century artist like Jackson Pollack, however, is striking. Both the expectations of the artist and the interpretation of the audience are radically different than at any time before. In the postmodern world, no one

---

occasionally helpful, Buttrick's disdain for the authority of Scripture so compromises his methodology as to render the book barely useful for an expositor.

expects Pollack to convey *meaning*, only *feeling*. If the question one asked of a Rembrandt was, "What does it mean?" the question one asks of a Pollack is, "What does it mean *to me*?" Similarly, the literary world asks the same question. As illustrated in the story that opened this chapter, literary critics who subscribe to this theory deny that the goal of reading a literary work is discovering the author's intent.

The communication model required three discrete and tangible elements for communication to occur: a source, a signal, and a receptor. Modern criticisms of art, literature, and even the Bible have mangled that model by declaring the source irrelevant or even unnecessary. All that matters is the signal and the receptor. The receptor is freed from any attempt at decoding what the source encoded, and communication, therefore, is moot. This approach first denies that communication is actually possible, and then renders it unnecessary.

The problem, of course, is that this view of the text does not work in the real world. Without doubt, the very ones who deny that students of the Scriptures can know the intent of the authors do not work from that assumption in their daily lives. What if they told that theory to the company that holds their home mortgage? If modern literary critics treated their mortgage contracts like they treat the Bible, they would be free to make a monthly payment based on their experience and interpretation rather than on what the contract actually says. Imagine someone who is delinquent in his payments telling the collection agency that inevitably calls for payment that discerning the intent of the contract's author is impossible, and besides, meaning is less important than experience. I am confident that a foreclosure notice would be forthcoming regardless of the debtor's theories about hermeneutics.

Would a scholar who denies that knowing authorial intent is possible want his pharmacist to believe that? Druggists are not free to *interpret* the prescription as they experience it. Instead, they must strive to determine *precisely* what the doctor has written. The intent of the doctor who wrote the prescription is *everything*.

The pharmacist has only one task regarding the prescription: decode the author's intent and carry out his instructions.

Similarly, no father who buys an unassembled bicycle for his child's birthday ought to apply this hermeneutic to the assembly instructions. In fact, many parents have perhaps lamented that the directions did not reveal the author's intent clearly *enough*, but no dad who cares about the safety of his child and his own reputation with his family would think that the directions do not matter. In his brashness or self-confidence, he might ignore them, but he does not reinterpret them.

THE SECOND CHALLENGE TO TEXT-DRIVEN COMMUNICATION

Although most conservatives are wary of the challenge to text-driven preaching arising from those who deny that one can discern the author's intent, a more insidious dispute comes from within the ranks of conservatives and even would-be expositors. Far too many who hold the text with a reverence ignore the process by which that text is communicated. In other words, in their devotion to the sacred signal, they ignore the human means that God uses to convey that meaning. Bearing in mind that communication occurs with more than mere words, we must be willing to use every tool at our disposal to communicate the truth as God has given it. My mother's clearing of her throat communicated as much to me as any words she could ever have said. My wife's smile does too, though it is a much more pleasant experience, to be sure. In other words, although words are central to our proclamation of truth, words are not the only instruments we have to convey it. God has given us a great toolbox by which we make an *emotional* connection with our audience as well. Through conveying emotion, we can denote urgency, joy, sorrow, hope, grief, solemnity, faith, or any other appropriate emotion that further highlights the meaning of God's original message.

To prove the point, one need look no further than the biblical prophets themselves. Having received the word from God, they were then responsible to convey it to their audience *in the most effective means at their disposal*. If all that mattered was delivering the data, then they would have merely spoken words, but they did not. They also conveyed emotion. Jeremiah is the *weeping* prophet. Ezekiel used elaborate one-man performances *that God prescribed* for him—laying siege to a model city, cooking on a dung fire, refusing to cry when the Lord took his beloved wife from him. Isaiah walked throughout the land barefoot and naked for three years. David's dance before the Lord signified something. Jesus wept over Jerusalem, showed anger in the woes He pronounced on the Pharisees, demonstrated tenderness in His reception of children, and shared humor in His hyperbole. In other words, effective communication—even of the biblical text—involves a lot more than merely saying the right words. If the words were all that mattered, the personal presence and delivery of the preacher would be superfluous. Pastors could e-mail their sermons to their parishioners and let them read them.

The very notion of congregations merely reading the sermon rather than hearing the man of God orally and personally deliver it should send a chill through any church. We intuitively, and by experience, know that listening to a man of God skillfully deliver a sermon is far superior to reading it. We *connect* because our tools are not limited to words on a page. We can include pitch, volume, facial expressions, gestures, posture, listener involvement, eye communication, dress, and appearance to open doors of reluctance and disenchantment. We can actually adjust the delivery style on the spot, something we could never do with a written text.

Christian preachers have long tipped their clerical hats to Aristotle's rhetorical categories of *logos*, *pathos*, and *ethos*. As David Larsen writes,

> Communicators through the centuries have walked in the steps of Aristotle and his *Rhetoric*. Perhaps we have been

too slavish to his system, and certainly we who preach must reexamine our debits and credits. We need to remember that Aristotle did not reinvent the law of contradiction. Yet it is not likely that we shall better Aristotle's classic divisions of discourse: *logos*—the message; *ethos*—the speaker; and *pathos*—the audience.[8]

Secular classical rhetoricians like Quintilian and Cicero have paid homage to these divisions as well as Christians from Augustine to the present. A line of orators and preachers through the centuries, by their consensus view of Aristotle's categories, has borne witness that more than the words count. A preacher who has been married five times might preach the greatest sermon about the home imaginable, but his *ethos* will undermine his *logos*. Likewise, a pastor can preach a sermon in which everything he says is true and challenging, but if he is monotone and dry, his *pathos* overwhelms his *logos*.

Preachers who aspire to preach the truth of God's Word in the most effective manner dare not concentrate on the *logos*—the exegesis and hermeneutics of exposition—while ignoring their own passion in communication or their overall integrity. All of these things carry content.

Sometimes, in their zeal to give the glory to God alone, some preachers will diminish their own role in the preaching event by not giving enough thought to the way they communicate. They almost fear to preach with passion lest someone accuse them of being too dramatic and focusing on themselves rather than on God or His Word. It is as though they feel like they are not actually preaching unless they give the Holy Spirit an obstacle to overcome.

Solomon Stoddard, Jonathan Edwards' grandfather and greatest influence, dismissed this view:

---

8. D. Larsen, *The Anatomy of Preaching: Identifying the Issues in Preaching Today* (Grand Rapids: Baker, 1989), 35.

> *The reading of sermons is a dull way of preaching.* Sermons
> when read are not delivered with authority and in an affecting
> way. . . . When sermons are delivered without notes, the looks
> and the gesture of the minister is a great means to command
> attention and stir up affection. Men are apt to be drowsy
> in hearing the word, and the liveliness of the preacher is a
> means to stir up the attention of the hearers, and beget suit-
> able affection in them. Sermons that are read are not deliv-
> ered with authority, they savor the sermons of the scribes,
> Matthew 7:29. Experience shows that sermons read are not
> so profitable as others.[9]

Put simply, to reach the mind with the content of the text,
the preacher has to go through the gateway we usually refer
to as the "heart." The emotions play an enormous part in the
communication of truth. Most of us have had the unpleasant
experience of listening to a sermon with which we found over-
whelming agreement, yet it either bored us or, in some cases in
which we found the preacher's manner condescending or arro-
gant, it even angered us. Imagine that: even a message with
which we concur may anger us by the manner and emotion
with which the preacher delivers it.

By the same token, however, the preacher who learns how to
use his communication skills to disarm or engage his audience
can get the gates of the mind to open to the message he delivers. Though the preacher does not pursue *emotionalism*, he
must not flee *emotion*. God Himself designed the human mind
and will so that emotions move and influence them. The biblical
prophets used the power of emotion to deliver their messages,
as did Jesus and the apostles. Why should a twenty-first-century
preacher not do the same?

The preacher must reach the mind through the heart and
not vice versa. People are not led to trust Christ by taking out a

---

9. S. Stoddard, *The Defects of Preachers Reproved in a Sermon Preached at Northamp-
ton, May 19, 1723* (New London, CT: n.p., 1724; repr., Ames, IA: International
Outreach, n.d.), 20–21. Emphasis in original.

yellow legal pad and listing the pros on one side and the cons on the other, and then feeling conviction, repentance, and joy once they have rationally considered it. To the contrary, the Lord uses the sorrow of conviction to drive the sinner to Christ. In similar fashion, God's goodness leads to repentance; godly sorrow also leads to repentance. Although the rational mind is and should be engaged, it does not operate in a vacuum. God uses the passion of the messenger to stir the passions of the listener and confront his mind with the urgency of a decision to accept or reject the message.

The two errors of communication that we have discussed are strangely complementary. Ironically, liberals often do a great job with communication from the point of the signal, though they ignore the source and the authorial intent. Conservatives, on the other hand, expend great effort at embracing the authority of the text and understanding authorial intent but often fail to use all the tools God has provided them in driving that truth home to their listeners. Frequently they spend so much energy on levels one and two of the communication models that they forget that they must do everything they can to get that message to their listeners. Liberals emphasize connection with the audience, whereas conservatives believe that giving them the biblical data is enough.

In the following chapter in this book, Jerry Vines and Adam Dooley argue correctly that the preacher must match the emotional content of the text. I concur completely and argue further that a failure to preach the emotional content of the text is as much an abdication of expository responsibility as failure to preach the theological content. God designed them to go hand in hand because he designed human beings to respond to emotion as well as data. Authorial devices such as irony, sarcasm, rebuke, repentance, sorrow, and joy can be conveyed through behaviors coupled with words much more effectively than with words alone.

CONCLUSION

Unlike much contemporary preaching, text-driven preaching begins with a conviction about inspiration itself, that we speak because God has spoken and that God's revelation is knowable and communicable. A preacher whose sermons are driven by the text holds a conviction that he can discern the intent of God's meaning through the words of the biblical authors whom God inspired. Beyond that, he must also seek to communicate the truth that he has discerned in the biblical text in such a way that it accurately conveys the meaning—both the lexical and *emotional* content.

The preacher whose sermons are lashed to the text cannot be content to present lexical and cultural analysis arranged in homiletical fashion. He must be convinced that, like the biblical prophets, he can use behaviors, illustrations, and even nonverbal techniques to fulfill his goal of faithfully presenting the content of God's Word to his audience. He uses the gate of the "heart"—that is, the emotions of the audience—to reach the mind.

Preaching that uses multiple channels of communication to meet the goal of helping others receive the intended meaning of what God originally conveyed to the authors of the Bible is not only true to the meaning of the text as given by God and sensitive to the needs of the audience to apprehend that meaning; it also glorifies God more than any other kind of preaching because it respects both the form and the substance of God's revelation.

10

DELIVERING A
TEXT-DRIVEN SERMON

Adam B. Dooley and Jerry Vines

A t first glance, marketing genius Louis Cheskin's concept of "sensations transference" has little or nothing to do with delivering a text-driven sermon. Further investigation, however, reveals greater congruence than one might initially realize. By arguing that people transfer sensations about the package of a product in a supermarket to the product itself, Cheskin began looking for new ways to make his products more appealing. In the late 1940s, convincing consumers to buy margarine seemed like a hopeless effort. Cheskin, however, believed that the appearance of margarine was a greater obstacle than the substance of margarine. He curiously hypothesized that people transferred bad sensations to the food. In order to test his hypothesis, Cheskin colored margarine yellow so that it would look like butter. He then invited several homemakers to an event where margarine was interspersed among the butter on the food tables. After the luncheon, while rating the food, everyone concluded that the "butter" was just fine.

Sensing that he was on to something, Cheskin changed the name of his product to Imperial Margarine and put an impressive crown on the package. He wrapped yellow sticks of margarine in foil because of its association with high quality. The rest is marketing history because the sale of margarine skyrocketed to the point that it even surpassed butter sales. Mere coincidence is a poor explanation for the dramatic change in receptivity of the public.

Other examples abound. For example, adding more yellow to a can of 7-Up leads people to report a more lime or lemon flavor. Taking peaches out of a can and putting them in a jar makes people think they taste better, and thus, they are willing to pay a little more. Faces like Hector on a can of Chef Boyardee ravioli, Orville Redenbacher, and Betty Crocker all portray life-like human faces that are easy for the consumer to relate to. As strange as it sounds, these packaging techniques predispose consumers to be more positive about the products they buy. That does not mean, however, that clever packaging allows companies to produce bad products. It simply means that people will give the validity of a product a chance if the package is appealing.[1]

If Cheskin is right, and people do not make any distinction on the subconscious level between a package and the product in the package, why would a preacher of the gospel refuse to package his message in such a way as to gain a hearing? Or why would he do anything, even on the subconscious level, to hinder an audience's ability to perceive correctly the message of a biblical text? Because of a deep conviction about the quality of the Bible and its message, at the very least, the act of preaching requires preachers to package sermons in order to reflect that quality. Most books on preaching have at least a chapter or section on delivery; these emphasize avoiding distracting habits that hinder communication, as well as using proven techniques that engage people.

---

1.   See M. Gladwell, *Blink* (New York: Little, Brown, 2005), 160–65.

Despite the common sense of this approach, some question the morality of using the skills of communication theory. Long ago, Michael Bell accurately articulated the tension that many still feel today:

> The theologians are lined up on one side of a gaping chasm, the communicators are lined up on the other side, and both are throwing stones at one another. The theologians insist upon the necessity of preaching, complain about "gimmickry" and Madison Avenue "tricks" and shout across the chasm, "We are preaching the Gospel not selling soap and cars." The communicators shout back, "Take a look around. We are selling soap and cars a whole lot better than you are 'selling' the Gospel."[2]

Likewise, Dean Dickens surmises, "Ever since that ancient but inevitable marriage between 'sacred preaching' and 'worldly rhetoric,' numerous ministers have feared that the preached word would eventually be the mate prostituted."[3]

Second Corinthians 4:2 (NKJV) is pertinent to this issue: "But we have renounced the hidden things of shame, not walking in craftiness nor handling the word of God deceitfully, but by manifestation of the truth commending ourselves to every man's conscience in the sight of God." Some might assume that sharpening delivery skills would constitute "craftiness" and "deceit." Second Corinthians 4:5 continues, however, "For we do not preach ourselves, but Christ Jesus the Lord." The irony of Paul's statement in v. 5 is that failing to use persuasion skills that prevent the preacher from being a distraction is actually closer to manipulation than doing so. Annoying habits, whining voices, and overpowering human personality can actually hinder an audience's ability to receive the biblical message.

2. M. Bell, "Preaching in Our Mass Media Environment," *Preaching* 4 (January–February 1969): 5.
3. D. Dickens, "Now Heerreessss . . . Brother Johnny: Studies in Communication and Preaching," *SWJT* 27 (1985): 19.

Those who dismiss the validity of using any persuasion techniques in preaching often question the moral and ethical bases for such approaches. However, this may be a reaction to preachers who are more like manipulators than persuaders. The discerning factor is making certain that the technique used does not detract from the message by drawing attention to the messenger. As with any method reflecting the right motive, the goal is to equip the preacher to speak so flawlessly that people do not notice him and are free to focus on the message. Success in this area will minimize the messenger and exalt the message to the glory of God and for the good of the listener. Defining rhetoric as any means that one might use to communicate truth, Raymond Bailey warns,

> Those who abandon rhetoric to the modern medicine men surrender to the advertisers, politicians, and religious demagogues the cumulative knowledge of the centuries regarding what motivates and attracts people. Rhetoric is inherently an indifferent instrument which may be employed for justice or injustice, good or evil.[4]

With this is mind, we now turn our focus toward avoiding abuses that will rob the preached Word of its power. If the art of rhetoric is just a tool that can be used for good or evil, what determines the difference?

THE IMPORTANCE OF *PATHOS*

Most books and articles about sermon delivery deal primarily with the mechanics of communication rather than ascertaining the biblical essentials that proper delivery requires. Many reason that a sermon is biblical as long as its message corresponds

---

4.   R. Bailey, "The Art of Effective Preaching," *Preaching* 4 (July–August 1988): 11.

to the original meaning of the text. Although the content, or *logos*, of a biblical passage represents the front lines for ensuring doctrinal fidelity, discerning and demonstrating the emotive intent of the Scriptures is also necessary to avoid biblical misrepresentation. In addition, utilizing rhetorical persuasion techniques outside the parameters of *pathos* increases the likelihood of a man-centered presentation of the gospel that draws attention to the messenger. Unfortunately, too many preachers fail to realize that *pathos* in preaching is more than a passionate presentation of truth. Although energy is important for effective sermon delivery, the preacher is not free to impose his own emotional design on the message he proclaims. To the contrary, *pathos* that does not correspond to the emotive mood of the biblical author is dangerously manipulative. Just as we are not free to tamper with the inspired *logos* of the Bible, neither are we at liberty to alter its *pathos*.

If writing sermons were God's primary means of communicating the gospel, sermon delivery would require little attention and *pathos* would be hard to communicate. Since, however, we cannot divorce the message of salvation from the messenger, understanding the biblical author's meaning for a text requires not only accurate communication of the *logos* of Scripture but also the *pathos* of Scripture. Such an obligation means that those who preach must give attention to *what* they say and *how* they say it. Both must be a reflection of the Bible's original intent within a given biblical passage. Anointed persuasion will declare what the author says with the same *pathos* with which he says it.

In recent years, renewed interest in expository preaching is surfacing, with the primary emphasis being on the *logos* of Scripture. Although this attention is important, there has been little concentration on the *pathos* of preaching. Terry Mattingly observes, "In most congregations, the word 'sermon' means a verse-by-verse explanation of scripture, perhaps enlivened with occasional illustrations from daily life. Thus, most people hear academic lectures at church, then turn to mass media to find inspiring tales of heroes and villains, triumph and tragedy, sin and redemption, heaven and hell."[5]

Unfortunately, the neglect of *pathos* in preaching leads many to abandon the expository method altogether. Lucy Lind Hogan and Robert Reid illustrate the contemporary frustration of neglecting *pathos* due to an apparent overemphasis on the *logos* of a text: "Many of the approaches that have been labeled the New Homiletics have distanced themselves from *logos* by emphasizing *pathos* in their interest to create an affective experience for listeners."[6] This perceived overemphasis is unfortunate because it leaves many homileticians creating a false dichotomy between preaching passionately and preaching exegetically. A strong emphasis on *logos*, however, does not necessitate the neglect of *pathos* in sermon preparation or sermon delivery. In fact, unlocking the richness of a text's *logos* requires wrestling with the emotive structures that reveal its *pathos* as well. Biblical preaching demands that neither is neglected. Gregory Hollifield emphasizes this point:

> The Bible pulsates with emotion. Few sermons that attempt to expound a biblical text ever seem to lay a finger on its pulse. Often the emotions provoked by the typical sermon, whether topical, textual, or expository, fail to grow out of the text. The preacher who desires to exegete the Scriptures accurately and attractively can do so by giving greater attention to the emotional dimension. The inspired text itself can establish the parameters for the emotional content and delivery of the sermon, meaning that the emotions of the sermon are informed by careful exegesis.[7]

Because the *pathos* of Scripture is often discernable exegetically, ignoring emotional intent is just as manipulative as ignoring *logos*. Bryan Chapell concurs:

---

5. T. Mattingly, quoted in G. K. Hollifield, "Expository Preaching that Touches the Heart," *Preaching* 19 (2004): 18.
6. L. L. Hogan and R. Reid, *Connecting with the Congregation: Rhetoric and the Art of Preaching* (Nashville: Abingdon, 1999), 41–42.
7. Hollifield, "Expository Preaching that Touches the Heart," 18.

Our manner should reflect Scripture's content. Because we convey meaning not merely by what we say but also by how we speak, accurate exposition requires us to reflect a text's tone as well as define its terms. Sometimes this requires a voice reminiscent of the thunder on Sinai and other times the still small voice at Horeb.[8]

Thus, exegeting the emotion of Scripture requires careful attention. God not only inspired the words of Scripture, but He also inspired the presentation and the passion of those words. Proper interpretation of a text's emotive intent is necessary for correct understanding of a its meaning. Grant Osborne correctly emphasizes the need for emotional exegesis by stating,

> We must also recognize the important place of emotive or expressive speech in the Bible. Certainly the emotional feeling with an epistle is an important aspect of its total meaning. In fact, it could be argued that the true meaning is lost without the portrayal of the emotions to guide the interpreter. There is no depth without the personal element, no grasp or feel for a passage without the underlying tone. This is especially essential for the preacher, who wants to lead first himself and then the congregation into the intensity of the text, to awaken those slumbering passions for God and his will that were so essential to early Christian experience but often have been set aside by the pressures of modern life.[9]

Osborne further explains that the interpreter "must perform a paradigmatic and syntagmatic study of emotional coloring."[10] In other words, measuring the biblical author's use of words on a scale of intensity will aid correct communication.

The point here is simply that Bible preachers must commit to study and proclaim faithfully the *pathos* and *logos* of Scripture. No dichotomy exists between these two elements

---

8. B. Chapell, *Christ-Centered Preaching: Redeeming the Expository Sermon* (Grand Rapids: Baker, 1994), 93.
9. G. Osborne, *The Hermeneutical Spiral* (Downers Grove: InterVarsity, 1991), 99.
10. Ibid., 100.

because each sheds light on the other. Accurately communicating Scripture requires emotion in the pulpit. We must appreciate the proper use of *pathos* as the fullest expression of solid exegesis and biblical content rather than a substitute for it. The key, however, is yielding to the right emotion as determined by the text instead of the preacher. Jeremiah 20:9 reads, "Then I said, 'I will not make mention of Him, nor speak anymore in His name.' But His word was in my heart like a burning fire shut up in my bones; I was weary of holding it back, and I could not." Notice that the Word of God drives the emotion of the prophet as he proclaims. The *pathos* of Scripture will magnify its content rather than distort it. The divine Author will naturally empower preaching that illuminates a biblical text according to its original inspiration.

A SURPRISING OBSERVATION

Unfortunately, many pulpits not only lack expository preaching, but they also neglect the Holy Spirit's empowerment even when exposition is taking place. "'Exposition' so-called can be a cold-blooded, lifeless affair. It is possible for a preacher to follow the expository method and never preach in the power of the Holy Spirit."[11] Most contemporary preaching models place little emphasis on both the inspiration and the empowerment of the Holy Spirit during sermon preparation and delivery. Consequently, powerless sermons produce ministries that bear little fruit for the kingdom. Rhetorical skill, although not inherently bad, is no substitute for the supernatural power of God. Arturo Azurdia describes the current dilemma: "I believe the greatest impediment to the advancement of the gospel in our time is the attempt of the church of Jesus Christ to do the work

---

11. R. K. Hughes, "Preaching God's Word to the Church Today," in *The Coming Evangelical Crisis* (Wheaton, IL: Crossway, 1995), 67.

of God apart from the truth and power of the Spirit of God."[12] One reason for this lack of power, though many others exist, is the absence of *pathos* in preaching that coincides with the original passion of the Holy Spirit. The proclaimer of God's Word is most persuasive when he encourages the Holy Spirit to speak as He originally moved the biblical authors to write.[13] One cannot experience the power of the Holy Spirit in preaching apart from the Word's proclamation, nor can powerful proclamation of the Word take place apart from the Holy Spirit. From beginning to end, the assignment to preach the Word requires guidance from the Holy Spirit, both in preparation and delivery. Rather than succumb to the transparent meaning and emotion within, the preacher must honor the transcendent *logos* and *pathos* that is without. This understanding requires a dramatic paradigm shift.

Ideally, with regard to *logos* and *pathos*, the goal of the preacher is to reflect the content and emotion of the Scriptures within his own life. When impossible, at the very least the preacher must separate himself from the message in order to proclaim its *logos* and *pathos* despite his inconsistency. The result is persuasive preaching empowered by the Holy Spirit.

Take, for example, the unfortunate possibility that Pastor X has a disagreement with his wife on the way to church. Visibly frustrated and perturbed, he suddenly realizes that today's sermon is about the love of God being revealed in the life of Christians. At that moment, he is hateful and negative, both of which contradict the love of God. Yet in a few moments he will stand to preach 1 John 4:7–9: "Beloved, let us love one another, for love is of God; and everyone who loves is born of God and knows God. He who does not love does not know God, for God is

---

12. A. Azurdia, *Spirit-Empowered Preaching* (Ross-shire, Great Britain: Mentor, 1998), 29.

13. For a helpful discussion on the role of the Holy Spirit in preaching, see G. Heisler, *Spirit-Led Preaching: The Holy Spirit's Role in Sermon Preparation and Delivery* (Nashville: Broadman & Holman, 2007).

love. In this the love of God was manifested toward us, that God has sent His only begotten Son into the world, that we might live through Him." Here, the fundamental crossroads between persuasion and manipulation opens up. Those with a high view of Scripture would never dream of changing the *logos* of the message simply because of the misfortunate timing of a marital disagreement. However, the call for authenticity might lead some to conclude that communicating the emotion of love would be manipulative and hypocritical because these emotions are at that moment inconsistent with the preacher's current *pathos*.

If dismissing the meaning of a text is not permissible, dismissing the emotion of the same text is equally unacceptable. If the preacher has no right to impose his own meaning on a text, neither should he impose his own emotion on the same text. Dismissing the intention of the Holy Spirit is reckless and violating with regard to either *logos* or *pathos*. Thus, bending the emotions of a biblical text to match the emotions of the preacher is a form of manipulation. The most persuasive preacher will alter his emotions when necessary in order to avoid manipulating the *pathos* of a biblical text. Hollifield concurs:

> A rudimentary knowledge of the dynamics of pathos can serve the preacher who wishes to bring his exposition of the Scriptures to life. Recovering the mood of the text, regulating his own emotions by submitting to those of the text, and recreating those emotions within the listening audience will influence what he says, how he says it, and how it is received. The resulting difference might be compared to listening to a song in "surround-sound stereo" rather than from a static-filled transistor radio.[14]

A high view of Scripture demands that the text, rather than the preacher, be the primary focus of any sermon. Although transparency is important, exegetical faithfulness ranks more

---

14. Hollifield, "Expository Preaching that Touches the Heart," 23.

importantly. Every preacher must decide between communicating what he feels emotionally and what the text communicates emotionally if any inconsistency abides between the two. The ramifications of this premise are immense. Pursuing accurate portrayal of Scriptural *pathos* with the same intentionality of communicating the Bible's *logos* requires the submission of the heart as well as the mind. Just as the preacher is not the source for the cognitive message of a sermon, neither is he the standard for the emotional substance of the message. Consequently, yielding to the authorial intent of Scripture necessitates that preachers plan to reveal the *logos* and *pathos* of every text regardless of beliefs or feelings that may be contrary to it. Stated simply, being transparent in the pulpit can be manipulative if such openness hides or contradicts the *pathos* of the biblical author. Certain circumstances will require faithful preachers to ignore their personal disposition for the sake of interpretive fidelity.

DISCOVERING *PATHOS*

Conceding the need for passionate preaching that reflects the general mood of a biblical text necessitates questions about discovering *pathos*. Illuminating the *logos* of a passage is challenging, despite the sound hermeneutical steps that are available, but discerning *pathos* can be even more difficult. Admittedly, the feelings of every text do not surface easily, if at all. In such cases, preachers must be careful not to ignore and render powerless the possible interpretations of *pathos*. Wise communicators will lay their fingers on the emotional pulse of their text in order to grasp fully the complete meaning of its *logos*.

Hollifield cites text selection, grammatical construction, historical context, literary genre, and character development as triggers that unmask the emotive intent of a passage.[15] The issue

---

15. Ibid., 19–20.

of text selection will naturally be a reflection of one's approach to preaching. A conviction that "all Scripture . . . is profitable for doctrine, for reproof, for correction, and for instruction in righteousness" (2 Tim 3:16) manifests a practice demonstrating that every text has value. In other words, to say that all Scripture is inspired but fail to preach difficult texts because the *pathos* is not apparent is contradictory. Many preachers profess their belief in the inspiration of the Bible while they practice the insufficiency of it. Hershael York laments, "By skipping over books or passages that are difficult or seem dated, [preachers] plant the suggestion in the minds of their churches that the Bible is a buffet from which one may pick and choose what suits him or her."[16] Varying levels of emotional correlation will require more or less inducement by the preacher, but this should not discourage efforts to preach the whole counsel of God.

Grammatical construction will also assist the process of uncovering the emotive language in a text. Looking for energized words that are pregnant with emotion provides direction for pinpointing what will become the focal *pathos* of sermon delivery. Certain passages of Scripture present emotional language that is easily detectable. In Rom 1:18–32 the apostle Paul straightforwardly writes about the anger of the Lord against those who profess to be wise and become fools. In addition to explicitly stating that "the wrath of God is revealed from heaven against all ungodliness and unrighteousness of men, who suppress the truth in unrighteousness" (v. 18), Paul also uses phrases like "gave them up," "lusts of their hearts" (v. 24), "dishonor their bodies" (v. 24), and "exchanged the truth" (v. 25). Sensing Paul's personal *pathos* is also relatively easy when reading words and phrases that describe the sins of humanity. They include "vile" (v. 26), "against nature" (v. 26), "leaving the natural use" (v. 27), "burned in their lust" (v. 27), and "shameful"

---

16. H. York and B. Decker, *Preaching with Bold Assurance* (Broadman & Holman, 2003), 20.

(v. 27). Romans 1:29–32 concludes the passage with descriptive language of intense anger and righteous indignation against those who deny the Creator,

> being filled with all unrighteousness, sexual immorality, wickedness, covetousness, maliciousness; full of envy, murder, strife, deceit, evil-mindedness; *they are* whisperers, backbiters, haters of God, violent, proud, boasters, inventors of evil things, disobedient to parents, undiscerning, untrustworthy, unloving, unforgiving, unmerciful; who, knowing the righteous judgment of God, that those who practice such things are deserving of death, not only do the same but also approve of those who practice them.

To preach this passage without a sense of urgency, lament, and even righteous anger will fall short of Paul's tone and emphasis. Clearly offended by humanity's transgressions against God's holiness, the apostle becomes a model of holy indignation and frustration for the preacher.

Understanding the historical context of a text releases the preacher to probe the possible feelings of a given circumstance. This technique is extremely helpful when the *pathos* of a passage does not appear on its grammatical sleeves. In an effort to clarify, Stephen Olford points to 1 Kgs 11:1–13 as a needed example that reveals the value of historical context:

> This narrative passage clearly presents the turning of King Solomon's heart after other gods. You see the initial causes (vv. 1–4), the developing condition (vv. 5–8), and the devastating consequences of King Solomon's "heart problem," a heart problem that is contrasted with his father David's faithfulness (vv. 9–13). Now, we've already moved into homiletical expression, but that's just to summarize the text. What we seek to illustrate here is the importance of the setting or context. This passage occurs at a significant point in 1 and 2 Kings. Chapters 1–10 of 1 Kings describes a king that is glorious, wise, healthy, and powerful. This is a man who has

experienced abundant privileges and blessings, even having "the Lord God of Israel" appear to him twice (v. 9). The
temple has been built and dedicated. The kingdom is strong
and expanding. After this text, things start to fall apart. God
raises adversaries against Solomon (11:14, 23). Jeroboam is
introduced, and the rebellion of Israel takes place. When one
views a summary statement such as 2 Kings 17:5–23 (21–23),
one can see that the movement towards tragedy began in
the wake of Solomon's sins and God's response. Jeroboam
is attributed with driving Israel "from following the Lord"
(2 Kings 17:21), and his rise was part of the consequences
of Solomon's sin. So the context reveals the seriousness of
Solomon's sin, both in the light of the glorious period of time
in chapters 1–10, and the development from 11:14 to the end
of 2 Kings.[17]

Admittedly, the narrative of 1 Kgs 11:1–13 is void of explicit
emotive content (aside from the clear statement of God's anger
in v. 9). The historical context, as well as the literary context,
reveals a sense of anger, regret, and disappointment, all of
which reinforce the seriousness of sin that is evident in the passage. Aside from the historical setting, both before and after
1 Kgs 11:1–13, discerning the emotional emphasis of these
verses would be difficult. By way of caution, relying on the
historical context to interpret the *pathos* of a passage should
always reinforce rather than detract from the obvious grammatical meaning present within the text.

Considering literary genre is also essential for correctly deci-
phering the emotive intention of a biblical text. Elliott Johnson
defines literary criticism as "the study and evaluation of imaginative writings describing the structure of different genres,
considering themes, mood, tone, plot motifs, image patterns,
vocabulary, conventions, etc."[18] Although understanding genre

---

17. S. F. Olford and D. L. Olford, *Anointed Expository Preaching* (Nashville: Broadman & Holman, 1998), 113–14.
18. E. Johnson, *Expository Hermeneutics* (Grand Rapids: Zondervan, 1990), 309.

as a means of classification is important, the preachers should also appreciate it as an invaluable tool of hermeneutics as well. Osborne argues that "genre plays a positive role as a hermeneutical device for determining the *sensus literalis* or intended meaning of the text. . . . It is an epistemological tool for unlocking meaning in individual texts."[19] Consequently, misunderstanding the genre of a text can be devastating. Because distinctive rules within each biblical genre govern our presuppositions about a given passage, failing to recognize the parameters of form can skew our perception of the author's *pathos*. Greidanus contends that "a form sets our expectations and guides the questions we ask."[20] E. D. Hirsch concurs: "An interpreter's preliminary generic conception of a text is constitutive of everything that he subsequently understands, and this remains the case unless and until that generic conception is altered."[21]

This understanding helps the preacher interpret a text correctly and proclaim it effectively, both logically and emotionally, according to the intention and design of the original author. It also enables the preacher to consider the best method of presentation that will evoke the original *pathos* of the passage. Elizabeth Achtemeier says, "Because the story of God's salvation of humankind is presented to us through the heart-stirring genres of the Bible, it therefore follows that if we are to proclaim that story, we should do so in words and forms that will produce the same telling effects."[22]

Examples of genre's importance abound. For example, handling a narrative text has different rules of interpretation than a poetic text. York is helpful:

---

19. G. R. Osborne, "Genre Criticism—Sensus Literalis," *TJ* 4 (1983): 24.
20. S. Greidanus, *The Modern Preacher and the Ancient Text* (Grand Rapids: Eerdmans, 1988), 17.
21. E. D. Hirsch, *Validity and Interpretation* (New Haven, CT: Yale University, 1967), 74.
22. E. Achtemeier, *Creative Preaching: Finding the Words* (Nashville: Abingdon, 1980), 46.

John 21 records the story of Jesus' encounter with Peter, relating the details of Jesus' appearance to him and the other disciples in Galilee. Jesus appeared to the hapless fishermen and suggested they cast their empty nets on the other side of the boat. Following this suggestion, verse 11 records that they caught 153 large fish. Now here is the question: *how many large fish did they really catch?* . . . While they may or may not have caught others that they did not number, the count of *large* fish is precise: 153. . . . The number occurs in a *story*—a narrative text that nowhere indicates it should be taken figuratively, allegorically, or as myth. . . . We should accept, then, that their nets were filled with 153 large fish, not 152 or 154. The text is clear.

But what about poetry? Would we apply the same standards of interpretation to a poetic statement like Psalm 50:9–10 in which God speaks and says, "I have no need of a bull from your stall or of goats from your pens, for every animal of the forest is mine, and *the cattle on a thousand hills*" [emphasis added]? When the psalmist writes these words as though spoken by the Lord, are we to conclude that God owns the cattle on *exactly* 1,000 hills—not 999 or 1,001? Of course not. We understand intuitively and from the text itself that the real meaning of the verse is that God owns *everything*. Our point, then, is that the *form of writing* affects our understanding of its meaning.[23]

A final avenue for emotional insight is character development. Considering the holistic nature of a biblical character's mind, will, and emotions unlocks the hidden experiences of their *pathos*. Hollifield urges, "When the inspired writer gives details to indicate the emotional states of a character, the preacher should take advantage. These details may well be the way that the writer chose to lead his audience to identify with the character."[24] Henry Mitchell offers a practical illustration:

Take special care to preselect the lesson to be taught, and to identify the character who learns it. Then be sure so to present

---

23. York and Decker, *Preaching with Bold Assurance*, 59–60.
24. Hollifield, "Expository Preaching that Touches the Heart," 20.

that person that the audience will be drawn to identify with her or him and so experience its way through that saving truth. As stated, the narrative must be entertaining, but this high art has reason to be performed as gospel only if the artist has some clear notion of how the Holy Spirit might use it to generate growth in the hearers. They must be moved from point A to point B along a lived path whose ultimate end and model is Jesus Christ. For instance, the tale of Jacob wrestling with God is a gold mine for teaching folks who have unresolved interpersonal conflicts and guilt. But they will presume that the message is given to "somebody else" unless Jacob is so introduced that they like him and identify with him, so as to live out his lesson and go through his change from cheater to chosen vessel.[25]

Notice the emphasis on authorial intent in Mitchell's example as he aspires that hearers learn the "lesson" of Jacob. The key to utilizing the emotive tool of character development is submission to the biblical author's intention for each character. In other words, a failure to consider whether the author intended for a character to be the focus of audience identification violates sound hermeneutical principles. Greidanus, seeking to avoid this error, contends that "problems can be solved, however, by going back to the original relevance of the passage: How did the original hearers understand the passage? Did the author intend his hearers to identify with a certain character?"[26] He concludes, "By going back to the passage's original relevance, one both honors the author's intention and acquires the needed control for responsible understanding and transmission."[27]

Considering the primary emotional emphasis of a passage is largely an Aristotelian contribution. Hollifield remarks, "Generally, Aristotle's insights on the role of *pathos* in oratory help the preacher by reminding him that the judgments of

---

25. H. H. Mitchell, "Preaching on the Patriarchs," in *Biblical Preaching*, ed. J. W. Cox (Philadelphia: Westminster, 1983), 41.
26. Greidanus, *The Modern Preacher and the Ancient Text*, 179.
27. Ibid.

people are not entirely rational by nature. Emotions play a role in their formation."[28] Thus, the goal of the aforementioned evaluative measures is to discover the primary emotional catalyst upon which the sermon builds. Although minor moods will surface in most passages, the preacher's general concern should express and evoke the major mood he identifies in a text.

DEFENDING *PATHOS*

Understanding the Bible's emotive design underscores the importance of good communication skills. David Hesselgrave contends, "It seems we cannot do anything without communicating something. To stand is to stand somewhere. And both the 'standing' and the 'somewhere' communicate."[29] Therefore, intentional study of *pathos* communication proves to be of great value to the preacher. Corbett and Connors affirm,

> Making a conscious study of the emotions and being aware that we are appealing to someone's emotions will not necessarily make us more adept at this kind of appeal. But conscious knowledge of any art makes it more likely that we will practice the art skillfully. The person who learned to play the piano by ear will not be hurt by studying music; but that person might very well be helped to play better.[30]

Affirming the need to plan facial expression, gestures, body language, and vocal variety begs a number of questions concerning just how far ministers of the gospel should go to capture the true meaning of Scripture. The goal of every communication skill is to make certain that a human messenger does not violate or diminish the *logos* of a biblical text. This being the

---

28. Hollifield, "Expository Preaching that Touches the Heart," 20.
29. D. Hesselgrave, *Communicating Christ Cross-Culturally*, 2nd ed. (Grand Rapids: Zondervan, 1991), 431.
30. E. P. J. Corbett and R. J. Connors, *Classical Rhetoric for the Modern Student*, 4th ed. (New York: Oxford University, 1999), 84.

case, one is equally wise to consider the necessary means to ensure the accurate portrayal of Scripture's *pathos*. If one goal of the preacher is to ascertain that an audience believes what a text teaches, a complementary ambition will also seek to help hearers feel the emotion of Scripture as well. Even this, however, has not been assumed without resistance.

Robert Ferguson illustrates a general suspicion about eliciting emotion:

> Manipulation can occur whenever the preacher uses language and/or stories designed to evoke an emotive response. Please do not misunderstand me: emotions are created by God and are involved in our religious faith commitment. However, to specifically design sermons to pull emotional strings so that "decisions" are made is ungodly, unbiblical, and unChristlike.[31]

Granted, Ferguson does not forbid the use of emotion in preaching. His conclusion, however, that pulling emotional strings is unbiblical simply does not align with Scripture.

When Nathan proposed a hypothetical scenario before issuing the indictment "Thou art the man!" to an unsuspecting King David, he was intentionally pulling emotional strings. When Paul defends his apostleship in 2 Corinthians 11 and 12, sarcasm sprinkles his disappointment in order to evoke embarrassment and regret within the Corinthians. First Thessalonians 2:7–12 elicits endearment as Paul reminds the infant church of the motherly love and the fatherly admonishment he shared with them. These are passages with intense emotion designed to change belief and behavior.

Integrity does not require a refusal to pull the strings of *pathos* evident in these verses. To the contrary, just the opposite is true. A failure to elaborate on and evoke the same emotion from a contemporary audience is a subtle but significant form

---

31. R. U. Ferguson Jr., "Motivation or Manipulation in the Pulpit," *Preaching* 6 (May–June 1991): 11.

of manipulation. Admittedly, a preacher is not free to decide for himself the emotions he should elicit, but neither is he free to determine the emotions he will ignore. Because the focus of sermon delivery is on accurate communication of both the message and the intensity of a biblical passage through a human messenger, the ability to use persuasive communication strategies is essential.

Just how much planning is permissible though? Is it okay to plan to be angry? What if crying illuminates the meaning of the text? Should a preacher really plan to cry? If laughing can accurately communicate the joy of a text, should the preacher plan to do so? These are difficult questions because intrinsically those concerned about their integrity resound, "No!" However, if the ultimate goal is to correctly communicate a *pathos* that correlates with the biblical text, why should the answer be no? Most consider submitting to the *logos* of Scripture both permissible and necessary, even when that requires the altering of personal views and beliefs. If Scripture is the true authority, why is submission to its *pathos* any different? Granted, being so captured by the *pathos* of a biblical passage that you, the messenger, exude the correlating emotion is without question the ideal scenario. Those who preach regularly, however, know that conditions for text-driven proclamation are not always textbook. Thus, preaching with emotions that transcend personal emotions is sometimes necessary in order to communicate biblical truth comprehensively. Walter Kaiser explains,

> We must have the Holy Spirit incite us to declare with boldness the truth we have discovered in the Word of God. From the beginning of the sermon to its end, the all-engrossing force of the text and the God who speaks through that text must dominate our whole being. With the burning power of that truth on our heart and lips, every thought, emotion, and act of the will must be so captured by that truth that it springs forth with excitement, joy, sincerity, and reality as an evident token that God's Spirit is in that word. Away with the mediocre, lifeless, boring, and lackluster orations offered as pitiful

substitutes for the powerful Word of the living Lord. If that Word from God does not thrill the proclaimer and fill the servant who delivers it with an intense desire to glorify God and do his will, how shall we ever expect it to have any greater effect on our hearers?[32]

Although it goes without saying that the best opportunities unfold when the preacher and the passage he proclaims resonate in emotional harmony together, honesty demands consideration of what to do when such a correlation is absent from the preaching situation. Prerequisite to this question is another. Namely, does God care that much about emotion? After preaching in Nineveh to pagans that he hated, the prophet Jonah sulked outside the city. The effect of God's word had already taken hold, but Jonah refused to celebrate it. Even though Jonah proclaimed exactly what God instructed him, God is obviously not satisfied. Jonah 4:4 indicates that *pathos* does matter: "Then the LORD said, 'Is it right for you to be angry?'"

It does seem apparent that at times it will be necessary to work up emotions in order to communicate accurately a text of Scripture. Jay Adams observes the need:

> To experience an event in preaching is to enter into that event so fully that the emotions appropriate to that event are felt, just as if one were actually going through it. When a preacher says what he relates in such a way that he stimulates one or more of the five senses, thus triggering emotion, then the listener may be said to "experience" the event. In that way, the event will become "real" to him, which means it has become concretized (or personalized), memorable, and, in the fullest sense of the word, understandable.[33]

To avoid manipulation in this regard requires careful attention to the motive behind every emotion that does not transparently

---

32. W. C. Kaiser Jr., *Toward an Exegetical Theology* (Grand Rapids: Baker, 1981), 239.
33. J. Adams, *Preaching with Purpose* (Grand Rapids: Baker, 1982), 86.

reflect the *pathos* of the preacher. Manufactured *pathos* that does not glorify God and benefit the listener constitutes unethical means. Being constrained to the *pathos* of Scripture prohibits outlandish emotional appeals that seek the good of the individual addressed but fail to propagate the glory of God due to inconsistency with the biblical text. Efforts to exalt self above Jesus Christ are a form of manipulation because of its attempt to diminish God's glory. The apostle Paul disdained drawing attention to his rhetorical skills in 1 Cor 2:1–5. Preachers must be careful, when seeking to evangelize others through preaching, not to be guilty of flashy techniques or discourses that distract from the message of salvation. When individuals make conclusions about a preacher's eloquence rather than the glory of God in a text, they fail to see the power of the gospel.

Likewise, by its very nature, biblical *pathos* will always seek the good of the listener and should, therefore, be emulated. Preachers are not free to distort the biblical text just to "get" people saved. Looking upon a person as just another notch on one's belt is unacceptable. This form of manipulation merely uses people as part of a numbers game in order to make the preacher appear to be successful. Doing so leads a noble desire to persuade down the path of ministerial abuse. Evangelism should always be honest and biblically transparent both in content and presentation. Stripping verses of Scripture out of context in order to evangelize is not biblical persuasion, nor is it helpful to one's audience.

Arguing for the need to preach with biblical *pathos* does not, however, negate the importance of exercising caution when applying these principles. Ideally, a preacher's personal *pathos* will correspond to the emotive intention of the biblical passage he preaches. Though this is not always reality, it should be the preacher's goal nonetheless. Continually preaching with transcendent emotions that are foreign to personal experience will produce powerless sermons. Though circumstances will occasionally require the adjustment of personal *pathos*, the difficulty of doing so should not be underestimated. Although it is true that the Bible should determine and drive the emotion of every sermon, it remains equally true that the Scripture should also alter the preacher's disposition. Stated differently, the Bible will continually challenge preachers toward authenticity as it confronts and recreates their current feelings and emotions. P. T. Forsyth was correct in saying, "The Bible is the supreme preacher to the preacher."[34] A habitual failure to exhibit naturally the sincere emotions of Scripture reveals a lack of spiritual maturity that preaching requires. An awareness of the need to alter personal disposition at times is not a license to preach regularly with *pathos* that does not resonate personally. The consistent, overall pattern of ministry is to preach in harmony with both the emotional and logical intentions of Scripture.

DELIVERING *PATHOS*

The discussion of sermon delivery in light of biblical *pathos* reminds us that what the preacher says and how he says it are important. Using various mechanics of good communication allows the preacher to honor not only the *logos* of a text but also its *pathos*. Vocal rate, volume, and pitch are worthy of our attention because each communicates emotion. Visible gestures with the face, hands, and body also reinforce the desired emotion of a message.

Measuring one's rate of speech is as simple as dividing the number of spoken words by the minutes elapsed during delivery. Acceptable rates vary between 120 and 160 words per minute. Increasing delivery speed communicates a sense of excitement or celebration, whereas a decreased rate conveys a more serious, somber tone along with emphasis. The key is variety and avoiding unnecessary extremes. Speaking too quickly suggests nervousness and lack of ease, whereas moving too slowly is a strain to the listener's ear.

---

34. P. T. Forsyth, *Positive Preaching and the Modern Mind* (Grand Rapids: Eerdmans, 1964), 11.

Along these same lines, volume variety enables the preacher to capture the *pathos* of a biblical text in a discernable way. The preacher should govern the volume of his voice by the content of his message. Changing decibel range draws attention to both the importance and the mood of key points in a sermon. Without a variety in sound level, emphasis by means of volume will be missed. Loudness communicates moods of anger, celebration, rebuke, praise, joy, and such. In contrast, softness portrays reflection, regret, peacefulness, amazement, or disbelief. Depending upon the emotive structures of a biblical text, both the faint whisper and the loud exclamation can be extremely effective and reflective in representing the original author's mood.

Although similar to vocal volume, pitch is the movement of the voice up and down the scale in different registers with various inflections. Utilizing pitch allows the preacher to express sarcasm, conviction, doubt, or questions. Rising inflections suggest uncertainty or incompleteness, whereas downward inflections indicate certainty, completeness, and emphasis. In the same way, flat inflections communicate frustration or disappointment. Gradually changing one's pitch is a powerful way to reflect calmness, repose, contemplation, and command over material. Likewise, abrupt changes reveal intensity and excitement. These emotional triggers are powerful means to present the Bible's *pathos*.

Outside of communicating with the voice, the preacher's body is also a tool for reflecting the emotive intention of the Scripture. Ignoring nonverbal indicators will undermine the best efforts to communicate the passion and feelings of passage. For example, if the voice captures the *pathos* of a text, but the preacher's facial expressions do not correspond with his words, confusion will triumph over clarity. Smiling during an exposition on the judgment of God diminishes the seriousness of the message, just like sarcasm will veil the jubilation of John 3:16. Gestures with the hands will create distance between the messenger and congregation or invite them in. Good posture conveys strength just as much as slouching conjures an image of weakness. Body movement indicates confidence and purpose, whereas stiffness implies nervousness or boredom. Because the text is the primary criteria for determining what emotions one will communicate, one must be sure that the expressions visible to the audience reinforce the content and mood of the message. The sermon does not begin when the preacher opens his mouth but as soon as he steps on the platform.

CONCLUSION

Preaching God's Word remains one of the greatest privileges outside of knowing Christ personally. Though transparency in the pulpit is desirable, it is not the distinguishing factor that ensures persuasion rather than manipulation. The most powerful preaching will take place when there is a correlation between the emotive intention of the biblical author and the contemporary preacher. The ultimate goal must be to honor the true design of the text, despite contradicting circumstances. Stephen Olford was correct to insist, "True preaching is an incarnational mystery. . . . You cannot detach the messenger from his message if preaching is going to be redemptive, and therefore, life changing."[35] With this in mind, all who are committed to the message of Scripture must renew their commitment to the means of Scripture when it comes to preaching. Because the Bible is persuasive, preachers should be persuasive. Because biblical *pathos* runs like an emotive thread throughout the Scripture, understanding emotional persuasion as a legitimate homiletical means will separate good delivery from great delivery.

---

35. Olford and Olford, *Anointed Expository Preaching*, 233–34.

11

APPLYING A TEXT-DRIVEN SERMON

Daniel L. Akin

In Jas 1:22, the half brother of Jesus charges his readers, "But be doers of the word and not hearers only, deceiving yourselves." He then proceeds to answer the all important "why question" in v. 25, "a doer who acts—this person will be blessed in what he does."

In the Bible, belief and behavior are never separated. What we believe will determine how we live. The famous North Carolina evangelist Vance Havner was fond of saying, "What you live is what you really believe; everything else is just so much religious talk."

Text-driven preaching that is faithful to Scripture not only will expound the text but also will, of biblical and theological necessity, apply the text. Unfortunately, this is an area of some homiletical confusion, and the church has suffered greatly as a result. On the one hand, topical and felt needs preaching gives significant attention to application, but it fails to expound the text and thus provide the necessary biblical and theological grounding for application. On the other hand, some expositors of the Bible offer only a running commentary on the text, neglecting to show the relevance of the text for the eagerly listening audience who are desperate for a word from God that will (1) educate the mind, (2) motivate the heart, and (3) activate the will. Howard Hendricks says, "Application is the most neglected yet the most needed stage in the process. Too much Bible study begins and ends in the wrong place: It begins with interpretation, and it also ends there."[1] He then shocks our hermeneutical and homiletical sensibilities with a startling image: "Observation plus interpretation without application equals abortion. That is, every time you observe and interpret but fail to apply, you perform an abortion on the Scripture in terms of their purpose. The Bible was not written to satisfy your curiosity, it was written to transform your life."[2] Walt Kaiser also recognizes the fact that application can be banished to the sidelines, and painfully he lays the blame at the feet of us who have the assignment of training preachers. He writes,

> A gap of crisis proportions exists between the steps generally outlined in most seminary or Biblical training classes in exegesis and the hard realities most pastors face every week as they prepare their sermons. Nowhere in the total curriculum of theological studies has the student been more deserted and left to his own devices than in bridging the yawning chasm between understanding the content of Scripture as it was given in the past and proclaiming it with such relevance in the present as to produce faith, life, and bona fide works. Both ends of this bridge have at various times received detailed and even exhaustive treatments: (1) the historical, grammatical, cultural, and critical analysis of the text forms one end of

---

1. H. Hendricks and W. Hendricks, *Living By the Book* (Chicago: Moody, 1991, 2007), 289. These authors provide a simple three-step process for faithful Bible study. (1) Observation: What do I see? (2) Interpretation: What does it mean? (3) Application: How does it work?
2. Ibid., 290.

the spectrum; and (2) the practical, devotional, homiletical, and pastoral theology (along with various techniques of delivery, organization, and persuasion) reflected in collections of sermonic outlines for all occasions forms the other. But who has mapped out the route between these two points?[3]

In this chapter the goal is to provide such a map that crosses the bridge from exposition to application and to demonstrate its essential nature in a healthy and holistic homiletical strategy. The place to begin is with a good, solid definition and description of what we are after.

WHAT IS TEXT-DRIVEN APPLICATION?

When I taught at Southern Seminary, I had the joy of supervising an outstanding student of preaching as he pursued his Ph.D. degree. His name is Scott Blue and he serves our Lord as both a teacher and pastor. He is a remarkable individual in that he completed his Ph.D. in record time, receiving the highest possible grades for his work. This accomplishment is further enhanced by the fact he is a quadriplegic. Dr. Blue wrote his dissertation on "Application in the Expository Sermon." He also coauthored a superb article with Hershael York addressing the same theme.[4] Having worked closely with both men, Blue as his Ph.D. supervisor and York as a cherished colleague, and discussing this important issue for many hours, I want to draw on their excellent treatments, especially in terms of a definition and description of application.

Application in text-driven preaching can be defined as "the process whereby the expositor takes a biblical truth of the text

---

3. W. Kaiser, *Toward an Exegetical Theology* (Grand Rapids: Baker, 1981), 18.
4. H. York and S. Blue, "Is Application Necessary in the Expository Sermon?" *SBJT* 3, no. 2 (Summer 1999): 70–84. Blue's dissertation is titled "Application in the Expository Sermon: A Case for Its Necessary Inclusion."

and applies it to the lives of his audience, proclaiming why it is relevant for their lives, and passionately encouraging them to make necessary changes in their lives in a manner congruent with the original intent of the author."[5] To this excellent definition I would add that the application should be God-centered and Christ-focused, fitting into the grand redemptive storyline of the Bible and the pattern of creation, fall, redemption, restoration. Let me unwrap this definition/description.

First, text-driven application is grounded in biblical truth gained through a historical-grammatical-literary-theological analysis of the biblical test. Application, of necessity, flows from our exegesis and exposition. The order is not optional. It is essential. Practical application must find its foundation in biblical exposition.

Second, text-driven application must be based on the author's intended meaning found in the text. Authorial intent determines and dictates application. Because we believe the ultimate author of Scripture is the Holy Spirit of God, we dare not trifle or manipulate the plain sense of Scripture to fit any preconceived agenda with respect to how we want to apply our sermon. This is homiletical malpractice worthy of pastoral disbarment.

Third, text-driven application should demonstrate the relevance and practical nature of biblical truth for the listeners in their present life context. The Bible does not need to be made relevant. It is relevant now and forever as revealed, eternal truth. However, it is the responsibility of the preacher to unfold and make clear the Bible's relevance. I particularly like the way Louis Lotz puts it:

> Good preaching begins in the Bible, but it doesn't stay there. It visits the hospital and the college dorm, the factory and the farm, the kitchen and the office, the bedroom and the classroom. Good preaching invades the world in which people live, the real world of tragedy and triumph, loveliness and

---

5. Ibid., 73–74.

loneliness, broken hearts, broken homes, and amber waves of strain. Good preaching invades the real world, and it talks to real people—the high-school senior who's there because he's dragged there; the housewife who wants a divorce; the grandfather who mourns the irreversibility of time and lives with a frantic sense that almost all the sand in the hourglass has dropped; the farmer who is about to lose his farm and the banker who must take it from him; the teacher who has kept her lesbianism a secret all these years; the businessman for whom money has become a god; the single girl who hates herself because she's fat. Good preaching helps them do business with God.[6]

Fourth, text-driven application must include practical illustrations, examples, and suggestions so that the audience can adopt and model their lives after the biblical truth being taught. The best place to begin, in my judgment, is with biblical examples. The Old Testament in particular contains a reservoir of resources. One should then proceed to the here and now, taking into careful consideration the specific context in which one ministers the word. In this sense there is a cross-cultural contextualization in good preaching that must not be ignored, especially when we find ourselves in an increasingly missiological context, even in America. The brilliant missiologist David Hesselgrave is extremely helpful at this point:

> Contextualization can be defined as the attempt to communicate the message of the person, works, Word and will of God in a way that is faithful to God's revelation, especially as it is put forth in the teachings of the Holy Scripture, and that *is meaningful to respondents in their respective cultural and existential contexts.* Contextualization is both verbal and nonverbal and has to do with the theologizing, Bible translation, *interpretation and application,* incarnational life-style, evangelism, Christian instruction, church planting and growth,

---

6. L. Lotz, "Good Preaching," *RefR* 40 (Autumn 1986): 38.

church organization, worship style—indeed with all those activities involved in carrying out the Great Commission.[7]

Fifth, text-driven application must persuade and exhort listeners to respond in obedient faith to the truths of Holy Scripture. York and Blue state, "Sermon application must persuade listeners that they should conform their lives to the biblical truths presented and encourages them to do so, warning them of the negative consequences of failure in this regard."[8] Jay Adams adds that preachers "make scriptural truths so pertinent to members of their congregations that they not only understand how those truths should effect changes in their lives but also feel obligated and perhaps eager to implement those changes."[9]

WHY IS TEXT-DRIVEN APPLICATION NECESSARY?

Application in preaching helps us answer two important questions based upon the exposition of God's Word: (1) So what? and (2) Now what? In other words, how does the Bible speak to me today and what do I do about it? So important is this component of preaching that the father of modern exposition, John Broadus, said,

> The application in a sermon is not merely an appendage to the discussion or a subordinate part of it, but is the main thing to be done. Spurgeon says, "Where the application begins, there the sermon begins." . . . Daniel Webster once said, and repeated it with emphasis, "When a man preaches to me, I

---

7. D. Hesselgrave, "Contextualization That Is Authentic and Relevant," *International Journal of Frontier Missions* 12 (July–August, 1995): 115, emphasis mine. Also writing in a missiological context, Stan Guthrie adds, "The message must be tailored or contextualized in such a way as to remain faithful to the biblical text while understandable in and relevant to the receptor's context." S. Guthrie, *Missions in the Third Millennium: 21 Key Trends for the 21st Century*, rev. and expanded ed. (Waynesboro, GA: Paternoster, 2000), 129.
8. York and Blue, "Is Application Necessary in the Expository Sermon?" 73.
9. J. Adams, *Truth Applied: Application in Preaching* (Grand Rapids: Ministry Resources Library, 1990), 17.

want him to make it a personal matter, a personal matter, a personal matter!" And it is our solemn duty thus to address all men, whether they wish it or not.[10]

Text-driven application is necessary because it requires a decision on the part of the listener. Further, if done well, it provides a specific action plan that allows the Spirit of God to take biblical truth and make it a part of who we are and are becoming in Christ (Rom 8:28–29).

Text-driven application is necessary then for at least five reasons.

First, it is one of the main purposes for God's revelation. God wants us to know Him, love Him, and obey Him. The act of proclaiming biblical truth is incomplete without the call to obey.

Second, it brings balance to the information element in preaching. Knowing precedes doing, but knowing must lead to doing, or biblical exposition will come up short of its intended goal.

Third, it focuses Scripture on the genuine needs of the congregation. Sin brings separation, sorrow, pain, and death. Ours is a hurting world. Application speaks to those needs and provides the healing balm of divine truth.

Fourth, it makes biblical principles specific to real life situations. Addressing the whole person with the whole truth of Scripture is what good application does.

Fifth, it provides the necessary bridge between the world of the Bible and the world in which we live. Application shows us that our problems ultimately are the same as those of the ancients. Sin is our problem and Christ is the answer. Some things remain the same across the centuries.

My friend and colleague Wayne McDill, professor of preaching at Southeastern Baptist Theological Seminary, provides helpful insight concerning the "right use" and necessity of text-driven application. He writes,

---

10. As quoted in J. Broadus, *A Treatise on the Preparation and Delivery of Sermons* (New York: A. C. Armstrong and Son, 1894), 230.

Application is more than just taking the sermon truth and attacking the congregation with it. Application presents the implications of biblical truth for the contemporary audience. It is a call for action, for putting the principles of Scripture to work in our lives. It deals with attitudes, behavior, speech, lifestyle, and personal identity. It appeals to conscience, to values, to conviction, to commitment to Christ.[11]

The great Reformation theologian John Calvin also saw the essential and necessary nature of text-driven application. He said it would impact just how and what we teach to the congregation in our charge and under our watchcare:

What advantage would there be if we were to stay here a day and I were to expound half a book without considering you or your profit and edification? . . . We must take into consideration those persons to whom the teaching is addressed. . . . For this reason let us note well that they who have this charge to teach, when they speak to a people, are to decide which teaching will be good and profitable so that they will be able to disseminate it faithfully and with discretion to the usefulness of everyone individually.[12]

We would do well to heed his admonition.

HOW DO WE DO TEXT-DRIVEN APPLICATION?

Timothy Warren is most certainly correct: "[Preaching] is not complete until God's people think and act differently for having heard the Word expounded."[13] Text-driven preaching has as its

---

11. W. McDill, *The 12 Essential Skills for Great Preaching* (Nashville: B&H, 1994), 187.
12. Quoted in P. Adam, *Speaking God's Word* (Downers Grove: InterVarsity, 1999), 132–33.
13. T. Warren, "A Paradigm for Preaching," *BibSac* (October–December 1991): 143.

goal a community of believers who think and live differently as a result of their confrontation with the Word of God. Changed lives is what we are after, and nothing less will satisfy the faithful expositor. Pastor Rick Warren is direct and to the point:

> I'll say it over and over: The purpose of preaching is obedience. Every preacher in the New Testament—including Jesus— emphasized conduct, behavioral change, and obedience. You only really believe the parts of the Bible that you obey. People say, "I believe in tithing." But do they tithe? No? Then they don't believe in it.
>
> That is why you should always preach for response, aiming for people to act on what is said. John did this: "The world and its desires pass away, but the man who does the will of God lives forever" (1 John 2:17 NIV). And in 1 John 2:3 (NIV), "We know that we have come to know him if we obey his commands."[14]

As we prepare to set forth our method, several observations should guide our process. Let us again draw on the insights of Pastor Warren. I will closely follow him at some length, as I believe you will see it is worth it.

Basic Observations for Application in Preaching

1. **All behavior is based on a belief.**

   What you believe will determine how you act. Creed and conduct go hand in hand. For example, if you get divorced because you are unhappy, it is because you believe that disobeying God will cause you less pain than staying in your marriage. It is a lie, but you believe it and you act on it. When somebody comes to you and says, "I'm leaving my husband, and I'm going to marry this other man because I believe God wants me to be happy," they just told you the belief behind their behavior. It is wrong, but they believe it.

---

14. R. Warren, "Preaching Tips That Will Change Lives," *Ministry Toolbox* 246 (February 15, 2006).

2. **Behind every sin is a lie I believe.**

At the moment you sin, you are doing what you think is the best thing for you. You say, "I know God says to do that, but I'm going to do this." What are you doing? You are believing a lie. Start looking for the lies behind why people in your church act the way they do. When you start dealing with those, you will start seeing change. Titus 3:3 (NIV) declares, "At one time we too were foolish, disobedient, deceived and enslaved by all kinds of passions and pleasures." When you live in sin, you're living in deception and believing a lie.

When you look at your congregation, you may not see the lies they believe, but you do see their behavior. You know they are unfaithful; you know they are uncommitted; you know all these things. The tough part is figuring out the lie behind the behavior. The wiser you get in ministry, the quicker you will start seeing the lies. You will grow and become more discerning, because you will start seeing patterns over and over.

3. **Change always starts in the mind.**

You have got to start with the belief—the lie—behind the behavior. Romans 12:2 (NIV) commands, "Be transformed by the renewing of your mind." The way you think determines the way you feel, and the way you feel determines the way you act. If you want to change the way you act, you must determine (change) the way you think. You cannot start with the action. You have got to start with the thought. Remember Prov 23:7!

4. **To help people change, we must change their beliefs first.**

Jesus said, "You will know the truth, and the truth will set you free" (John 8:32 NIV). Why? Because to help people change, you have got to help them see the lie they are basing their behavior on. That is why when you know the truth, it sets you free.

5. **Trying to change people's behavior without changing their belief is a waste of time.**

If you ask a person to change before his mind is renewed, it will not work. He has to internalize God's Word first. God's Word has got to become a part of who he is.

Your belief patterns are in your mind. Every time you think about a belief, it creates an electrical impulse across your brain. Every time you have that thought again, it creates a deeper rut. If you want to see change in your church, you must help people get out of their ruts and change their autopilot. For example, let us say I go out and buy a speedboat with an autopilot feature on it. I set the speedboat to go north on autopilot, so the boat goes north automatically. I do not even have my hands on the wheel. If I want to turn the boat around, I could manually grab the steering wheel and, by sheer willpower and force, turn it around. I can force it to go south, but the whole time I am under tension because I am going against the natural inclination of the boat. Pretty soon I get tired and let go of the steering wheel, and it automatically turns around and goes back to the way it is programmed.

This is true in life. When people have learned something over and over, being taught by the world's way of thinking, they are programmed to go that way. What if a man is programmed to pick up a cigarette every time he is under tension? But one day he thinks, "This is killing me! I'm going to get cancer." So he grabs the steering wheel and turns it around forcibly, throws the pack away and says, "I am going to quit!" He makes it a week without a cigarette, a week and a half, two weeks, but the whole time he is under tension because he has not changed the programming in his mind. Eventually, he is going to let go and pick up a cigarette again.

If you want to change people radically and permanently, you have to do it the New Testament way. You have to be transformed by the renewing of your mind. Just telling people, "You need to stop smoking . . . You need to stop doing this . . . You need to stop doing that" is not going to work. You have got to help them change their belief pattern.

6. The biblical term for "changing your mind" is "repentance."

What do most people think of when they hear the word "repent"? They think of a guy on the street corner with a sandwich sign saying, "Turn or burn. You're going to die and fry while we go to the sky." They think of some kook.

But the word "repentance" is a wonderful Greek word—*metanoia*—which means "to change your mind." Repentance is changing the way we think about something by accepting the way God thinks about it. A modern way of describing repentance is "paradigm shift." We are in the paradigm-shifting business. We are in the repentance business. We are about changing peoples' minds at the deepest level—the level of belief and values.

7. You do not change people's minds; the applied Word of God does.

First Corinthians 2:13 (NLT) helps us keep this in focus: "We speak words given to us by the Spirit, using the Spirit's words to explain spiritual truths." In real preaching, God is at work in the speaker.

Zechariah 4:6 (NIV) says, "'Not by might nor by power, but by My Spirit,' says the Lord Almighty." So keep in mind that you do not change people's minds; the Word of God applied by the Holy Spirit does.

8. **Changing the way I act is the fruit of repentance**.

Technically, repentance is not behavioral change. Behavior change is the result of repentance. Repentance does not mean forsaking your sin. Repentance simply means to change your mind. John the Baptist said in Matt 3:8 (NIV), "Produce fruit in keeping with repentance." In other words, "OK, you have changed your mind about God, about life, about sin, about yourself—now let's see some fruit as a result of it."

9. **The deepest kind of preaching is preaching for repentance**.

Because life change happens only after you change somebody's thinking, then preaching for repentance is preaching for life change. It is the deepest kind of preaching you can preach.

Repentance is the central message of the New Testament. What did the New Testament preachers preach on?

- John the Baptist: "Repent, for the kingdom of heaven is near" (Matt 3:2 NIV).
- Jesus: "Repent and believe the good news" (Mark 1:15 NIV).
- What did Jesus tell his disciples to preach? "So they went off and preached repentance" (Mark 6:12 NAB).
- What did Peter preach at Pentecost? "Repent and be baptized every one of you" (Acts 2:38 NAB).
- What did John preach in Revelation? Repent (Revelation 2–3).

Warren concludes,

I believe that one of the great weaknesses of preaching today is that there are a lot of folks who are afraid to stand on the Word of God and humbly but forcefully challenge the will of people. It takes courage to do that, because they may reject you. They may reject your message; they may get mad at you and talk about you behind your back. So now, I have a personal challenge for you—life application. Are you going to use the Bible the way it was intended or not? Will you repent of preaching in ways that were not focused on application that could change people's character and conduct?[15]

15. Ibid.

These are sobering and challenging words from a seasoned veteran of preaching, but they help us see how necessary text-driven application is. Faithful expositors are not only responsible to explain and expound the meaning of the text; they are also responsible to apply the text, preaching for a life-changing verdict from the audience. We are called to be doers of the Word and not just listeners of the Word. Therefore, we must instruct and inspire our people in applying Holy Scripture to their everyday lives. Let us turn to a model for accomplishing this all-important objective.

Guiding Principles for Doing Application

First, your application should be Theo/Christocentric. No one has said this better than Dennis Johnson, who writes,

> Preaching must be *Christ centered*, must interpret biblical texts in their *redemptive-historical contexts*, must aim for *change*, must proclaim the *doctrinal center* of the Reformation (grace alone, faith alone, Christ alone, God's glory alone) with passion and personal application, and must speak in a language that connects with the *unchurched* in our culture, shattering their stereotypes of Christianity and bringing them face to face with Christ, who meets sinners' real needs—felt and unfelt.[16]

Drawing upon the insights of Timothy Keller, a pastor in New York City, Johnson adds, "What both the unbeliever and the believer need to hear in preaching is the gospel, with its implications for a life lived in confident gratitude in response to amazing grace."[17]

This observation is crucial and must drive all aspects of biblical proclamation. Jesus is the hero of the whole Bible. He is the Savior in that He delivers us from the penalty of sin (justification), the power of sin (sanctification), and the presence of sin

---

16. D. Johnson, *Him We Proclaim: Preaching Christ from All the Scriptures* (Phillipsburg: P&R, 2007), 54.
17. Ibid., 55.

282 ◆ Daniel L. Akin

(glorification). Text-driven application is particularly interested in sanctification. Our people must understand that they are saved by Jesus and that they grow into Christlikeness through Jesus.

Mark Driscoll, a pastor in Seattle, calls this the "Christological Question" in preaching:

> How is Jesus the Hero-Savior? The Bible is one story in which Jesus is the hero. Therefore to properly teach and preach the Bible we have to continually lift him up as the hero. Any sermon in which the focus is not the person and work of Jesus will lack spiritual authority and power because the Holy Spirit will not bless the teaching of any hero other than Jesus. . . . There is an ongoing debate as to the purpose of the sermon and whether it should focus on converting the lost or maturing the saved. The apparent conflict between preaching for seekers and preaching for believers is resolved simply by noting that both need to repent of sin and trust in Jesus to live a new life empowered by the Spirit.[18]

Second, weave your application into the outline or movements of your sermon. In other words, let the outline of your message be the application points of your sermon. State them in complete sentences that are clear and concise, in the present tense, and in harmony with the plain meaning of the text of Scripture. A simple example from Col 3:18–21 will help us see what we are after. The context is the lordship of Jesus Christ wherein His Word dwells richly in each of us (Col 3:16). The subject at hand is the Christian family where a directive is given to each member of the family. Text-driven application wed to a text-driven exposition would look something like this:

Title: When Christ Is Lord of the Home
Outline:
    I. Wives submit to your husbands (3:18)
    II. Husbands love your wives (3:19)

---

18. M. Driscoll and G. Breshears, *Vintage Church* (Wheaton, IL: Crossway, 2008), 101–2.

III. Children obey your parents (3:20)
IV. Fathers [Parents] encourage your children (3:21)

We should recognize that some applications of a text will more readily apply to the mind (belief) and other applications will more readily apply to the will (behavior). Some will actually speak to both. The key is that the application is true to and faithful to the meaning of the text.

Third, aim for specific action on the part of your people. Fuzzy thinking is deadly to any aspect of a sermon. This is especially true when it comes to application. Using the imagery of the Bible we must remember that we are preaching to sheep (Psalm 23; John 10). Sheep need very specific and particular guidance and direction. We must not assume that they will just "get it" on their own. This is one of the deadly weaknesses of the so-called New Homiletic. We cannot hope our people will "fill in the blanks" of sermon applications. Practical steps that are challenging but attainable by God's grace and Christ's strength is our goal. We cannot beat them over the head with "oughts" without also providing "hows." Challenge your men to be leaders in the church and home, to be godly husbands and fathers, but make sure you show them how.

Fourth, tie application to illustration and provide some practical examples of Scripture at work. Again, the text must drive this union. Some examples will appeal to the mind and be deeply theological. Others will move the heart and give attention to the practical. Warren says,

> If you want your people to share their faith with others, then tell stories about people in your church who are already doing that. If you want your people to care for the sick, tell stories about people in your church who care for the sick. If you want your people to be friendly to visitors tell stories about people who were friendly to visitors.[19]

---

19. R. Warren, "Put Application in Your Messages," *Ministry Toolbox* 317 (June 27, 2007).

Fifth, state your application in the form of a universal principle. Look for what is true anywhere, anyplace, anytime, and under any circumstances. There is an ultimate principle to remember: the solution to any problem is a person and His name is Jesus. As you state your universal principle, be in line with the needs, interests, questions, and problems of today. This is the key to relevance. The chart below visualizes what we mean:

THERE ARE TWO HISTORIES AND YOU MUST BRIDGE THE HORIZONS:

ORIGINAL HISTORY   **OUR HISTORY**

Colossae AD 60–63   **COLOSSIANS**   Your context in the 21st century

Truth revealed out ⟵ Eternal truth that ⟶ Truth reborn
of "the then"   bridges the two worlds   into "the now"

Your principles must be in harmony with the general tenor and totality of Scripture. The analogy of faith is crucial here: "Scripture will not contradict Scripture." As you state these principles, be specific enough to indicate a course of action. Always ask any text these 13 questions:

1. Is there an example for me to follow?
2. Is there a sin to avoid/confess?
3. Is there a promise to claim?
4. Is there a prayer to repeat?
5. Is there a command to obey?
6. Is there a condition to meet?
7. Is there a verse to memorize?
8. Is there an error to avoid?
9. Is there a challenge to face?
10. Is there a principle to apply?
11. Is there a habit to change—that is, start or stop?
12. Is there an attitude to correct?
13. Is there a truth to believe?

Sixth, saturate your mind in terms of the many relationships of life. Examine the text with relations like education, social life, business, church, values, thought life, worldview, marriage, family, and sex in view. Release your mind to run freely and explore the various possible relationships the text speaks to. Be realistic and think concretely and not abstractly. Work to see the text vicariously through the eyes of those you shepherd. Hans Finzel in *Unlocking the Scriptures* highlights four broad categories with specific considerations under each:

A. WITH GOD

1. A truth to understand
2. A command to obey
3. A prayer to express
4. A challenge to heed
5. A promise to claim
6. A fellowship to enjoy

B. WITH YOURSELF

1. A thought or word to examine
2. An action to take
3. An example to follow
4. An error to avoid
5. An attitude to change or guard against
6. A priority to change
7. A goal to strive for
8. A personal value or standard to hold up
9. A sin to forsake

C. WITH OTHERS

1. A witness to share
2. An encouragement to extend
3. A service to do
4. A forgiveness to ask
5. A fellowship to nurture
6. An exhortation to give
7. A burden to bear
8. A kindness to express
9. A hospitality to extend
10. An attitude to change or guard against
11. A sin to forsake

D. WITH SATAN

1. A person to resist
2. A device to recognize
3. A temptation to resist
4. A sin to avoid and confess
5. A piece of spiritual armor to wear[20]

Seventh, remember the meaning of the text is always one but the applications are many. Jerry Vines and David Allen have rightly argued, following E. D. Hirsch, that there is a distinction that must be made between "meaning" and "significance" (what we would call application). They note, "When the biblical exegete comes to a text of Scripture, he can proceed on the premise that there is a determinate meaning there. His job is to discover this meaning through exegesis. Having done this, there remains the further task of applying this meaning to modern man. . . . We propose then that a text has one primary meaning with multiple significances or applications of that meaning."[21]

Eighth, consciously put into practice the application(s) gleaned from the exegesis of the text. Never forget that you have not applied until you have appropriated and put into practice what you have learned. Indeed, the application and practice of the text will serve as a commentary on your understanding of the biblical truth. It will be extremely difficult for you to apply to others what you have not first applied to yourself. Granted, no one can apply everything, but you should diligently and intentionally be working to apply something. What are you trusting God for right now? In what ways are you looking to Jesus and

---

20. H. Finzel, *Unlocking the Scriptures: Three Steps to Personal Bible Study* (Portland: Victor, 2003), 64.
21. J. Vines and D. Allen, "Hermeneutics, Exegesis and Proclamation," *CTR* 1, no. 2 (Spring 1987): 315–16. Vines and Allen's insight does not negate the intriguing possibility of a fuller meaning or what is called *Sensus Plenoir*. For an excellent treatment of the issue, see D. Moo, "The Problem of *Sensus Plenior*," in *Hermeneutics, Authority, and Canon*, ed. D. A. Carson and J. Woodbridge (Grand Rapids: Baker, 1995), 179–211.

appropriating His grace? What is your action plan to experience change in what you think and how you live? These are questions you should ask yourself before you put this to your audience. Howard Hendricks provides a helpful comparison as to where we have been/are but hope to be/move:

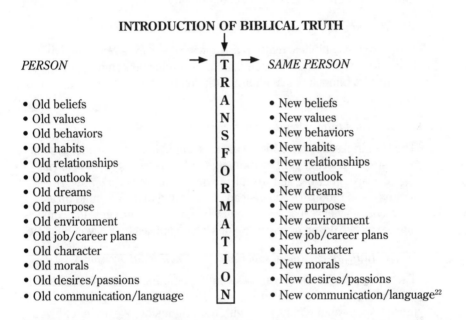

INTRODUCTION OF BIBLICAL TRUTH

PERSON → **T** → *SAME PERSON*

• Old beliefs	• New beliefs
• Old values	• New values
• Old behaviors	• New behaviors
• Old habits	• New habits
• Old relationships	• New relationships
• Old outlook	• New outlook
• Old dreams	• New dreams
• Old purpose	• New purpose
• Old environment	• New environment
• Old job/career plans	• New job/career plans
• Old character	• New character
• Old morals	• New morals
• Old desires/passions	• New desires/passions
• Old communication/language	• New communication/language[22]

Ninth, beware of the challenges and problems to application. Howard Hendricks warns us of what he calls "substitutes for application."[23] He raises five, and a quick survey and digest of each one is beneficial for our study.

1. *We substitute interpretation for application.*

    It is easy to settle for knowledge rather than change. That is tragic because as the Hendrickses say, "According to the Bible, to know and not to do is not to know at all." Jesus said, "Why do you call me 'Lord, Lord,' and do not do what I say?" (Luke 6:46). The implication is clear:

---

22. Hendricks and Hendricks, *Living By the Book*, 313.
23. Ibid., 291–97. I follow their analysis very closely in this section, quoting them directly at some length.

either stop calling me "Lord," or start doing what I tell you. You cannot have one without the other. James 4:17 reminds us, "Anyone, then, who knows the good he ought to do and doesn't do it, sins" (NIV). The person who knows the truth but does not act on it is not simply making a mistake—making a poor judgment—he is committing sin. In God's mind, knowledge without obedience is sin. The fact that we have knowledge only increases our accountability.

2. *We substitute superficial obedience for substantive life change.*

Here, we apply biblical truth to areas where we are already applying it, not to new areas. The result is no noticeable and genuine change in our lives. A blind spot remains, and the truth never affects that part of our life needing change.

3. *We substitute rationalization for repentance.*

The Hendrickses note, "Most of us have a built-in early-warning system against spiritual change. The moment truth gets too close, too convicting, an alarm goes off, and we start to defend ourselves. Our favorite strategy is to rationalize sin instead of repenting of it." We build up a healthy supply of responses so that, whenever the truth gets too convicting, we have a dozen or more reasons why it applies to everyone but me.

4. *We substitute an emotional experience for a volitional decision.*

There is nothing wrong with responding emotionally to spiritual truth. However, if that is our only response, then our spirituality is nothing more than a vapid empty shell with nothing inside. We are after a volitional response to God's truth. We are after substantive, life-changing decisions based on what the Scriptures say. We must not be satisfied with just being exposed to the truth of God or convicted by it; we must be *changed* by it. Real change always takes place in the will.

5. *We substitute communication for transformation.*

"We talk the talk, but we don't walk the walk." We think that if we can speak eloquently or convincingly about a point of Scripture, we are on safe ground. We have fooled others into believing we have got that biblical truth down. But God is not fooled. He knows our hearts. He knows our actions. First Samuel 16:7 says, "God sees not as man sees, for man looks at [and listens to] the outward appearance, but the LORD looks at [and listens to] the heart" (NASB). Hebrews 4:13 adds, "Nothing in all creation is hidden from God's sight. Everything is uncovered and laid bare before the eyes of him to whom we must give account" (NIV). God is not impressed with our words as fellow humans might be. The Lord looks at the heart, and nothing is hidden from His sight.

Tenth, be on guard against "the heresy of application." This particular danger is so prevalent, we will dedicate a short section to it, drawing extensively on the outstanding article by Haddon Robinson titled "The Heresy of Application."[24]

THE DANGER OF HERESY IN TEXT-DRIVEN APPLICATION

Haddon Robinson says, "More heresy is preached in application than in Bible exegesis." He points out that "preachers want to be faithful to the Scriptures, and going through seminary, they have learned exegesis. However, they may not have learned how to make the journey from the biblical text to the modern world. They get out of seminary and realize the preacher's question is *application*: "How do you take this text and determine what it means [I would say 'applies'] for this audience?"

Sometimes we apply the text in ways that might make the biblical writer say, "Wait a minute, that's the wrong use of what I said." This is heresy of a good truth applied in the wrong way. He notes that this heresy looks like a sermon from Ruth on how to deal with in-laws. Ruth was not given to solve in-law problems!

Robinson notes there is a devastating effect on our congregation in terms of how they, themselves, will handle the Word of God:

> One effect is that you undermine the Scriptures you say you are preaching. Ultimately, people come to believe that anything with a biblical flavor is what God says. The long-term effect is that we preach a mythology. Myth has an element of truth along with a great deal of puff, and people tend to live in the puff. They live with the implications of implications, and then they discover that what they thought God promised, he didn't promise.

---

24. E. Rowell with H. Robinson, "The Heresy of Application," *Leadership* 18, no. 4 (Fall 1997): 21–27.

Affirming the steps to application we have offered, Robinson notes, "In application we attempt to take what we believe is the truth of the eternal God, which was given in a particular time and place and situation, and apply it to people in the modern world who live in another time, another place, and a very different situation. That is harder than it appears."

Indeed, "the Bible is specific—Paul writes letters to particular churches; the stories are specific—but my audience is general." Robinson then provides guidelines or principles for avoiding heresy in application leading to what he calls the "Ladder of Abstraction." He proposes two questions that we should put forth to each text we examine: (1) What does this teach about God? (2) What does this teach about human nature? To this, we would add, what does this text teach me about Jesus?

He explains how to get at this issue:

> [T]ake the biblical text straight over to the modern situation. In some cases, that works well. For example, Jesus says, "Love your enemies." I say to my listeners, "Do you have enemies? Love them."
>
> But then I turn the page, and Jesus says, "Sell what you have, give to the poor, and follow me." I hesitate to bring this straight over because I think, *If everybody does this, we'll have problems, big problems.*
>
> Some texts look as though they can come straight over to my contemporary audience, but not necessarily. I need to know something about the circumstances of both my text and my audience.

Robinson correctly warns us again, "A text cannot mean what it has not meant. That is, when Paul wrote to people in his day, he expected them to understand what he meant. . . . I cannot make that passage mean something today that it did not mean in principle in the ancient world. That's why I have to do exegesis. I have to be honest with the text before I can come over to the contemporary world." Robinson goes on to apply his "Ladder of Abstraction" to a most unusual text he locates in Leviticus. (Actually, the text he cites is found in Exod 24:19; 34:26.) His insight is very helpful:

> Leviticus [*sic*] says, "Don't boil a kid in its mother's milk." First, you have to ask, "What is this all about?" At face value, you might say, "If I have a young goat, and I want to cook it in its mother's milk for dinner tonight, I should think twice."
>
> But we now know the pagans did that when they worshiped their idolatrous gods. Therefore, what you have here is not a prohibition against boiling a kid in its mother's milk, but against being involved in the idolatry that surrounded God's people or bringing its practices into their religion.
>
> If that's the case, it does no good for the preacher to bring this text straight over. You must climb the ladder of abstraction a couple of levels until you reach the principle: You should not associate yourself with idolatrous worship, even in ways that do not seem to have direct association with physically going to the idol.

In other words, look for what is true anywhere, anyplace, anytime, and under any circumstance. Work in the text until you capture, on one hand, the vision of God that is there and, on the other, the portrait of fallen man that is there.

Robinson expounds on what we are talking about:

> One thing I always do with a passage is abstract up to God. Every passage has a vision of God, such as God as Creator or Sustainer.
>
> Second I ask, "What is the depravity factor? What in humanity rebels against that vision of God?"
>
> These two questions are a helpful clue in application because God remains the same, and human depravity remains the same. Our depravity may look different, but it's the same pride, obstinacy, disobedience.
>
> Take 1 Corinthians 8, in which Paul addresses the subject of eating meat offered to idols.
>
> The vision of God: He is our redeemer. Therefore, Paul argues, I will not eat meat, because if I wound my brother's weak conscience, I sin against Christ, who redeemed him.
>
> The depravity factor: People want their rights, so they don't care that Christ died for their brother.

Robinson goes on to challenge us to be honest with application, both in terms of the text and our audience. He says,

> We want to have a "Thus saith the Lord" about specific things in people's lives, but we can't always have that. So we need to distinguish between various types of implications from the text. Implications may be necessary, probable, improbable, or impossible. . . .
>
> Too often preachers give to a possible implication all the authority of a necessary implication, which is at the level of obedience. Only with necessary implications can you preach, "Thus saith the Lord." This will help us to avoid legalistic prescriptions in our application of the text!

In his closing thoughts, Robinson provides a pastoral word to those called to preach the inerrant Scriptures:

> People who are good at exegesis tend to spend a lot of time in that and may not know when to quit. Those folks would be well served to spend extra time on how to communicate the fruit of their research.
>
> Others are into the communication side. They're always relevant, but they desperately need to spend more time in the biblical text to let it speak to them.
>
> The Spirit answers to the Word. If I am faithful to the Scriptures, I give the Spirit of God something to work on that he doesn't have if I'm preaching *Reader's Digest.* . . .
>
> That's the greatness of preaching. Something can always happen when a preacher takes God's Word seriously.

CONCLUSION

The *Westminster Directory for Public Worship* reads, "The preacher is not to rest in general doctrine, although never so much cleared and confirmed, but is to bring it home to special use by application to his hearers."[25] To do this effectively, we must

---

25. Quoted in E. Alexander, *What Is Biblical Preaching?* (Phillipsburg: P&R, 2008), 29.

know the Scriptures and the culture, the world of the Bible and the world in which we find ourselves. Eric Alexander says it well:

> We are thus to be contemporary in our application. For that reason, it is important that we know the world and the pattern of thinking in the world in which we live. For that reason too it is important that we know the world in which our congregation lives. Evangelicals have traditionally been strongest in knowing the Scripture, and weakest in knowing the world. Others have mostly been stronger in knowing the world and weakest in knowing the Scripture. But there is no reason why these two things should be mutually exclusive.[26]

Of course, to do this well, we will need to ask of the Holy Spirit of God who must first apply the biblical truth to the heart of the man of God. Hear Alexander once more:

> Now of course we will recognize and acknowledge that it is the Holy Spirit who is the true applier of the Word. That is a vital, central, basic truth for all our thinking. It is the Holy Spirit who takes the Word of God and uses it as the sword that pierces to the dividing asunder of soul and spirit. But that does not excuse us from the labor of asking, "How ought I to apply these truths to my own conscience and then to the conscience of this people?[27]

The great puritan John Owen would add, "A man preacheth that sermon only well unto others, which preacheth itself in his own soul. If the word does not dwell with power in us, it will not pass with power from us."[28]

---

25. Quoted in E. Alexander, *What Is Biblical Preaching?* (Phillipsburg: P&R, 2008), 29.
26. Ibid., 30.
27. Ibid., 29.
28. Ibid., 28. Concerning this chapter, let me also commend two books that provide excellent treatments on the importance of application: D. Doriani, *Putting the Truth to Work: The Theory and Practice of Biblical Application* (Phillipsburg, NJ: P&R, 2001), and H. Robinson and C. B. Larson, gen. eds., *The Art and Craft of Biblical Preaching: A Comprehensive Resource for Today's Communicators* (Grand Rapids: Zondervan, 2005).

CONCLUSION

Ned L. Mathews

The text-driven preacher is mentally, spiritually, and dispositionally under the control of the *ethos* and authority of Scripture. He is a text-driven man in and out of the pulpit, and it is his fervent desire to be so. For him, no other literature is so arresting in interest, authentic in essence, and compelling in influence, as that of the Bible. Certain effects follow from this. I will highlight four.

First, the text-driven preacher is not culturally driven either in his perspective of reality or his pulpit proclamation. The reason is simple. He derives neither his ministry mandate nor his missionary incentive from the conventions or customs of the age but from the timeless and therefore always relevant imperatives of Scripture. Like the apostle Paul, not only is he aware of the need to keep his message and ministry relevant to the concerns of the culture, but also he knows that one gains attention by being culturally sensitive in order to declare the truth that people *need* whether or not they *want* it. Like Paul, he is driven by the desire to engage and, when necessary, confront the culture with the challenging and life-changing message of the Word of God. And, again, like Paul, he will not compromise that message in order to gain the approval or admiration of the culture even if that means that he and his message are rejected by many (see Acts 17:22–31).

Second, the text-driven preacher is not driven by systematic theology in developing his doctrinal formulations.[1] Why? To paraphrase an old aphorism, he is not willing to put his theological "cart" before his scriptural "horse." Although committed to biblical theology[2] and grateful for the contributions of gifted teachers of systematic theology, he derives his *authority* for preaching from Scripture alone. This is because the text-driven preacher views theology through the prism of Scripture, not the other way around. He is therefore not given to preaching his theological perspectives, whether representative of Calvinism, Arminianism, or theologies of whatever stripe. He preaches "thus saith the Lord," not "thus saith Calvin" or "thus saith Arminius." He preaches not these perspectives because he is convinced that the result of viewing the Bible through the prism of systematic theology, as many unfortunately do, is likely to spiritually impoverish his listeners leaving them (and him) hindered and even prevented from receiving fresh insights into previously misunderstood or even underappreciated biblical texts. For the text-driven preacher, then, the goal is not to squeeze a text of Scripture so that it fits a theological system; it is rather to let Scripture shape and determine his theology, even if this requires that he, and those who hear his sermons, must live with some degree of tension in theological understanding.[3]

Third, text-driven preachers are text driven in their lives as well as in their preaching. This does not mean that they

---

1. See the introduction and chapter 5 of this work for elaboration on this point.
2. See chapter 8 of this work.
3. Perhaps the preacher and his people would be best served if they spends their time in deeper study of Scripture rather than attempting to resolve century-old polemical theological arguments.

worship the Bible (deemed "bibliolatry" by some) or that they are the sort of people who adorn their homes with the texts of Scripture (though some may). It does mean, however, that the text-driven preacher takes seriously the same injunction given by Paul to Timothy to *"continue* in what you have learned and have firmly believed" (2 Tim 3:14, italics added) because the source of what he had "firmly believed" was "the sacred writings" (2 Tim 3:15). Furthermore, such a commitment to Scripture had enabled Timothy to become "competent"[4] for ministry since he was thereby being "thoroughly equipped for every good work" (2 Tim 3:17).

Text-driven preachers will therefore *continue* to learn and grow in faith through their study of the written Word of God. They do so because they know that their confidence in Scripture is completely justified, that Scripture is the primary source for understanding Holy Spirit–inspired living *and* preaching and that the biblical texts are clearly inspired by God (2 Tim 3:16).[5] Moreover, text-driven preachers know that the Scriptures are derived from God Himself through the prophets and apostles and that they are thus the means by which persons are made "wise for salvation through faith in Christ Jesus" (2 Tim 3:15). The text-driven preacher, accordingly, must remain in *continuous training* (2 Tim 3:16) in his study of the Scriptures in order to become competent in declaring God's Word. And what is the result of such a commitment? It is the satisfaction of knowing that there will be no stagnation in the development of competency when this training becomes a lifelong discipline.[6]

---

4. The Greek is ἄρτιος. The closest English equivalent would be the word "qualified." Translations render the word as "efficient" (NEB), "competent" (NASB), and "proficient" (NRSV). This meaning is amplified by the words "thoroughly equipped" (NIV).

5. Peter puts this another way but with a similar conclusion. "For no prophecy was ever produced by the will of man, but men spoke from God as they were carried along by the Holy Spirit" (2 Peter 1:21 ESV).

6. See chapter 4 for a fuller treatment of this.

The words that make up the text of Scripture are therefore not void of life-changing power. Thus, they should not be considered as nothing more than the arcane religious expressions of an ancient people that hold little or no interest or relevance for modern or postmodern people. They are rather the very words of God himself though necessarily written in the words of men. Of course, the words of Scripture do come to us from a time frame other than ours, a different "horizon," as Anthony Thiselton has put it.[7] Accordingly, they require a hermeneutic that is based on accurate exegesis and application to our own time as David Black indicates in chapter 6 of this work.

Fourth, the text-driven method is the norm for biblical hermeneutics. We see in Scripture a consistent pattern for that. For example, Matthew's Gospel is replete with the argument that Jesus, in his life and death, fulfilled the prophecies concerning the promised Messiah. In fact, it is apparent that the entire veracity of Matthew's Gospel is supported by the testimony of Scripture. Again and again, he reminds his readers of fulfilled prophecy in the life of Jesus with the words, ". . . now this took place to fulfill what was spoken by the Lord through the prophet" (or similar words in 12 other places in his Gospel). It is clear then that Matthew's understanding of Jesus' life and mission is informed and shaped by the written Word of God. Likewise, the text-driven preacher can do no better than to follow the example set forth by the writers of the New Testament when he bases his own preaching on the authority of Scripture.

But there is a greater testimony of this than what is provided even by the authors of Scripture. It is Christ Himself who is the sublime and consistent model. We see him as a 12-year-old sitting in the temple in discussion with the learned teachers of the Torah and confounding them with his understanding of it.

---

7. A. Thiselton, *The Two Horizons, New Testament Hermeneutics and Philosophical Description* (Grand Rapids: Eerdmans, 1980), 11, 15, 17, 20.

We follow Him after His baptism as He is "led up by the Spirit into the wilderness" for His encounter with Satan (Matt 4:1–11; Luke 4:1–13). We observe as He negates each suggestion of Satan with the authority of Scripture. Moreover, Jesus clearly sees the text as the actual written Word of His Father. By the Sea of Galilee, on the occasion of His Sermon on the Mount, the Lord announces the inviolability of the complete text of the Torah in asserting that "not an iota, not a dot, will pass from the law until all is accomplished" (Matt 5:18 ESV), thereby suggesting that His listeners should be guided by the text of Scripture if they would understand who He is and what He was doing. Again and again, Jesus hears Scripture as the voice of His Father. And when the time comes for the Lord to plainly declare to both detractors and supporters the nature of His mission (Luke 4:16–21) He simply lets the text of Isaiah speak for Him (Isa 61:1–2). He tells His disciples repeatedly that He is going to the cross and that afterward He will rise again as it is "written of Him" (Matt 26:24 NASB). When dying on the cross, He identifies what is happening to Him by quoting Ps 22:1 word by word. His sense of timing for the salient acts of His messianic mission is determined by Scripture as seen, for example, by His arrangement, at all costs, to be in Jerusalem at the time of Passover for the event of His crucifixion (Luke 9:51). And after His resurrection, He conducts a walking Bible study for His two companions by showing them from the Scriptures that the sufferings of the Messiah were accurately predicted by "Moses and all the prophets" (Luke 2:25–27). So, as Jesus was clearly a text-driven man in word and deed, it follows that His disciples and His preachers should also be text driven in word and deed.

The goal of text-driven preaching then is not to find a better homiletical method; it is at its best the means of producing disciples who, like their Lord, are text-driven people. What we are offering in this book therefore is a fresh cry for relevancy in regard to the comprehensive and perspicuous themes of Scripture. We do this by insisting that preaching must be driven by the text of Scripture so that we and our listeners will hearken once again to *the interests of God,* especially in regard to the themes of creation and redemption.[8]

Text-driven preachers are therefore purpose driven. Haddon Robinson writes that expository preachers start with the purpose of delivering "[the] definite units of God's Word to [their] people."[9] Robinson adds, however, that "[w]hether or not a man can be called an expositor starts with his purpose and with his honest answer to the question: 'Do you, as a preacher, endeavor to bend your thought to the Scriptures, or do you use the Scriptures to support your thought?'"[10] He explains,

> This is not the same question as, "Is what you are preaching orthodox or evangelical?" Nor is it the same as, "Do you hold a high view of the Bible or believe it to be the infallible Word of God?" As important as these questions may appear in other circumstances, a passing grade in systematic theology does not qualify an individual as an expositor of the Bible. Theology may protect us from evils lurking in atomistic, nearsighted interpretations, but at the same time it may blindfold us from seeing the text. In his approach to a passage, an interpreter must be willing to reexamine his doctrinal convictions and to reject the judgments of his most respected teachers. He must make a U-turn in his own previous understandings of the Bible should these conflict with the concepts of the biblical writer.[11]

In our day, much has been made of the need for churches to be purpose driven. But the term "purpose driven" is elastic in application. *Whose* purpose is to drive our churches? This is an important question for many have observed an astounding

8. That creation and redemption, in the broadest sense, are the primary themes of Scripture and therefore reflective of the interests of God may be discerned from a close study of Revelation, especially chapters 4 and 5. For Jim Hamilton's extended elaboration of this, see chapter 8.
9. H. W. Robinson, *Biblical Preaching, The Development and Delivery of Expository Messages* (Grand Rapids: Baker, 1980), 20.
10. Ibid.
11. Ibid., 20–21.

breadth of theological diversity in pulpits and pews. Others have concluded that what is happening in many churches is far more influenced by culture than by biblical theology. Accordingly, even heresy abounds in some quarters. The interests of God are rapidly being eclipsed by the interests of a consumer-driven mentality, even in our worship services. The result is a Christian culture that is, as some have said, "a mile wide and an inch deep." The time has come for the remedy. That remedy is the kind and scope of text-driven preaching that is described in this book.

NAME INDEX

Achtemeier, E.   *168, 257*
Adam, P.   *101, 276*
Adams, J.   *263, 274*
Akin, D.   *7, 55, 133*
Albee, E.   *222–23, 224*
Alexander, E.   *292–93*
Allen, D. L.   *6–7, 104, 116, 125, 153, 286*
Alter, R.   *160*
Ambrose   *41*
Anaximenes   *15, 17*
Anderson, M.   *45*
Aristotle   *5, 14–15, 17–19, 29–30, 35, 238, 259–60*
Augustine   *3, 41–42, 239*
Austin, J. L.   *83*
Awbrey, B. E.   *53*
Azurdia, A. G.   *58–59, 251*

Bailey, R.   *246*
Bar-Efrat, S.   *160*
Barnhouse, D. G.   *48*
Barr, J.   *102–3*
Barrett, C. K.   *139*
Basil   *41*
Bates, C.   *58*
Bauckham, R.   *201, 202*
Baxter, R.   *46, 81–82, 87–88*
Beale, G. K.   *194, 202, 213*
Beaugrande, R. de   *115*

Beecher, H. W.   *80–81*
Beecher, L.   *80*
Beekman, J.   *106, 110, 113, 116, 125*
Bell, M.   *245*
Bennett, B.   *5, 57*
Berlin, A.   *161*
Bernard of Clairvaux   *4*
Black, D.   *6, 117, 119, 136, 139, 141, 142, 143, 144, 146, 147, 148, 149, 151–52, 153, 154, 298*
Blomberg, C. L.   *141, 177, 184*
Blue, S.   *271, 274*
Boers, H.   *115, 119*
Boice, J. M.   *48*
Booth, W.   *15*
Bounds, E. M.   *70*
Breshears, G.   *282*
Briggs, C. A.   *160*
Broadus, J. A.   *46, 105–6, 107, 109, 274–75*
Brooks, J. A.   *147*
Brown, C.   *118, 146*
Brown, F.   *160*
Brown, J.   *46*
Bruce, F. F.   *139*
Bullinger, E. W.   *175–76*
Bunyan, J.   *46, 96–97*
Buttrick, D.   *2, 24–25, 234–35*

Templeton, C.   *94–95*
Thiselton, A.   *298*
Thompson, J.   *104*
Thornwell, J. H.   *46*
Tilton, E.   *80*
Tov, E.   *160*
Trible, P.   *161*
Truett, G. W.   *23*
Turner, M.   *142*
Twain, M.   *114–15*
Tyndale, W.   *42*

van der Merwe, C. H. J.   *161*
Van Gorder, P.   *2*
Vanhoozer, K. J.   *161*
Vaughan, C. J.   *46*
Vines, J.   *7, 57, 69, 107, 241, 286*
Vogel, R.   *6*

Wallace, D. B.   *148*
Walsh, J. T.   *161*

Warren, R.   *277, 280, 283*
Warren, T.   *108, 276*
Webber, E. R.   *43, 47*
Wells, D.   *90–91*
Wesley, J.   *56, 78, 93*
Whitefield, G.   *47, 56, 78*
Wilder, J.   *56*
Willhite, R. K.   *52*
Wilson, G. H.   *161*
Winbery, C. L.   *147*
Witherington, B.   *139*
Witten, M. G.   *91–92*
Wright, A. G.   *199*
Wright, D. F.   *43*
Würthwein, E.   *160*
Wycliffe, J.   *80*

York, H.   *6, 226, 254, 257–58, 271, 274*

Zwingli, U.   *4, 44*

SCRIPTURE INDEX